DEAR MRS. WRIGHT

For Pat ~
Be inspired and
inspiring.
Love,
Jan

DEAR MRS. WRIGHT

A Teacher's Memoir
Inspired by Students' Letters

Jan Wright

Vintage Press
Whidbey Island
Coupeville, Washington
USA

First edition

Cover Design by Terry Hansen

Printed in the United States of America

Vintage Press
Whidbey Island
Coupeville, Washington

ISBN# 978-1-7375962-0-2
LCCN: 2021914901

For more information, contact:
jan@DearMrsWright.com
or visit:
www.DearMrsWright.com

DEDICATION

For all my students, especially those to whom I promised to write this book.

For all the teachers and staff members who taught me so much, thank you!

For my grown sons, David and Brian. After all the times you put up with the projects I did for my students whom I often called "my kids," you have always been the best part of my life, my true and most dearly loved kids.

And for my grandson, Kryten, who listened as I read early drafts of this book to him and told me to keep writing.

Table of Contents

Note to Readers xi

PART ONE - The Novice Teacher

Jumping into the Fire, Florida, February - June 1972
1. Where Do I Start? 5
2. Camping Trip 9
3. Southern Surprises 14
4. Andrew 18
5. Gum 26
6. Lice 30
7. Tornado 41
8. Black and White 47
9. Joy to the World 54

A Fresh Start, Virginia, 1972 - 1973
10. Perfect 59
11. The Name Game 68
12. Schedules 76
13. Figaro 80
14. Black Mollies 84
15. The Math Lesson 90
16. The Helping Teacher 94
17. Extension 100
18. Observations 104
19. Celery 110
20. Farewell Feast 115
21. Smile 121
22. Autumn Bounty 127
23. The Pedestal 132

24. Radiator 137
25. Gifts 143

DECADES IN THE MIDDLE

PART TWO - The Seasoned Teacher

Transitions, Calilfornia, 1999, 2000
26. Moving 157
27. Portables 165

Shifting Focus, California, 2001 - 2002
28. Past and Present 171
29. The Art Room 176
30. A Scientist 181
31. A Day Like No Other 189
32. Welcome Back, Steven 199
33. Circle of the Muse 204
34. Football 211
35. Mosaic 214
36. Gumdrops 219
37. I Don't Care 223
38. Rodney 230
39. Cooperative Learning 238
40. Spring is in the Air 247
41. Sex Education 254

Endings and Beginnings, California, 2002 - 2003
42. Getting Ready 263
43. Planning for Success 268
44. Tiffany 272
45. Grade Level Meeting 278
46. Microscopes 282

47. Partners 287
48. Creative Solutions 292
49. Eyeballs 297
50. Exploratorium 304
51. Observation Fiasco 311
52. Mentor 316
53. Medical Emergency 320
54. Letter from the District 325
55. Graduation 327
56. Last Day 332

Excerpts from Letters 335
Epilogue 341
Acknowledgments 343
About the Author 345

Note to Readers

This narrative is based on my personal memories of real events, but I cannot claim complete accuracy. First, to protect their privacy, I have changed the names of most of the characters in this book. More than that, however, memories form the basis of my story, and human memory is fallible. I no longer remember the exact words of any conversation, but I have created dialogue and some unverifiable details in my story to paint a whole picture, given those vagaries of memory.

PART ONE
The Novice Teacher

Jumping into the Fire

East Milton, Florida
February – June 1972

Chapter 1
Where Do I Start?

February 11, 1972

With soapy sponge in hand, I stepped back and admired the gleam of the red '65 El Camino truck with its white camper top. I brushed off the handful of fire ants crawling across my bare foot, stepping away from the emerging ant hill in the newly wet sand. Since moving to the panhandle area of Florida, I'd learned to avoid the nasty stings of these little red devils. Ducking beneath the fine-haired, silver moss that dripped down from the weeping willow tree, I continued around the truck, searching for spots I might have missed. Satisfied, I threw the sponge into the bucket just as the phone in my kitchen began to ring.

I sprinted into the duplex.

"Hello?" I said, trying to quiet my breathing, wondering who was calling at this hour on a Friday afternoon.

"Miz Wright . . ." I recognized his voice immediately. We had spoken to each other many times over these past several months while I searched for a full-time teaching position and took the occasional substitute jobs. "This is Mista Jameson." I could picture his beefy, ruddy face, his sparse comb-over, and his jaunty bow tie as he leaned back in the well-used leather chair behind his massive mahogany desk.

"How y'all doin' this fine Friday aftanoon?" he intoned in his distinctive, bayou drawl so prevalent in the Panhandle area. I often got distracted by the relaxed, lilting sound of his southern accent as he spoke.

"Hello, Mr. Jameson. My husband and I are doing well, thank you. How are you today?" I responded.

"Fine, jes' fine, Miz Wright. Well now, I jes' got a call from Mista Davis ova' at his school," he continued. "Looks like he has a sixth-grade teacha' ova' thea' who left and will not be comin' back." My attention riveted on his words instead of his accent. "We gonna have an openin'."

He paused. I figured he was a man who knew the value of his hiring power and exercised it for the benefit of friends first and newcomers, like me, dead last. My grip on the receiver tightened. "I wuz wonderin', Miz Wright, if ya might be interested in a full-time job 'til the end of the school yea'?"

"Yes!" I answer without hesitation, too eager to question the details of his offer.

"Let's see. It's nearly fo' o'clock now. Y'all need to do an interview at the school. Betta do it now, befo' ever'one leaves for the weekend," he said with paradoxically slow deliberation.

In the middle of a school year, this job possibility came as an unexpected gift. I finished all the requirements for my teaching credential in August. However, to my disappointment, the required physical copy of the credential did not arrive by mail until the end of September, too late for me to be hired for the regular school year.

Standing in the small, remodeled-on-the-cheap, yellow and avocado green kitchen in my shorts and bare feet, I reached over and grabbed a napkin from the kitchen table and a pencil from the window sill. I squeezed the yellow wall phone receiver between my ear and shoulder and jotted down the school address and the principal's name. As I hung up, I glanced out to the El Camino I had been washing and the camping gear piled beside the front door, glad my husband had let me drive him into the Navy base that morning, so I could do the errands. I felt a tingle of anticipation. Could this be it? Was I about to become a teacher with my very own class?

I dashed into the bedroom, pulling off my wet clothes as I went. I grabbed my powder blue sleeveless dress out of the closet and dragged it over my head, ran a comb through my long, straight hair, slipped my feet into my sandals, applied some lipstick to my lips and a smudge to each cheek, and I skipped out the door in less than five minutes.

Only a few cars remained in the parking lot when I arrived. A smiling young woman in a frilly white sundress met me at the main entry door and introduced herself as Miss Sutherland, the vice principal/art teacher. She ushered me down the hall and into a cluttered office where a frazzled, middle-aged man got to his feet, putting his cigarette out in an over-full ash tray. He wore a rumpled, sweat-stained, white shirt, opened at the neck, with his tie loosened. "This is our principal, Mr. Davis," she said. Her smile broadened across her face as she backed out the door and disappeared down the hallway.

Mr. Davis moved a pile of books off a chair across from his desk and asked me to sit. Then he rounded his desk and plopped down in his seat. He shuffled through a few papers until he found what he needed. Reading from his notes, he said, "Let's see, you graduated with a Master's Degree in Elementary Education from the University of West Florida just this September. Mr. Jameson tells me you've done some substituting since then." He looked up at me through tired eyes.

"Yes, sir," I replied.

"Let me get right to the point. We need a sixth-grade teacher." Without skipping a beat, he continued, "Can you start on Monday?"

After two summers and a long year of scraping together the money for classes and school supplies, and after five months of intermittent substituting and disappointment, I was being offered a real teaching job. Then, with a gulp, I remembered the camping trip. My husband and I planned to leave in an hour for a weekend on a tiny island in the bayous. *How can I possibly be ready to teach on Monday?*

I took a deep breath and said, "I would very much like to take the job. Is there any possibility I could start a few days later?"

"No. We need someone right now," he said in a firm voice. "This class has been without a teacher for two weeks already. Are you interested in the job or not?" he pushed.

"Yes," I responded, placing my worries about the weekend into the back of my thoughts.

"All right. Let me show you to the classroom, and then you need to go over to the district office to sign some papers." He rose from his paper-piled desk.

At a quick pace, the principal walked me down the hall and turned the corner heading to the far end of another hallway. We stepped through the open door into what would become my new sixth-grade classroom. A haphazard sea of desks, all sorts and sizes, assaulted my eyes. Books and papers lay strewn on the back counter beneath a wall of open windows, on the desks, and in crumpled heaps on the floor. The room smelled stuffy. The acrid smell of preteens who hadn't yet been introduced to deodorant lingered in the air. Directions for a Valentine's Day art project, precisely lettered and drawn in white chalk, covered the blackboard on the front wall.

Standing on a chair at the far side of the room, the woman I'd met earlier stapled bright colored sheets of student art onto the wall, the only sign of student work in the room. She grinned as she turned around and stepped down from the chair.

"Mrs. Wright will be taking over the class, Miss Sutherland," offered Mr. Davis.

"How wonderful!" she replied. "They really are a good bunch of kids when you get to know them. I was the substitute for the past week, but I am usually the art teacher at this school. I'm just finishing up a few things before I go home. I'm so glad you'll be joining us."

"Mrs. Wright needs to get over to the district office right away to get the papers signed," said Mr. Davis. "Give her some manuals and send her on her way, Miss Sutherland. I need to get back to my office," he sighed. "See you on Monday morning, Mrs. Wright."

He turned and started to walk out the door. "Uh, what time does school start?" I asked after him.

"You need to be here when the buses arrive at 6:45," he threw back over his shoulder as he continued into the hall.

Miss Sutherland glanced at her watch and began to collect teacher's manuals from various locations as she walked around the perimeter of the classroom. Two sat on the back counter, one on a large round table in the back corner, and one lay on a dilapidated book case behind the table. She stacked the well-worn, dog-eared books on top of an untidy teacher's desk at the front corner of the room. I felt a sense of panic beginning to rise. I asked, "But, where do I start? How will I know where the students are in each subject?"

"I don't really know. I did mostly art projects with them last week," she responded. She searched through the scattered papers on the desk and found the previous teacher's lesson plan book. "Maybe this will help." She piled it on the top of the stack.

Opening up a drawer in the teacher's desk, she pulled out a couple more manuals and looked up at me with what seemed like an apology on her face. "Here, let me help you out to your car," she said.

Driving out of the parking lot, smiling so hard it almost hurt, I shouted out loud to myself, "I got a teaching job! Wahoo!"

Then it hit me. *Yikes! I'm leaving to go camping in less than an hour.*

Chapter 2
Camping Trip

After signing the papers at the district office, I rushed home, grinning all the way. When I pulled up in front of the duplex, a mud-spattered black truck I didn't recognize sat in my regular parking spot. While the radio blared a song by Led Zeppelin, a young man slouched in the driver's seat, nodding his head in time to the music, eyes shut, oblivious to my arrival. From the Navy sticker on the bumper, I figured he brought my husband home from the base.

Just as I jumped out of our El Camino, Jerry burst through the front door, dressed in his civilian clothes, with two sleeping bags in his arms. I dashed toward him.

"Oh, there you are. Where have you been? We're ready to go," he said, brushing past me.

"Jerry, I got a job! I'm going to teach!" I cried, an irrepressible smile reaching into my words.

"Great!" he responded. "I knew you would. They finally hired the best. Now, get the rest of your stuff for camping. They're waiting for us." He dumped the sleeping bags into the back of the waiting truck and leaned over to arrange the rest of the camping gear. The guy in the driver's seat, absorbed in his music, still didn't open his eyes or acknowledge either one of us.

"I just need to change my clothes. There are some books on the front seat we need to take with us," I replied. "Will you get a couple of paper bags to put them in?"

Jerry turned and walked back toward me. "Books? On a camping trip?" he asked.

"Yes, I start teaching on Monday morning," I said, in a breathless rush, heading for the door.

"Monday morning?" he repeated, as he followed me inside. "But, how are you going to do that? We don't get home until Sunday night."

"I know, I know. I'll just have to make my lesson plans while we're camping. I'll figure it out," I said. "Hey, who's that guy in the truck?"

"That's Tim. He's the mechanic I told you about, the one who organized this camping trip."

An hour after I'd been hired to teach, we carried groceries, all our camping gear, and my teacher's manuals to the edge of the river next to a small, beat-up, old, aluminum fishing boat already filled with several six packs of beer. With a raised eyebrow, my husband's new acquaintance, Tim, asked me, "Do you really *need* to bring all those books? It'll take an extra trip to manage all that gear."

"Yes, absolutely! I can't leave anything behind. I'm starting a new job, teaching, on Monday," I assured him.

"You're gonna be a teacher?" he replied with a sneer. "Great. You'll be a lot of fun camping," he finished sarcastically.

Looking irritated, Tim set out to ferry us across a lazy little bayou. I sat in the center, holding my bags of books tight on my lap with one hand and holding onto the side of the boat with the other hand. The old motor sputtered to life, chugging to pull our weight through the water. Half way across, I saw snakes slithering past us. The sight elicited a dire warning from Tim. "Be careful not to fall in. Poisonous water snakes ball up in nests. Hah! They can kill a human in minutes," he smirked, as he rocked the boat just enough to be a tease.

Relieved to land on the tiny island, a mere sand bar in the middle of the steamy, slowly meandering, snake-infested river, I wondered what other creepy critters, including the two-legged kind, I would encounter.

I didn't recognize any of the Navy guys or girls already setting up camp, so I followed my husband to a spot where he put down our tent. I set my bags of books next to it. We made a couple of trips back and forth to the boat to carry supplies, and then Tim and Jerry set off to go back for the rest of the gear. I began to put up our small tent, sweating in the unrelenting heat and humidity.

Evening settled upon us. Camp set-up complete, the crackling campfire drew us into a circle. Cold beers were handed out while hot dogs were stuck onto sticks for roasting. A few casual introductions were made. The guys seemed to know each other, but not many of the girls. Young enlisted men, just out of high school, the guys complained about duties at the base and bragged about pranks they had played. Jerry enjoyed adding his own stories into the mix. The girls flirted with the young men, becoming more outrageous as the night wore on and the beer cans emptied. At the mature old age of twenty-four, I was an outsider to this rowdy group of campers from the Navy base and their girlfriends. Sharing my enthusiasm about my new teaching job felt out of place in this group, so I kept it to myself.

I listened to their stories and increasingly drunken bravado. At last, I leaned over and whispered in Jerry's ear, "Do you mind if I go to bed?"

"Now?" he responded.

"Yeah. You stay. I don't mind. I need to get up early to work on my lesson plans," I replied with an apologetic shrug.

"Okay, see you soon," he said, as he kissed me good night.

They partied late into the night. I lay on my sleeping bag, thinking about my classroom. I wanted to clean it and make some changes to the barren space. I imagined the students I would meet on Monday.

As soon as the sun came up the next morning, while everyone else slept off their hangovers, I dragged my sleeping bag out of the tent and spread it out on top of the sand, placing the bags of books in the middle. I sat down cross-legged and began to examine my teaching materials. Impatient to begin, I picked up the previous teacher's lesson planning book.

In the natural beauty of a steamy Florida morning, with the birds singing their break-of-day songs and the insects buzzing, I set the plan book on my lap and turned to yesterday's date, February 11.

Blank. The whole week. Oh, right, substitutes taught then.

I turned back a page, then another, and then another. Under the heading for reading, I found, "We had a good time reading today." *What kind of lesson plan is that?* Nothing. No objectives, no methods, no anticipatory sets, none of the elements I had been taught were so essential. *I just need to know what page they're on, darn it!*

Jerry emerged from the tent, yawning, his hair sticking out in disarray. "Jerry, the previous teacher didn't even list any plans for reading groups. Look at this last entry for math: 'page 12.' Could they be on page 12 after more than half a school year? Page 12? Unbelievable. There's a lot written under social studies. Maybe that's what they did all day long, social studies. Can you believe that? Social studies. And, there's not a single mention of science. Shoot! This is impossible."

He stared at me with eyes squinting in the morning sunshine and replied, "I just need to take a leak."

"Oh, right. Sorry. I know, too much, too early. I'm wound up about this. Never mind me. You go back to sleep."

In the mounting humidity, sweating, the worry grew. *What am I going to do with a room full of sixth graders for a whole day, let alone a whole week?* I searched through the teacher's manuals, scanning the guides for all the subjects, getting a sense of sixth-grade curriculum, trying to work my way toward something specific to do for the first few days.

Hours later, someone started up the campfire, and I could smell the coffee brewing. Sounds of rustling inside our tent told me Jerry was stirring again. At last, he sat up and peered out at me. "Are you still at it?"

"There's more here in these manuals than I could ever read. This is awful. I have no idea where to start in these books."

"What did you do when you substituted?"

"I followed the teacher's plans."

He thought for a moment and said, "Didn't you always bring a bag full of extra stuff with you, just in case?"

"Good idea," I said, shifting my eyes to look up. "Maybe I can adapt some of those."

"You'll do fine. You always do."

I felt frustrated at his lack of sympathy for my struggle, even though I loved his support for me. "But it takes hard work, Jerry," I said in an exasperated tone.

"You can do it, Jan. You'll do fine."

Jerry predicted it. I figured out a list of activities to help me get to know my students and begin to assess where to start teaching. Miss Sutherland introduced me to the class and then left me on my own. For my first assignment, I wrote on the blackboard: "Dear Mrs. Wright," and then I asked my class to write a letter to introduce themselves to me.

At the end of the day, Miss Sutherland returned just in time to supervise the Valentine exchange she had organized the previous week.

That first nerve-wracking day of teaching melted into a blur. I don't remember much about what we did, nor a single significant thing I learned from the letters they wrote to me. By the end of the second day, however, I managed to learn the names of all my students. I had a total of forty-three kids. I discovered they ranged in age from eleven to almost sixteen years old. On Friday, I had to complete a form required to monitor integration compliance, listing each child by race, thirty-two white and eleven black students, and noting whether or not they rode the bus to school.

By the middle of the second week, my informal evaluations revealed that these kids fell far behind in sixth-grade skills. The enormous task ahead overwhelmed me. I filled up the teacher's plan book with detailed lesson plans in a desperate attempt to address my students' academic needs.

I tried out a variety of curriculum ideas, while my students tested my patience and my boundaries, wanting to know just how much they could get away with. Could they get me to leave, as all the others had before me? But, unlike the others, I was young, determined, and dedicated. No matter how difficult, I would not give up on *my* kids.

Chapter 3
Southern Surprises

Locked out? It was the end of my second week of teaching and the door wasn't open as it had been all the days before. I realized, with surprise, I'd never been given a key.

The early morning sunlight filtered through the dusty windows at the end of the hallway. Alone, I tapped my toe in anxiety. All the other doors were open, yet mine was closed. Perspiration beaded on my temples at the start of another sultry day. I juggled the huge armload of papers and heavy manuals and reached for the door knob. It didn't budge. I had just walked the mile and a half to school at a rapid pace, so I was a little ahead of schedule, but I was anxious to get inside to prepare for the busy day ahead. Puzzled, I took a deep breath.

Stacking the books and papers on the floor beside the classroom door, I tried the door handle again. No, it was definitely locked. I straightened the crumpled blouse sticking to my sweaty waist and then set off to find help.

I peeked into each of the empty rooms along the hallway as I strode toward the front of the building in search of the principal, the man I'd met just two short weeks earlier when he offered me this teaching job. My mind had been absorbed with planning the important activities ahead, not practical issues like securing a key.

Mr. Davis met me on the way out of his office with keys in hand, a grin on his face. "I'll bet you'd like to get into your classroom this morning, wouldn't you, Mrs. Wright?"

"Yes, I would," I responded, trying to keep the irritation out of my voice. "Why was my door locked?"

"Oh, you'll see," he smiled, leaving me hanging for an explanation. When we reached my classroom door, he fumbled with his overfilled key ring, finally managing to insert the correct key into the lock. At last, with a flourish, he swept the door open wide, standing back to watch my reaction. On a round table at the front of the classroom, sat a huge cage containing a hissing, snarling, and very much alive, raccoon, the first I'd ever seen, and it was not the least bit tame or happy.

"Wow!" I exclaimed wide-eyed.

Mr. Davis said, "Ricky and Jeremiah came to me after school yesterday to see if I'd help them get it into your classroom to surprise you."

Ricky and Jeremiah, one red-haired, freckle-faced, white student, and one bushy-haired, coffee-colored, black student. Although each one had been taught how to fight with his fists in fearful anticipation of a need for self-defense before attending that first integrated school year, the jokesters were the best of friends whose parents, I discovered later, didn't know their son's school buddy was of a different race. Under their infectious exuberance and natural leadership, my entire class had gained a well-earned reputation for misbehavior long before my arrival as their new teacher.

According to my fellow sixth-grade teacher, Christine Riley, who taught across the hall from me, the previous teacher in my classroom had resigned because parents complained about her lack of classroom discipline and control. Christine said there had been quite a few substitute teachers, and none ever stayed longer than a single day, some not that long.

I knew these students were waiting to see if they could get to me. Could they send me packing as they had all the others? The raccoon was the latest of their teacher tests. What would I do with this newest challenge?

I stared at the bandit-eyed beast while it raged, spitting mad, as it strained at the confines of the wire cage placed center stage in the desk-crowded classroom. Were my students so different from this wild creature who obviously didn't want to be there? Something in my gut told me I had reached a make-or-break crossroad. *Can I trust my own intuitive ability and take advantage of my students' natural interest and curiosity to teach them something? Should I embrace the moment and dump my planned day to take advantage of the "gift" I've been given?*

Of course, Jeremiah and Ricky were among the first students off the bus that morning. Bouncing each other off the walls, they laughed and I heard Ricky yell loud enough to be heard above the din, "Hey Jeremiah, are you a bullfrog?" I smiled at the reference to the popular song by Three Dog Night. Both Ricky and Jeremiah sang out loud the familiar refrain about the bullfrog named Jeremiah. Their laughter infected the mass of students nearby.

Closing our classroom door, I positioned myself in the hallway, waiting with arms folded across my chest, forcing a neutral expression on my face as they approached.

"Hey, Miz Wright," Jeremiah yelled as he shot a conspiratorial look at Ricky.

The group of students heading in my direction came to a halt at the sight of the closed door, as unusual for them as it had been for me. They stared at me; a hush of anticipation blanketed the group. No one dared ask questions, letting me know they were all in on the prank.

I returned their stares. At last, I let the corners of my mouth turn up and broke into a wide smile. I opened the classroom door. "Come on in and take a look at our surprise guest!" I said, adding, "He's absolutely magnificent." The clamor in the hallway lifted a couple of levels as they poured into the classroom to see the "surprise" awaiting them.

The lessons inspired by that feisty raccoon, created on the spur of the moment, carried us well through the morning. We observed the wild creature in his cage, talked about what we knew, and made lists of what we wanted to learn. We sent a note to the librarian with a couple of students asking to borrow anything she could find about raccoons. We wrote descriptions, shared tales about their experiences with raccoons, and wrote our own poems and stories.

As lunchtime approached, Mr. Davis came in to remove our unexpected visitor. My students groaned in disappointment.

"Awwww, cain't he stay?" Andrew inquired from the front row. "I wrote a poem 'bout that there raccoon, Mr. Davis."

16

"Really? I'd like to read your work, Andrew."

"Miz Wright says it's good."

"I'm sure it is, Andrew. Sorry kids, Ricky's dad is waiting for the raccoon, so I've got to take him now. Ricky, you want to help me carry this thing?"

"Yes, sir!" Ricky replied.

"Mr. Davis," I said, in a tone I hoped sounded authoritative, "please thank Mr. Smith for taking the time to bring such a treat for our class." Murmurs of agreement ran through the room. "I'm sure Ricky will be glad to share with his parents what he's written."

Ricky beamed with pride as he exited the room with the principal, the raccoon spitting and hissing once again as they jostled the cage through the doorway, Jeremiah's animated face following their departure.

When the day drew to a close, the room emptied of students who packed themselves into the various buses that would take them to their separate and disparate homes. Jeremiah and Ricky lingered in the back of the room together. I gathered my papers and began to stack the manuals I would take home for the weekend. They sauntered toward me at last, stopping near my desk. Jeremiah, eyes down cast in uncharacteristic shyness, drawled, "Miz Wright, …uh, …uh, … today with the raccoon was cool. Right?"

"Yes, gentlemen. Very cool," I said with a chuckle.

"See you on Monday, Miz Wright!" Ricky grinned.

"Yeah, see you on Monday," I responded with a satisfied smile.

They exited the room with their customary joking, shoving, and a loud chorus of "Joy to the World"—the bullfrog version.

I sighed.

Maybe I surprised them as much as they surprised me. We seemed to have forged a tentative alliance. This might yet become a functioning sixth-grade class. My students would return on Monday morning, and now they knew I would be there too, ready to teach them.

Chapter 4
Andrew

"**M**ornin' Miz Wright," Andrew yelled across the hallway. His head and shoulders towered over a mass of students on their way to class. "I did my homework!" He waved his paper high, eyes alight with sheer joy, as he lumbered his way through the crowd on his determined path toward me. "My dad helped me."

"Andrew's daddy does his homework. Andrew's daddy does his homework. You cain't even do it by yourself," taunted a pint-sized, curly-haired spitfire of a third-grade girl as she and her two friends bumped and poked him.

Barreling past them with ease, he continued on his course toward me, still waving his paper above his head. "Wanna hear my story, Miz Wright? Got it right here!"

A blond-haired tyke whose lunch pail clattered to the floor in the wake of Andrew's passing, yelled at him, "Watch it! I got a mind to . . ."

"Sorry Frankie, I help you, I help you," cooed Andrew, as he turned and bent over to pick up the lunch pail, backing into a trio of fourth grade girls, knocking a stack of books onto the floor behind him.

"ANNNDRREWWW!" wailed the girls. "Watch where you're going."

"I sorry, I sorry," he mumbled. He whirled around to reach for the books.

"Let go my books, Andrew!" shouted the tallest of the three. "Get yourself to class, boy."

He arrived, breathless, in front of me with a huge grin on his broad face, crumpled paper in hand. "Got my story for you, Miz Wright!"

I struggled not to reveal my amusement at his bumbling arrival and my relief that he'd reached his destination without further mishap.

"Oh, Andrew, I'm looking forward to reading it. I'm so proud of you for bringing your homework this morning," I replied.

His feelings were easy to read. He had an infectious smile that lit up his whole face when he was happy and a heart-wrenchingly sad expression when he was not. Andrew, a big boy, wide and tall, barely fit into his desk. He seldom sat still, always busy tapping his pencil on the various surfaces of the desk or bumping his knees underneath. His hand shot up frequently during class to add a comment or ask to go to the bathroom, and sometimes he just blurted out whatever was on his mind.

He must have been about fourteen years old, hard to tell for sure. He had the classic look of Down's syndrome: a flattened face, almond-shaped eyes that slanted up, and a tongue he often stuck out. When I met his father to discuss Andrew's school work, the wiry little old black man challenged me, insisting, "My son just has a little problem with his eyes. That makes him a bit slow, that's all, Miz Wright. He don't belong in no class for retarded kids like some folks say."

This proud man, adamant that his son would get the education he never did, was not about to let a brand-new teacher, a young slip of a white girl from California, tell him anything different. I had to respect that determination. So, there Andrew stayed, in my overcrowded class, barely able to read or write, and he had all the special attention and encouragement I could give him.

On this particular morning, the day began with our regular opening routine. An hour later, while the class worked in three reading groups, I stood at the far side of the room explaining directions to the Blue Group for a practice page that included the difference between the short *e* and short *i* sounds. It seemed like an easy assignment until I saw the puzzled looks on several faces.

"It's the difference between *pen* and *pin*," I pronounced with exaggerated facial movements.

To my ears, it sounded like Joey said, "Ahh don' git it. How do you know when to use one or t'other? They both say the same thang, *pay-en*."

"Yeah, they're both *pin*," said Sarah.

"No. You write with a *pen*, and a *pin* is a sharp thing that holds things together, like a tack. It's *pen* or *pin*. Like *ten* or *tin*," I said, enunciating perfectly, in my way of thinking. Still, they had the look of not understanding. Then it dawned on me. The oddity came from my accent, not theirs. "I see. You don't hear the difference, do you?" They shrugged and shook their heads.

Realizing a battle not worth fighting, I said, "Hmmm, guess you'll have to look at the context and memorize when to use *e* or *i*. Sorry about that, kids."

"Miz Wright, can I go to the bathroom?" Andrew called across the room, waving his hand frantically to get my attention.

I gave my automatic response, "Yes, Andrew, come right back."

He struggled to get himself untangled from the tight-fitting desk, ambled across the room, stopped occasionally to see what other students were doing, fumbled with the handle to get the door shoved open, and then disappeared for fifteen minutes. A similar routine occurred two or three times each school day.

Miss Sutherland, the vice principal/art teacher, who had been the substitute for this class the week before I took over, advised me to let him go when he asked. I tried talking to Andrew about making sure he used the bathroom during the morning recess and at lunch time. He assured me that he went at those times, too.

His father could give no helpful insight as to how to manage this constant absence from the classroom, even when I earnestly explained the importance for Andrew to be in class so he would not miss instruction. "He just needs to go, Miz Wright," he replied with a shrug when I brought up the embarrassing topic.

At the end of the day, the principal, Mr. Davis, marched into my classroom after school. Without preamble he began, "Andrew is spending entirely too much time in the hallway on his way to the bathroom. I want you to keep him in class. Don't let him go out except for recess."

"Even if he says he really needs to go to the bathroom?" I questioned.

"Yes, I want you to be firm with him and get these constant bathroom trips stopped. Starting tomorrow, do not allow him to leave your room during class no matter how often he asks," he said with a self-assured tone. With that, he turned and walked out of my classroom without further comment.

I sat at my desk, thinking about how to manage this ultimatum. No one had ever told me Andrew caused any problems in the hallway, yet I felt I had to follow the principal's directive.

I would have to let Andrew know what we expected of him. Having a private conversation with Andrew would not be an easy thing to accomplish. Naturally loud and without the usual social boundaries, I doubted I could get him into a whispered, side conversation.

The next morning, as students filtered into the classrooms from the various buses, I watched and waited for Andrew, willing him to walk a little faster, arrive a little earlier, to give us a chance to talk. Of course, it was not to be. I could see Andrew as he entered, looming above the rest in the crowded hallway, taking his time, good naturedly holding the door open for others, talking to younger students. "Y'all be good today."

A group of little girls giggled and elbowed past him, calling out, "Goofy Andrew, get a move on."

"Have a good day!" he sang out in reply.

He zigzagged from one thing that caught his attention to another. The multitude of students increased and ebbed around him. At last, he arrived in front of me. Noticing my presence, "Mornin' Miz Wright," he crowed. His face broke into a huge grin that reached his eyes.

"Good morning, Andrew," I smiled in return. "I need to talk to you." I could see no better time or place for this conversation, so I lowered my voice and spoke directly to him.

"Mr. Davis is concerned about how much time you've been spending out of class each day. He says you can't go to the restroom during class time any more. You need to go during recess and at lunch time only." I paused. "Do you understand what I'm telling you, Andrew?"

Andrew looked down at the floor, staring at his feet. "Yes, ma'am."

"All right, Andrew. Why don't you go to the bathroom right now, before we start class?" I suggested.

"I just went, Miz Wright," he replied as he sauntered to his desk and settled in for the morning.

We started our day. Amidst numerous distractions, I tried to keep my eye on Andrew to see how he was doing. All went well until, as recess time neared, he began to fidget. I could see his legs jittering up and down beneath his desk. *Ten minutes to go. Will he make it?*

Five minutes later, I told the class to hand in their papers and put their books away. Andrew, the first one out of his seat, rushed to my side. "I's ready, Miz Wright."

"Just a few more minutes, Andrew. Why don't you wait right here by the door with me?"

He rocked from side to side, shifting his weight from one foot to the other as the class prepared to leave the room. I opened the classroom door. The bell rang. Andrew made a bee line down the hall and out of sight into the boys' restroom. I sighed with relief. We successfully managed to get through the morning session.

Worry receded as the usual busy routine of the school day took over. With reading and language arts lessons finished, we tackled math.

Half an hour before lunch, Andrew raised his hand and asked, "Can I go to the bathroom?"

I stopped and looked at him. "Andrew, you need to wait until lunch break."

"Oh, right," he said as he gave me a sheepish grin. "I forgot."

Ten minutes later, Andrew's hand shot up again. He blurted out, "Can I go to the bathroom, Miz Wright?"

I replied slowly, "No, Andrew, lunch break is in twenty minutes. You need to wait." Worried, I hesitated, but I didn't want to defy the orders from my principal. Surely Andrew could make it until lunch time.

He sighed in resignation, dropped his head, and began to fiddle with the end of his pencil. It appeared to be broken. I watched him lean over to Sally and ask to borrow a pencil from her. She dug around in her desk and came up with a teeth-marked, stubby, yellow pencil with a chewed-up eraser on the end. She handed it to Andrew.

"Give that back to me before you go home, Andrew," Sally demanded. He gave her a nod and then spun the pencil around on his desk before picking it up to write. I glanced over at him a few minutes later. Squirming, he jostled his legs under the desk.

Jimmy Bob, standing at the chalkboard working with a small group of students on a long division problem, called to me, "Miz Wright, I got the right answer! Delilah's got it wrong."

"I got it right, Jimmy Bob. You don't know how to divide," retorted Delilah.

"I'll be right there," I replied. I made my way across the busy room to them.

We finished the last of the division problems, and the chatter in the room increased. I glanced at the clock. Time for lunch. "Put away your books and gather your lunch things," I announced. Students busied themselves getting ready while I placed my teacher's manual on my desk and grabbed my whistle and my lunch bag. The bell rang just as I reached the classroom door. Students spilled out into the hallway and lined up along the wall, talking and bumping each other as they jockeyed for position. I turned back toward the classroom and saw Andrew sitting at his desk, his head hung low. "Andrew," I called to him, "It's time to go to lunch now. Come on and line up with us."

No response.

"Andrew?" I said, my concern rising.

The only student left in the room, I walked toward him. He sat very still, head bowed and eyes shut, a tear ran down his face and dripped off his chin onto his desk. Then I noticed the dark wet stain in his lap and down his pants legs. Feeling my own shame for pushing him to this embarrassing point, I said, "Just a moment, Andrew. I'll get you some help." With that, I walked over to the phone and dialed the office.

When the school secretary answered, I said, "Please tell Mr. Davis to come to my classroom right now." Anger increased the volume of my words as I finished, "It's very important."

Why did I listen to that man instead of standing up for my student? I stepped into the hall, closing the door behind me as I did.

"Miz Wright, can we go now?" questioned Bobby.

"In just a minute, Bobby. Just a minute," I replied.

When Mr. Davis arrived, I said with a tight voice, "Andrew needs your help in the classroom. I'm taking my class to lunch." I turned to walk the rest of my class down the hall to the cafeteria, leaving Mr. Davis to deal with Andrew.

Required to escort my class to our table in the school cafeteria, I also had to eat with them and manage their lunch-time behavior, including recess in the yard afterward. Allowed a five-minute break to go to the restroom, I had to ask another teacher to supervise the kids for me.

Just as the end-of-lunch-recess bell rang, Mr. Davis walked out to the yard, frowning. He joined me while I headed back toward the building. In a stilted voice, he said, "I called Andrew's father. From now on, you can let Andrew go to the bathroom whenever he asks."

I nodded in reply, not trusting my voice to respond to him, having berated myself during the entire lunch period for listening to him in the first place.

We filed back into the classroom for the afternoon session. Students shoved each other, teasing, recounting their hopscotch feats, or crowing about who had run the fastest in the game of tag. There were no basketball courts, no climbing apparatus, no lines painted on asphalt, not even a fence. The weeping willow trees, covered in dripping moss, created the visual border around the dirt field. Students made up their own games or sat beneath the shade of the trees in small groups, too hot to do more than talk.

Sally and Lillian shouldered through the door together. Giggling, they separated and found their seats. Sally slid into her desk and picked up the pencil she found in the center, the one she had loaned to Andrew earlier that morning. She glanced over at Andrew's empty desk. "Miz Wright, where's Andrew?" she asked in her bright little voice.

"His father came to pick him up, Sally," I responded, hoping no one would ask why he'd gone. I picked up our class novel from my desk to shift her attention.

"Oh," she replied. "Look, Miz Wright, he returned my pencil before he left."

"Yes, I see," I said.

"Yeah, that's why I give it to him. He's not too bright with school work, but he never forgets stuff like that," said Sally. The class began to settle down, waiting for me to start reading aloud the next chapter.

"I'd say Andrew is a pretty special young man," I said, feeling a strong need to protect him.

"He sure 'nough is!" she sang out. "Whatcha readin' to us this afternoon, Miz Wright? Andrew's gonna be sorry he missed it."

The room quieted; all eyes turned to me. Some of them must have known what had happened, but no one said anything about it. Chagrined, I opened the book and began to read to them, vowing to take the time to share the missing chapter with Andrew when he returned.

Chapter 5
Gum

"**D**wayne, are you chewing gum? Again?" I asked in exasperation.

The tall, acne-faced young man hung his head, as much to hide his smirk, as to show deference to his teacher when he responded, "Yes, ma'am."

Lisa shot him a coy smile as she smacked her own gum, reacting with exaggerated surprise when it burst. *POP!*

The class giggled.

"All right, how many of you are chewing gum this morning?" I asked.

A few hands raised, slowly. More followed, until almost a fourth of the class sat there grinning at me with their hands in the air. Of course, Jeremiah and Ricky had their hands up with smiles of defiance on their faces.

Now what? I thought.

"Is that all? Is that everyone who's chewing gum?" I said aloud. Two more hands crept up. With a calm I did not feel, I walked over to my desk, picked up a pen and a piece of paper, and started to write. Some of the hands began to sink.

"Noooo, put them back up," I said firmly while I continued to make my list. When I finished, I grabbed the trash can and walked up and down the aisles. Students spit their gum into the can. I stopped beside each student who hadn't raised a hand and gave each one the "look." I ferreted out one more gum chewer in this manner and added her name to my list. Thirteen students in all.

"You know there's a school rule about not chewing gum in class. I have warned you *twice* already," I said, almost whining in my attempt to sound serious.

The bell rang. "We'll take care of this after recess."

We filed out of our room along with the sixth-grade class directly across the hallway. Mrs. Riley and I emerged at the same time and met in the middle of a stream of children.

"I can't believe it! I just caught thirteen students chewing gum in my room!" I said in frustration.

"Jan, I told you before. You have to spank them," she replied with the authority of a seasoned teacher. "They disobeyed the rules. You need to show them who's boss. No doubt about it. Paddle the whole lot of them.

"Now, you run to the restroom while I watch the yard. And get right back, so I can go, too," she finished.

"Thanks, Christine, I'll just be a minute," I sighed.

I made my way down the hall toward the faculty restroom. As I turned the corner, Mr. Davis emerged from his office. "Good morning, Mrs. Wright."

"Good morning, Mr. Davis," I began. "Could I talk to you for a minute?"

"Sure, I'm on my way to find the custodian. Walk with me," he replied. "What can I do for you?"

"Uh, I just found some students chewing gum in my class," I answered. "In fact, thirteen students admitted to chewing gum."

He stopped and turned to look at me, "Let's go back and get the paddle. You can use the nurse's room."

"Errr, you want me to paddle sixth graders for chewing gum?" I asked.

"Of course. They will never respect you unless you do. Now's a good time to start," he replied as we slipped into his cluttered office. He picked up a big wooden paddle from the top of a stack of file folders and handed it to me. A long, sturdy, flat piece of plain wood, it had rounded corners and one end cut in the shape of a handle.

"After recess you line them up in the hall, right here, and take them into the nurse's office, one by one. Ask Miss Lola to stand as your witness." With that, Mr. Davis walked out of his office. I stared at the paddle, wondering how Mr. Davis had acquired it and how often he used it.

I grew up at a time when parents and teachers spanked children for misbehavior. My own grandmother used an old buggy whip on my brother and me. I never had a teacher education class on discipline, although it always came up as a new teacher's concern, and it most certainly was mine. Mr. Davis and my fellow teachers insisted that paddling led to respect for the teacher and, therefore, good behavior in my classroom. But, somehow, it just didn't feel right for me to spank students. I'd never spanked anyone. Yet here, in this school, paddling seemed to hold the answer to everything. The worse the offense, the more swats with the paddle. Chewing gum had to come in at the bottom of the list. *Could I do one swat for gum chewing? Maybe.* I felt pressured to try.

After recess ended, I lined up my class, with the thirteen offenders at the front of the line. I marched them down the hallway to the nurse's office, as I had been instructed. Miss Lola, the office aide, stood in the doorway, watching. Ellie, the first in line, one of the brightest students in my class and one of the best behaved, walked into the room and looked at me with questioning eyes.

"Sorry, Ellie," I started. "Turn around and put your hands on the table."

Nothing I'd been taught prepared me for this moment. I took the paddle in my two hands and aimed at her bottom. I pulled it back like a baseball bat and swung forward.

. . . *Thunk.*

It was not much of a hit.

Ellie snickered.

I cleared my throat. She quieted.

"Now, don't chew gum again in class," I said aloud. She straightened up and tried to hide her grin as she left the room.

I took a deep breath, called in the next student and committed to the process. My swing with the paddle got stronger with each successive child until I packed a mighty fine wallop. It's a good thing the toughest boys in my class lined up last in line.

THHHWAAACK!

There were no chuckles at the end.

I felt miserable, disgusted with myself.

From that day forward, gum was no longer an issue in my class. However, paddling was never again a part of my classroom discipline plan, either. No matter what other teachers or principals said or did, I knew this practice did not suit me. I realized, if I set a consequence for behavior, I had to be willing to stand by it and follow through. I also knew there had to be better ways to gain the respect of my students than hitting them.

Chapter 6
Lice

Tall, blond, good-looking enough for the girls to take notice, he had the start of a mustache, unusual for a sixth grader. One morning Billy came to school with a booklet. Joe, Bobby, and Lisa clustered around his desk, passing it around and chatting with him until time to take their seats. I began to take attendance. Billy set the booklet down on top of his desk with what looked like a deliberate attempt to get my attention, which I ignored.

A few minutes later, when the class began working on their reading assignments, I walked down the aisles, checking on student work, and came to Billy's desk as he knew I would. No homework papers on his desk, as usual, but his reader lay open.

"Good morning, Billy. I'm glad you're here today," I said to him.

He picked up the booklet he'd brought and looked up at me. In a voice that cracked, he said, "Miz Wright, can I work on this today? I wanna' get my license."

I took the Department of Motor Vehicles booklet from his hand, flipped through a few pages, and then leaned over to whisper, "When will you turn sixteen, Billy?"

"In May, but it will take me a while to read all this," he said with a frown.

I thought about it for a moment. He seemed motivated.

"All right. You can work on it at the library today, Billy." I set the booklet back on the desk. "If you want to underline some of the hard words, I'll help you with them," I assured him. There were no "cool" books written at his low reading level, but I wanted to encourage him to read, so we'd start with the DMV booklet.

Billy had a pattern of absences; he never came to school more than two or three days in a row. Sometimes he spent a day at school, followed by two or three days absent. I wanted to contact his parents with my concern about his inconsistent attendance, but Miss Lola, the office aide, told me they didn't have a phone number listed. When I asked Billy about his absences, he told me his parents needed him to work on the farm and sometimes to take care of his younger brothers and sisters. He said his family lived with an uncle, but they moved around a lot. They didn't have a phone, and neither did the uncle.

Billy took the notes I wrote to his parents, but he never returned with a response, only a shrug of his shoulders. I suspected they, like their son, could not read or write well. I wondered what would become of this young man and what I could do to help him. *If only I had more time to work with him.*

"Hi, Miz Sutherland!" yelled Andrew from across the room, a smile of delight beaming from his face.

I looked up to see the art teacher/vice principal stepping through the doorway, her eyes searching the room. I walked away from Billy's desk and met her at the front of the room. "Welcome. What can we do for you?" I asked.

"I need to talk to your class for a few minutes," she replied, a serious look on her face.

"Of course, go right ahead."

"Hello, Andrew," she started with a smile meant just for him. Then, in a somber tone, she addressed the class. "Boys and girls, I have an important announcement." Within seconds, the kids got quiet, everyone focused on her. "Some students at our school have head lice."

"Ughhh . . . " reacted Sarah. Several other students in the class groaned.

Feeling the same way, I shuddered with revulsion about the announcement. I pasted a neutral expression on my face and watched to see how Miss Sutherland would handle the class as their chatter increased.

She continued, calm and quiet. The kids settled in to listen to her.

"There will be a paper about lice for you to take home to your parents this afternoon. It's very important you give it to them."

Ellie raised her hand with a look of concern on her face.

"Yes, Ellie?" said Miss Sutherland.

"Doesn't having lice mean you're not clean?" she asked, voicing my exact thoughts. I had never known anyone who had lice.

Miss Sutherland explained, "No, it often means someone who has lice might have shared a comb, a brush, or a hat with someone else. That's why we ask you not to share those things with each other at school."

"How do you know if you have lice?" asked Joe.

"Lice can make your head feel very itchy. That's what you usually notice first, having an itchy head."

My own scalp felt itchy; I noticed students scratching their heads.

"Larvae, the babies, look like small grains of white rice stuck to your hair, close to the scalp. Adult lice are harder to notice, and they can travel from one person to the next."

Sally raised her hand.

"Sally?" responded Miss Sutherland.

"My cousin had lice once, and she gave 'em to me and my little brother. My mama poured kerosene on our heads to get rid of 'em," Sally expounded.

I listened to her statement with shock. I thought of the fire hazard and the risk to my little Sally.

Miss Sutherland took it all in stride. "It's better to use Nix on your hair and a special, very fine-toothed comb to get really close to the scalp, because the lice larvae, called nits, stick tight to the hair there," she finished.

"My sister and me had to use one of those combs when we had lice," interjected Lydia. "It's hard to comb your hair with it, 'specially if it's long. My mama shaved our heads."

Shaved their heads? Oh my. I ran my hand down a fistful of my own long, sleek hair.

The class was atwitter when she left us, and I let it go for a while. Again, I caught myself reaching up and scratching my head. *Ewww, head lice!*

Later that day, I took my class to the library for their half hour of wandering around to find a book to check out. Managing their behavior, always a chore in the classroom, became even worse in this unstructured environment, under the nose of Mrs. Dumphrey, the elderly librarian. She perched on a stool behind the check-out desk with arms folded, peering at us over the top of her white-rimmed glasses attached to a beaded chain that hung around her neck, silently noting our invasion of her space. Sitting there in her prim and proper navy blue dress that was covered in tiny white polka dots and topped with a starched white collar held together with a cameo pin, her gray hair tightly pulled back into a bun, she seemed formidable. I worked up a smile and gave her a slight nod of my head.

Tense, I hoped this time I could contain my students long enough to allow those who chose books to check them out. Besides, I wanted to spend some time with Billy and his DMV booklet.

"Hey, Miz Wright, is there a book on lice in this library?" asked Ricky.

I put my finger up to my lips, indicating he needed to use a quiet voice.

Jeremiah gave him a shove and laughed, "Whatcha wanna read 'bout lice for, Redhead?"

"I just wanted to see what they look like," retorted Ricky, as he shoved back.

"Ricky, Jeremiah, stop shoving each other," I said, moving to stand between them. "You could look in the health and science section over on that far wall." I pointed. "Or, maybe you could use the encyclopedias."

Both boys ambled away in the direction I had pointed out, still shoving, laughing, and singing their usual chorus of "Joy to the World."

"Shhh!" came from several girls they passed.

Mrs. Dumphrey glanced over toward us with an audible, "*tssk, tssk.*" She pulled an embroidered white hankie from inside her sleeve to dab at her temples. Her pinched face showed her disapproval. She returned to stamping a row of white stickers . . . *bam, bam, bam.*

I noticed Billy seated at a table with his DMV booklet, a group of girls clustered around him, giggling.

"Billy's sweet on Lisa. Billy's sweet on Lisa," sang Lydia, using a loud stage whisper.

Billy's cheeks turned a slight pinkish hue.

"He is NOT!" Lisa retorted, just a bit too loud.

"Billy's sweet on Lisa," continued Lydia, rounding the corner of the table with Lisa in pursuit.

I walked to the table and said, "Girls, leave Billy alone. Why don't you go find a book to check out?" I didn't dare look back to see Mrs. Dumphrey. I knew we traveled on thin ice with her.

The girls moved a few tables away, heading toward the stacks, and I could hear Lisa's loud whisper, "Ha, ha! You don't know anything. Billy asked his cousin to marry him!"

By this time, Billy's cheeks were a bright red, but he kept his eyes glued to the motor vehicle code in front of him. The girls scurried off into a row of books, tittering, and whispering.

"How are you doing with the DMV booklet, Billy?" I said, leaning in toward him.

After a long pause, he responded, "I got some words underlined for you, Miz Wright."

"Okay, let's take a look at them," I replied.

BANG!

I jumped. A couple of girls screamed.

Scattered giggles followed the noise explosion. Then came the expected expulsion by the annoyed librarian, "All right, pack up your things to go. Your library time is OVER!"

Mrs. Dumphrey scurried out from behind her desk and bustled around the room, shooing students toward the exit. Her gray-haired bun had sprung a few straggling hairs that stuck out at odd angles. The white rimmed glasses, now hanging from the chain around her neck, swayed from side to side. Another gold-rimmed pair of glasses, precariously askew, stuck out on the top of her head. Students began to laugh out loud and dashed toward the door.

Standing behind the farthest table, Sarah, the bossiest of my girls, stood with her feet planted wide, hands on her hips staring down at a tipped over, wooden chair. She demanded, "Pick up that chair, Jeremiah."

"I didn't do it!" shouted Jeremiah, a few feet away, with both hands in the air and a huge grin on his face. "I didn't do it!"

"Just pick up the chair!" Sarah continued, tossing her hair back out of her eyes.

"*Library time is over! Line up in the hallway right now,*" bellowed Mrs. Dumphrey.

"Why don't we ever get to check out books, Miz Wright?" whined Bobby. "I want to finish this one on race cars." Bobby shoved the book onto the shelf, causing several others to tumble to the floor.

"Just go get in line," I said. Feeling frustrated, I bent down to pick up the books and straighten the shelf myself. I turned around to see the chair still lying on the floor, Jeremiah and Sarah nowhere in sight. I started to walk over to pick it up, but Andrew beat me to it and righted the offending noise maker.

"I's got it, Miz Wright," he said. "That boy, Ricky, he knocked it over when Jeremiah chased him."

"Thank you, Andrew. Let's go get in line now."

Before I could manage to get my students back to our room, Miss Sutherland, with Miss Lola in tow, emerged from the third-grade classroom across the hall from the library. They were followed by two other women I didn't recognize.

Miss Sutherland waded through the sea of rowdy sixth graders toward me.

"Your class is next on our list," she said. "We need to check them for lice. We'll follow you into your room," she explained.

Once we were all settled back in our classroom, Miss Sutherland handed me a stack of papers. "These are the notices to go home today."

Miss Lola captured my students' attention when she clunked two boxes of tongue depressors and a box of latex gloves on the corner of my teacher's desk. We watched as Miss Sutherland and one of the other ladies picked gloves out of the box, pulling them on each hand with a snap.

Miss Sutherland stood in front of the class and said, "We will be coming down the rows and checking for lice."

Miss Lola picked up a trash can and the box of tongue depressors. She followed Miss Sutherland to the start of the first row. Taking two tongue depressors from the box, Miss Sutherland used them to pick through Joe's curly brown hair. Then she pulled forward on his ears, searching behind each one. "Lice often like to settle in the warmth behind the ears," she explained. I ran my finger behind my own ear, as did most of my students.

She looked up from Joe, tossed the tongue depressors in the trash can, grabbed two more, and moved on to Sarah's desk. The other two women moved toward the other side of the classroom to begin the same process. Up and down the rows they went.

Miss Sutherland and the other women kept working through the class until the lice hunt was over. The last student's head examined, Miss Sutherland and her entourage made their way to the door at the front of the room, where I waited.

"All right, your turn," she said to me, looking straight into my eyes. "Bend forward, and I'll check your head."

She wants to examine my hair in front of all my students! What if I have lice?

I gulped and bent forward, letting my long straight hair dangle in front of me, as if bowing to my whole class. They were silent, watching, as Miss Sutherland picked through my hair. Wishing I could be anywhere but right there, on display, in front of my students, it never occurred to me to refuse or to ask for privacy. Too recently a student myself, I dared not question Miss Sutherland's authority as a vice principal.

She pulled on one of my ears, inspected slowly and thoroughly, and then pulled on my other ear and did the same. Finally, backing away from me, she tossed the tongue depressors in the waiting trash can and removed her latex gloves with a snap. I straightened up, trying to regain a semblance of being the teacher-in-charge, pulling my hair back, squaring my shoulders, and standing up as tall as I could.

The women placed the trash cans, now filled with discarded tongue depressors, back on the floor by my desk. They took a moment to confer with each other in whispers.

Holding us in suspense, Miss Sutherland turned to address the class, "We didn't find any lice in your class today." Looking at me she continued, "Mrs. Wright, you be sure to send those papers home with your students."

"Yes, yes, I will," I mumbled with relief.

The women exited and the class broke into animated conversations with each other. I knew I would struggle to get us all back on track for the rest of the afternoon.

The next morning, I stopped to talk with Mrs. Riley, the other sixth-grade teacher. She was a native Floridian, older than I by twenty years or more, not young enough to be caught up in the current fad of miniskirts, like me. The only teacher I saw every day, we did yard duty at the same time, and she clearly claimed to be my guide and mentor in all aspects of the "way things are done at our school."

"Darn! I had six kids sent home from school yesterday with lice," she began. "How many did you have?"

"Uhhh, none," I said, trying not to sound smug.

"Well, these things can spread like wildfire in a school, so keep your eye out. And, watch out for your own hair. Don't lean in too close to your students with that long hair of yours!" she warned.

I gulped. *Holy cow!* I noticed Mrs. Riley's hair, pulled back with bobby pins away from her face, and I tucked my own hair behind my ears. *Oh, but none of my students had lice yesterday; I'll be okay.*

I went out to greet the arriving students. The full force of energy in children becomes apparent the minute the buses round the corner and approach the school. When that first driver opens the door, exuberance spills out and engulfs those of us whose quiet morning has just been shattered.

"Stop singin' that song in my ear!"

"Get outta my way!"

"You forgot your books!"

"Hey, Miz Wright!"

Eager to try out my new plans for math today, worry about lice faded as I faced the lively mass of youth headed my way.

Muggy and quite warm by the time classes began, the day would get hotter and stuffier and more uncomfortable. How did anyone expect me to teach, or more importantly, expect my students to learn in this heat without air conditioning? Mrs. Riley told me the PTA wanted to purchase window units last year, but they only raised enough money to do a couple of rooms. They argued about which classes would be air conditioned first, so they never did it. At all. And we were hot.

Taking attendance, I scanned the rows of students. I stopped at Billy's empty seat. Disappointed but not surprised, I wouldn't worry about finding time to work on reading with him today.

Sometime later that morning, the classroom door burst open, and a woman I didn't recognize strode into the room. She wore a light green jacket and matching skirt with a white blouse, white hose, and white saddleback shoes. A white head band held her short, mousey brown hair away from her pale face. She scanned the room. Her eyes locked onto Sarah, the tallest, most mature-looking girl in my class, standing at the far corner of our classroom reading a math challenge card out loud to a small group. The woman marched through all the desks and students, straight past me, and up to Sarah. She said, "Hello, Mrs. Wright. I'm Mrs. Beale."

The class, seeing her very public mistake, broke into peals of laughter. Sarah giggled and pointed back to me, saying, "That's Mrs. Wright."

Mrs. Beale turned around to stare at me in utter surprise.

I tried to suppress my own amusement, ignored the laughter, and moved toward her saying, "I'm Mrs. Wright. May I help you?"

Students hushed each other as they strained to hear what she had to say.

"I'm Mrs. Beale. The district office sent me to help you check your students for lice," she explained.

"Again? We did this yesterday," I said.

"Yes, we need to do a recheck," she replied.

"Can it wait a few minutes? We're just finishing up our math activities," I said.

"All right then. I'll be back," she answered. She picked her way back through the crowded classroom and disappeared through the door.

Laughter erupted again, and I could no longer hide my own chuckles.

"She thought Sarah was the teacher!" cried Ricky.

"Boy, was she fooled."

"That lady walked right past you, Miz Wright," marveled Andrew.

"Sarah's our new teacher!" sang out Lydia.

With some difficulty, I managed to get my students to finish the math practice activities and then return to their seats to work on the day's assignment from the math textbook.

After we were settled, Mrs. Beale reappeared.

Without preamble she began, "I'll start on this side of the room, and you can do that side."

Me? She wants me to pick through my students' hair. Geesh!

Mrs. Beale set a small box on my desk and picked out a pair of chopsticks. "They ran out of tongue depressors and gloves yesterday, so these will have to do."

I watched her for a moment. She moved from one student to the next examining hair using the same pair of chopsticks.

Pausing, she shot a glare at me. Uncomfortable, but giving in, I picked out a pair of chopsticks and walked over to the first student in the front row.

We worked through the room, while students worked on their math assignments, and a low buzz of conversation continued to swirl around us.

After a while, the hubbub in the room increased. I became aware of Mrs. Beale escorting Bobby out of the classroom. I followed them.

In the hallway, Mrs. Beale asked Bobby, "Your twin brother's in Mrs. Riley's class?"

"Yes, ma'am," he replied.

"We sent him home yesterday because he had lice, right?"

"Yeah."

"And, do you sleep in the same bed as your brother?"

"Yeah."

"I'm afraid you need to go home, Bobby. You have lice, too. I'll be giving your mother a call. We need to get this infestation stopped."

She gave me an I-told-you-so smile and said, "Mrs. Wright, I'll be back when I'm finished with Bobby. You keep checking for lice."

Bobby glanced back over his shoulder toward me, as Mrs. Beale accompanied him down the hallway toward the office. I stared after them, running a finger behind each ear to tuck my hair back, again.

I walked back into the classroom. All eyes rested on me. A chorus of inquiries began.

"What happened?"

"Does Bobby have lice?"

"Is he going home?"

Bobby's younger brother and sister also went home that day. Mrs. Riley's class had a total of eight students out for lice. Bobby was the only student "officially" sent home from my classroom with lice.

Billy's desk sat behind Bobby's, but I never found out whether Billy had lice. He never came back to class again. Ever. I received no notice, no phone call, nothing. I wondered what happened to this young man who wanted to get his driver's license and maybe marry his cousin.

Chapter 7
Tornado

The day dawned hot. Baking hot. I wished, once more, for air conditioning, so I wouldn't have to work in such muggy, sweltering conditions. Most mornings I opened the bottom layer of windows in my classroom to catch the slight morning coolness and the top row to let the heat escape. By mid-morning, when I could feel the temperature rising, I closed the windows to hang onto the illusion of cool comfort. I didn't want to test my theory by actually measuring with a thermometer. Besides, I didn't have one. Today, the concrete floor seemed the sole possible source of cooling relief, so I left the windows closed.

I dug around in the back of my teacher's desk drawer to find the tacks I'd hidden from my students, and then I walked to the round table at the back corner of the room carrying a bag filled with materials I had made at home the night before. I replaced folded, damaged, and missing word cards with new ones, so the next group would have the complete, useable set.

Next, I unrolled the new poster I had created to reinforce some grammar rules. I looked at my last chart, still hanging on the bulletin board. Pencil scribbles and doodles covered the bottom six inches of it, the edge curled up, since, of course, all the lower tacks were missing. I wondered how long the new poster might stay clean and how long the tacks would last.

I pushed myself not to give up. When I first started teaching, I noticed the complete lack of resources or stimulating learning materials in this room filled with wall-to-wall desks and students. I figured I could work with small groups while the other kids stayed occupied with self-monitoring activities. I had set up learning stations for students to rotate through with film projectors, manipulatives for math, word cards and game boards, and direction posters I'd hand-printed in neat letters. During class I had spent so much time running from station to station trying to keep them working, I could not complete my small group lessons, and general chaos ensued. Within days, the kids had destroyed or "lost" all the materials in the stations. The "fun" learning centers had failed; I dismantled what little remained of them.

I had then called my university contacts for advice. They'd helped me reassign students to more appropriate reading groups, borrow "new" old textbooks at more ability-appropriate levels, and set up revised lessons plans. I had made a new start.

This morning, months later, I stared in frustration at the damaged poster and reading cards wondering why these kids demolished the things I made for them. Didn't it matter to them how hard I worked for their benefit?

On this hot May morning, I felt dispirited, discouraged, and a bit hopeless. I still spent almost every waking moment of every day, seven days a week, working on my job. I planned lessons, always trying to figure out how to make progress against seemingly impossible odds. I graded papers, tons of papers, and I never got to many stacks at all, leaving me feeling guilty, always trying to catch up. I invented my own activities to supplement the inadequate textbooks. I worried about doing enough for my students, only to be disappointed when I found scattered, half-finished papers left behind at the end of the day, or textbooks opened and carelessly spread out, upside down, on the floor, or writing on the desks, or pieces missing from my newest game creation. I struggled to keep an academic focus while most of my students dedicated themselves to amusement, often at my expense.

My low spirits came with exhaustion as the end of the school year approached. I wondered if my students even cared about their education. How could I teach, if they didn't want to learn?

I seldom saw any other teachers. We never had staff meetings. The principal never came into my classroom to check on me. I had little opportunity to discuss ideas or concerns with peers, except on rare occasions with Christine. Every single day, I went into my classroom, shut the door, and all by myself kept forty-three kids occupied and tried to teach them something. All day long. I taught all the subjects, except one period of art each week, when Miss Sutherland came into our room to do the "fun stuff." I didn't even get lunch breaks away from kids. I did all my preparation and evaluation of classwork at the ends of long, tiring, student-filled days.

Feeling sorry for myself, I railed against being stuck in my hot, sultry classroom without air conditioning. I was not having a good start to my day.

Usually after lunch recess, limp from the steamy heat of the playground, I would keep the lights turned off in the classroom and read aloud to my students, giving them, and me, time to cool off and refocus on academic endeavors. This became the one activity during the day that might capture their attention. Maybe they thought it got them out of work, or maybe they just liked to hear me read to them. I guessed that few adults ever read aloud to most of these kids. I figured it could improve their vocabulary and strengthen their language skills, and it grew into a shared experience I could build upon. Besides, I loved reading aloud.

This day, however, a different lunch period unfolded. Especially hot, the air seemed quite still when lunch began. After eating in the cafeteria, I led all the children out to the playground while Mrs. Riley stayed to shoo the last few students on their way. I walked out to the far side of the field, aiming for the shadows of the magnolia trees. Mrs. Riley emerged and took up her post on the other side, closer to the school, but also in the shade. In fact, most of the kids scattered into every available shady spot ringing the empty dirt playground area.

After about ten minutes, I noticed the shadows begin to blur. I looked up to see a pewter sky dimming the sunlight. I watched with fascination as the darkening progressed, an extraordinary and unnerving transformation, in the middle of the day.

I noticed Miss Lola step outside the building, scan the field, and walk over to Mrs. Riley. They talked for a brief moment and then looked over at me. Miss Lola retreated, and Mrs. Riley turned and walked across the center of the dirt field toward me, a troubled look on her face. I met her part way. She looked up at the sky and then said to me, "There's a tornado warning. We better get these kids inside."

I knew what a tornado was, of course; I'd seen The Wizard of Oz. However, this "California Girl" knew little else about them. Earthquakes I could do, but I had never prepared for an emergency like this. Given no other instructions, except to take the children inside, I could see the gray sky becoming blacker by the moment, and it began to frighten me.

Mrs. Riley blew her whistle and then yelled at students to come in. I followed her lead and skirted around the playground, waving with my hands to direct the children into the building. Some dallied, loathe to leave the shelter of the trees, but not many complained about going inside before the bell rang.

"Looks like it's gonna hail any minute," commented Ellie.

"Hail?" I said.

"Tornado weather, Miz Wright," responded Lydia. "You watch that sky. If it turns green after a while, then we in big trouble. I seen it before like this."

Mrs. Riley and I herded all the children into the classrooms and shut our doors. They sat down at their desks, glancing out the windows behind them, nervous, talking to each other. I picked up our current class novel, Old Yeller. The next chapter featured the dog saving Travis from a bunch of wild hogs, a good one to keep their attention. So, without resistance from any of my more vocal students, I began to read aloud.

Although eerie and dark, I could just manage to see the print in the book, so I left the lights off. With some surprise, I realized the temperature felt cooler than fifteen minutes before. Deathly still outside, a few of my students continued to stare out the windows at the sky, while I drew others into the story as I read. Some kids appeared agitated; they drummed on a desk or picked at fingernails. I felt uneasy too, but I kept reading, trying not to let worry show in my voice.

All of a sudden, a strong dust-filled breeze picked up. The wind rattled the windows. I paused. In the back of the room, closest to the windows, Sarah began to moan. With the next gust, the windows clattered. We could see the wind picking up in strength. I could also see the fear etched on Sarah's face. Her moaning began to escalate into a loud wailing and several others began to make mewling, crying sounds, like the whimpering of fearful dogs.

Just as their volume began to ratchet up, I put the book down with a loud *bang* that startled them. Something switched on in my brain. I buried my own fear.

"Sarah, stop that crying right now!" I demanded.

"I'm scared," she sniveled.

"We're going to be all right. I know exactly what to do. We'll follow scientific principles. We need to equalize the air pressure between the inside and the outside. Sarah, stand up and get the windows open behind you. Steve, Jeremiah, Sally, go help her open the rest of the lower windows. Do it quickly. Theo, get the pole and start opening the upper windows. Linda May, you help him with that. Darrel, you go open our door."

The wind rattled the windows again with another cloud of swirling dust. The students jumped up to do as I asked.

"Now, those of you in the back three rows, come sit on the floor at the front of the room near me. We will be just fine. Opening the windows will reduce that pressure differential, and if the wind gets any worse, we will move out into the shelter of the hallway." I said it with such authority, I surprised even myself into believing it.

"Just stop the crying and the noise, sit up, and look at me. We'll get through this all right."

Students settled in close to me, away from the opened windows. The sky had turned an unnerving, blackish gray. Dust swirls continued to pick up, and the windows banged. Fully alert to the tempest outside and my children crowded in near me, I decided to continue reading for a while.

"Now let's find out how Travis manages his own scary situation with a pack of wild hogs," and I began to read again, transporting us into the world of Old Yeller.

I read that whole chapter aloud and then continued on to the next one. My students remained concerned, but calm and very quiet. The wind increased for a while, and I read just a bit louder. We got caught up in the story, and before we knew it, the wind subsided.

When the sky began to lighten, at long last, we returned to our regular schoolwork.

I sent them all home at the end of a long, distracted afternoon. When the last student hopped on the bus, I returned to my classroom. Alone, I sat down at my desk and let the tears of pent-up tension flow. I had made up the ploy about the science of air pressure to keep my students calm. I kept them close to me and did my best to keep their attention by reading with all the drama I could muster, but the tornado warning had really scared me, and I had no idea what I should have done in that situation. I needed to find out.

Later that evening, I learned that a tornado actually did touch down, less than half a mile from our school.

Chapter 8
Black and White

Many of my students didn't have a television in their house. Those who did might own one black and white TV set up for viewing in the main living area. So, I figured movies would be a special treat.

When I managed to squeeze in the time, I took a couple of hours to figure out the process for ordering films from the county Audio Visual department and sent in my requests for movies on weather and tornadoes to supplement the meager science education I could give my students.

Most teachers ordered all their films at the beginning of the school year, and there was often a long waiting list for movies. Since I had been hired in the middle of the year, my film orders came late, after all the other requests. Besides, if a teacher forgot to return a movie on time, it threw off the whole schedule.

The final weeks of school bore down upon us before Miss Lola carried them into our room: two round film canisters, one large blue tin about twelve inches in diameter and one smaller, silver gray tin about half that size. The kids cheered.

"When do we get to see 'em, Miz Wright?" yelled Andrew.

"Yeah, can we see 'em today?" asked Lydia.

I acknowledged their enthusiasm with a smile. "You remember the tornado we had a few weeks ago? Well, I have here, in the big can, a new, color movie about weather, including tornadoes. The smaller one is a bit older, a black and white film, just about tornadoes. As soon as I can reserve a time to use the school movie projector, we'll see them."

"Awww . . . I want to see 'em right now, Miz Wright," said Andrew, voicing the thoughts of the whole group.

Darrel put one foot on the bus step and turned back to holler to me, "Don't forget to sign up for the movie projector, Miz Wright!"

"I'm going right now, Darrel. See you on Monday!" I waved as the door closed and the bus pulled away. Then I made my way straight to the school office to find the projector sign-up sheet. I wrote my name on the only slot available, next Thursday afternoon.

I returned to my classroom and sat down at my desk. I penciled the movies into my plan book. At the end of another busy, long week, before I could work on the rest of my lesson plans, I needed to finish and turn in my transportation report, a requirement of the mandated busing for integration which had gone into effect the year before I started teaching in Florida.

Coming from all white schools and neighborhoods myself, I noticed the colors of faces when I first stepped into this classroom a few months ago, but as the days passed, the students became individuals with all of their own special characteristics. Skin color became the last of my concerns. Quite literally. Every week I had to record a count of how many black students and how many white students rode the bus during the week. At first, I had trouble with that task because I worked on it after they all went home. I had to remember who rode the bus and who didn't. I also had to know what race each student appeared to be. I would stare at the name in the list and try to visualize the student to determine what color to count. Black or white? I knew my students, but I had a hard time seeing them divided into races. I solved that issue one day by writing a B or a W beside each student's name. That made it easy. Black and white.

Once, in all those months, skin color raised up as an issue between a student and me. One day I made Darrel go to the end of the lunch line. As I started to walk away, I heard Darrel protest to another student, "She made me move to the back 'cuz I'm black." I stopped in my tracks, turned around, and walked back to him. I thought of the hateful signs I'd seen: the "Colored Entrance" to the theater in downtown Milton with an arrow pointed up the outside stairs to the stifling balcony and the "Whites Only" sign on the water fountain at the Memphis zoo. Neither sign seemed to be enforced at the time I saw them, but remained in place as degrading reminders of the near past and current underlying prejudice and undisguised injustice to a whole race of people.

"Darrel, I sent you to the end of the line because you shoved Tara out of the way at the front of the line. I will not tolerate pushing and shoving." He hung his head, scowling and still mumbling.

On an impulse, I held out my arm in front of his face.

"Darrel, look at my arm. Do you see that? I have both colors on my skin, black and white. I have freckles. I do not judge anyone on the color of skin." I walked away, in my naïve insensitivity, thinking I had made an important point with him.

Several days later, I heard Darrel, once again perturbed by something I'd done, mutter, "Ol' Freckle Face!" It was the first "bad" name I'd heard a student call me.

Since the end of the school year fast approached us, I had one other big question on my mind. My sixth graders were heading off to seventh grade at the junior high school. I needed to decide if any of my students would be retained, to repeat this grade level, a common practice of that time and place.

I walked across the hallway to seek advice from Mrs. Riley.

"Christine, you retaining anyone this year?" I started.

"Nope. Not this year. I had concerns about Barry, but I think he pulled himself up enough to go on," she replied.

"I'm not sure what to do about my students. None of them have reached grade level, particularly in math. The teacher before me just didn't teach it, and she didn't make much progress with reading either. I couldn't catch them up in the few months I had them," I said.

"You know you replaced Miss May, a colored teacher who came from a colored school, right? Those colored teachers just didn't get the education we whites did, and it became quite apparent once we integrated the schools last year," Mrs. Riley responded.

I almost winced at the disparaging tone in her voice.

"No one ever told me much about the previous teacher. I did learn that the parents of my students had concerns about the apparent lack of discipline in the classroom. I didn't know the teacher was black." I paused a moment, wondering why I didn't know this about the previous teacher. I never thought to ask, and no one ever brought up the subject of her race.

"Yeah, and she got another job right away, as soon as she left here. Staffs were desperate to integrate. I heard she got a job working in a detention class at East Pensacola Middle School."

"No kidding? I know that class. I worked with them twice a week for a month, as part of my Master's Degree program. Tough kids. Miss May got a full-time job there? That's a surprise, considering her supposed issues with discipline here."

"Yeah. Unreal, but predictable because she's black."

Uncomfortable, but not sure how to respond, I ignored the racist undertone in her remark. I changed the subject instead.

"So, I don't know what to do about my students and retention. They can't all repeat sixth grade, just to catch up. And then there's Andrew, who will never be on grade level, no matter how many years he's retained. I'm thinking I might pass all of them," I said.

"Yup. Let the next grade level teachers take care of bringing them along. It's not your fault they got so far behind."

"I guess I'll go talk with Mr. Davis," I answered, not having a lot of confidence in his advice, but feeling guilty about my lack of success with these kids.

"Just tell him not to put any extra students in *my* class next year! The incoming classes are big again, and I'm out of desks," she said. "Hey, do you know what you're doing next year? Will you be coming back here?"

"I don't know yet. I received a pink slip in May, like all the other probationary teachers. None of us will be hired back until later in the summer if they do hire us. Besides, my husband should be getting new orders soon, so I'm not even sure where we'll be."

"Yeah, I've seen a lot of Navy wives come and go. Good luck."

"Thanks, Christine."

The following week, busy with end-of-school chores, I did make an appointment with Mr. Davis to discuss passing all my students to the next grade level. He agreed, readily. He seemed relieved to send this particular group of kids on to the next school. I just felt defeated.

At last, Thursday afternoon arrived. Cheers again greeted Miss Lola when she opened the classroom door. She rolled in the movie projector and parked it in the front of the room. In a few minutes, she returned with the movie screen.

"Miss Lola, can you show me how to open and set up this screen before you go?" I asked.

She answered me in her relaxed drawl, "I just deliver it. I don't know how to work it."

"I know how to do it, Miz Wright," called out Jeremiah. "I used to do it all the time for my old teacher."

"Jeremiah the bullfrog!" chorused a handful of students.

"Okay. Thanks, Jeremiah. We'll figure it out together. Thank you, Miss Lola, for bringing it to us."

As one of the requirements for becoming a teacher in the 1970's, we learned to manage audio visual equipment, including threading and running a movie projector. However, it had been months since I last did it. I knew I could manage. Most machines have numbers to make sure you thread the film through each gizmo it needs to contact. If you skip one, it doesn't work right and you might split the film and have to tape it back together. It's important to engage the sprocket feet precisely in the holes along the edges of the film. Then, I could turn the light bulb switch and start the movie rolling. Once the lightbulb gets heated, I had to remember not to move the machine until it cooled down or the filaments in the bulb would break. It took days, or weeks, to order and receive an expensive replacement bulb.

When I managed to get the movie ready to roll, we settled in to watch. I had first chosen the shorter black and white film, just to make sure I could do everything right with the projector. As soon as I turned off the lights in the classroom, all eyes were glued to the movie. The narrator, a stern looking older white man wearing a white lab coat, sat at a science lab table, surrounded by beakers and "science stuff." His voice droned on and on, but the shots of the tornadoes kept our interest. The movie lasted twelve minutes, and students clapped at The End.

Next came the task of rewinding the film before putting it back in the film canister. Not sure what to do with this machine, I found the reverse button and turned it on.

Whoops! I made a mistake. I should have let the film run all the way out, raise the reel arms, and then threaded the two reels directly to each other. Instead, the movie began to run backwards, and the speech came out garbled.

Laughter erupted.

I turned off the machine.

"Aw, cain't we just watch it backwards, Miz Wright?" asked Bobby.

"Yeah, please, Miz Wright, please!" begged Ricky.

"PLEASE, PLEASE," the chorus of voices began.

I thought about it for a few seconds, and then turned the reverse knob again to applause from the kids. They hooted with laughter as the twisters untwisted and buildings un-blew apart. They mimicked with mirth the garbled sounds of the stuffy old scientist speaking backwards. We simply enjoyed the entertainment of it all. We shared twelve minutes of laughter and unplanned frivolity, not quite educational, but so very welcome.

I went home that evening feeling happy and connected with my black and white students through a silly black and white movie run backwards.

Later that night, my husband called to tell me he received his new orders to report to the naval base in Norfolk, Virginia just three days after school finished for me. We would have to get packed and ready to travel in a hurry. I would not be returning to this school.

Chapter 9
Joy to the World

The final bell rang, ending the school year. An exuberant bunch of kids joyfully departed for summer vacation. They streamed out of classrooms in a raucous mass with shouts of farewell.

"Good-bye, Bobby."

"Bye!"

"Bye, Darrel."

"Bye, Miz Wright!"

"Good-bye, Lydia."

"Byyyyyeeeee!!!!"

"Have a good summer, Andrew."

"Gonna see my cousins, Miz Wright!"

"Good-bye, Sarah."

"Good-bye, Mrs. Wright."

"Ricky and Jeremiah, you're always together! You two keep watching out for each other next year in junior high."

"GOOD-BYE, MIZ WRIGHT!"

"Good-bye . . ."

The room emptied, leaving me alone, staring at the wall-to-wall, mismatched, well-used, vacant desks. Silence descended. I took a deep breath, looking around the dingy, barren room.

I walked to the back table to stack books, smiling, and singing to myself the song that would always remind me of these students, Joy to the World. The bullfrog version, of course.

Relief! I would use the summer to move, settle into a new home, take a much-needed rest, and find a new job. Ready to start a clean new chapter in my teaching adventures, I continued to sing.

I'd miss these kids. After four months, I knew them, each and every single one, but I would never know what happened in their lives after that day. They would remain forever unchanged, etched into my memories, clearly evoked whenever I heard that song. This brief, intense time, our shared experiences, formed the very foundation of my life's work, and I wondered if I would ever be a truly good teacher.

A Fresh Start

Norfolk, Virginia
September 1972 – June 1973

Chapter 10
Perfect

The bees were flawless. Meticulously drawn, cut out of file folders, and colored in detail with felt tipped markers, each bee bore a student name, precisely lettered, across the black and yellow striped body. My husband and I had spent far too much time creating these works of art I called "name-bees," but I wanted to greet my students with colorful signs of their importance to me. Filled with hope, I envisioned the perfect beginning, starting out with my very own class from day one. Today I'd staple the "name-bees" onto the bulletin board to be ready for tomorrow, the first day of school.

Since my husband had taken our car to the Navy base at Virginia Beach to stand his watch in the middle of the night, I rode on public transportation to the school. I had studied the bus schedule and planned my arrival early enough to get some work done before the staff meeting. However, the ride into downtown Norfolk from our new apartment on Chesapeake Bay crawled along. The bus stopped, yet again, to pick up and drop off passengers. I shifted the paper grocery bags holding my books and the precious bees to check my watch. 8:50. My concern level raised. No time to go to my classroom. I didn't want to be late for the 9:00 staff meeting on this first official workday.

I'd met with the principal for orientation just the day before. He escorted me and the other two new teachers around the building and showed us our respective classrooms.

Lucky for me, the walls in my room should be completely painted by sometime today. I hope I can work around the painters this morning and get it all ready for students.

Other classrooms would be painted in the coming days and weeks.

I wonder why they didn't paint when the school was out for summer break. Why are they disrupting instructional time instead?

Two classes at a time had to be housed temporarily in the library, difficult for them, but also inconvenient for the rest of us, since the library would be closed.

The bus stopped again. An old woman with two large grocery bags struggled to climb the steps into the bus. "Let me help you with those, Minnie," said the bus driver as he got up to assist her. He placed her bags on the front seat, and she dug around in her purse searching for the bus fare on unsteady feet. Time ticked on.

We arrived at the bus stop near school at 9:00 on the dot. I still had a couple of blocks to walk, or rather, run.

How embarrassing to be the tardy new teacher! Maybe it will take a couple of minutes for the staff to settle in. Can I slip in without notice?

I bounded up the front steps of the school, burst through the front door, and raced down the quiet hallway to the library. I stopped short of the open door and caught my breath for a few seconds before stepping inside at the back of the room.

Dick Green, the principal, paused mid-sentence. Looking straight at me, he said, "Well, it's about time you joined us."

All heads turned to stare at me. My face felt hot, and I stammered, "...Uh, I'm s...so sorry to be late. The b...bus was late getting here."

"Well, find a seat and sit down," he replied in a stern tone. "Staff, this is the last of the new teachers, Mrs. Wright."

Some nodded in my direction, but I didn't notice many smiles of welcome.

Without much hesitation, Mr. Green continued with what he had been saying before I interrupted him. The meeting appeared to be well underway. Confused, I checked my watch again? It read only a few minutes past 9:00, late, but not *that* late.

I saw Nancy and Maria, the other two new teachers, beckoning me to an empty seat next to them. I tried to keep my bags quiet and made my way through the last couple of rows of people-filled chairs. "Excuse me," I whispered as I stepped over a purse and nearly knocked a coffee cup onto the floor.

I reached the relative security of the empty seat and plopped myself down, settling the bags around my feet. Mr. Green paused briefly, giving me a steady look before continuing once again.

I endeavored to focus on his words over the thudding rhythm of my heart. Sweating profusely in the early morning heat after the exertion of running from the bus, I unbuttoned my little cotton jacket and slid out of the sleeves in slow motion, trying not to draw any further attention to myself. At last, free of encumbrances, I could sit still, hoping the sweat stains on my sleeveless blouse weren't terribly obvious.

Nancy leaned over and slipped me some papers. "I got these for you," she whispered.

An agenda sat on top of the stack. Mr. Green was talking about the P.E. schedule, several items down on the list. I kept thinking about the time. *How could I have been so far off on my calculations and end up being so very late?* Hard to pay attention, I dwelled on the scolding by my new principal. In front of the entire staff.

Two hours later, when the staff meeting ended, I still felt frustrated at having missed so much in the beginning. The other two new teachers and I walked up the wide wooden stairs at the end of the hallway together, reviewing all the procedures for the start of school.

At last, I asked, "What time did this staff meeting start anyway?"

Nancy replied, "8:30."

"What? Didn't he tell us to be here at 9:00 for the staff meeting?"

"Yes, he did," she said with eyebrows raised.

"I specifically asked him what time the meeting started, didn't I? In fact, he repeated it twice!" I shot back. "How did you two manage to get here on time?"

"I just got lucky. I came really early to work on my room and saw some of the other teachers in the hall. They told me to come along with them to the meeting. Maria arrived fifteen minutes later."

"Did Mr. Green get on you for being late, Maria?"

"Yes, so embarrassing!"

"I hate being late. My bus took forever to get here! I worried I'd be a few minutes late and then I discovered I'm half an hour late? And, that principal! Good grief! Could he have embarrassed me more?" I fumed.

"I guess the only thing to do now is get to work in our classrooms and get ready for tomorrow. Are we even sure what time the school day actually starts? Is it at 8:35?"

"Yeah, it's written on the schedule he handed out at the beginning of the meeting. It's on one of those papers I gave you," Nancy answered.

"Thanks, Nancy."

The smell of fresh paint overwhelmed our senses and reminded us of major concerns ahead. We had to get our rooms ready for the opening of school amidst the crew of painters and wet paint on the walls.

The fifth and sixth grades occupied the second floor of the old two-story brick building in inner-city Norfolk, Virginia. Metal radiators dotted the halls. I wondered how effective the ancient heating system would be when the days turned cold. At the top of the stairs, Maria turned to the right while Nancy and I continued straight down the hallway toward our classrooms. When we reached Nancy's room, we could see that painters had not started there yet. I left Nancy to get settled and walked to the next door, the farthest corner of the building . . . to *my* room.

Drop cloths covered all the student desks crammed into one corner. Alone in the room I basked in the bright, cheery, new coat of pale-yellow paint, sun streaming through the bank of paneled windows on one side of the room. The view looked out into the branches of beautiful old trees that lined the street below. Paint fumes assaulted my nose, so I put my bags down beside the teacher's desk and walked over to the windows to see if I could open them. I touched the wood sash on the first window, noting the dried paint. I muscled the window up as far as I could reach and continued down the row, opening those I could manage, hoping to get some air circulation to dilute the smell.

I turned to survey the room. Apparently, the painters had finished, but it would take a lot of work to unstack the chairs and desks and move them into place.

Should I start with an arrangement of double columns of student desks or connected rows with a center aisle? The teacher's desk could sit at a diagonal in the front corner, away from the entry door.

School starts tomorrow, daunting, but thrilling to start a brand-new year with my own class. Best of all, I've only got twenty-six kids! This will be so much easier than the forty-three students I taught last year in Florida. I can be a real teacher this year.

I walked over to the shrouded teacher's desk and pulled off the paint tarp, setting it in a pile on the floor. I found the teacher's chair and dragged it over to the desk. I would deal with the student desks later. To start, I needed to organize my work space, take care of the paperwork handed out by the principal, find the student textbooks to distribute, and finish my lesson plans. Besides, I had those wonderful bees with all the student names to pin up on the bulletin board.

On the far side of the room, adjacent to the wall of windows, sat a built-in set of cabinets beneath the huge bulletin board wall, perfect for the welcoming bee display. Directly across the room from the windows a black chalkboard dominated the wall, but the yellow paint cheered up the rest of the room. That reminded me, I needed to find chalk, erasers, tacks, and all the other necessary supplies. On the fourth wall, to the left of the entry door, two open doorways flanked a bulletin board.

I walked into the first opening. The wooden floor creaked beneath my feet. I found myself in an old fashioned, wood paneled cloakroom that ran the length of that side of the room and opened out at the other doorway. There on the floor, beneath the long rows of hooks for student jackets, sat stacks of textbooks.

Good. One less thing to worry about.

A tall cabinet protruded from the middle of the wall, a closet for the teacher, a place to put my own coat. I opened it, breathed in the musty smell, and imagined the parade of teachers before me who had hung their own coats here, each a part of a proud educational history.

I walked back into the classroom, sat down at the teacher's desk, and began to open drawers. Each one was empty; I needed supplies. Remembering a supply closet we'd seen during the tour Mr. Green had given us, I walked next door to see Nancy. She was stacking textbooks on her students' desks.

"Oh, you put your desks in traditional rows," I said.

"We have to move out of our room for painting next week, so it's just easy to start the way they were when I walked in here yesterday. I won't even put up my bulletin boards until we move back."

"Gee, that's a pain! Hey, did you get your supplies yet?" I asked.

"Yes," she replied. "That's the first thing I did this morning, but I need a few more things on my list. Are you going to get yours now?"

"Yeah. Can you show me where that closet is?"

"Sure. Let's go."

We walked down the wide hallway, back toward the stairs, until we came to large wooden door. I saw no label to indicate its purpose, but Nancy turned the handle and opened it saying, "It's usually locked."

Inside I found a bountiful supply of everything I needed, so unlike the last school where I scrounged for the simplest of supplies. "Is there a check-out system or a limit to what we can take?" I asked.

"Selma, who teaches across the hall here, just told me to help myself to whatever I needed," Nancy replied as she started loading up with pencils and crayons.

"Wow."

After several more trips to the supply closet, I had everything I thought I'd need to start the school year and my desk drawers were neatly organized. I opened a package of large, light green construction paper and pulled out a single sheet. I placed it in the center of the top of my desk to brighten up the space and to use as a desk pad. On top of that, I set my brand-new teacher's lesson planning book. I opened the planner to the first page and wrote my name. Then I wrote the school year, 1972-1973 on the appropriate lines. I turned to the next page. The first blank week stared at me. I imagined filling each white square in this book with my plans. This whole year would be mine to create and orchestrate. I reached down into my bag and pulled out all the papers we had been given at the staff meeting, searching for the daily bell schedule. I decided to write the times in the margin of the pages for the first week. I began to envision how that first day would unfold with students.

The crackling sound of the loudspeaker in the classroom broke my reverie. "Lunch will be served by the PTA in the lunchroom in 10 minutes." I glanced at my watch, amazed how quickly time had passed and thought about how much more work I had to do to be ready for the morning.

Maybe I should skip lunch. But . . . I need to eat, and the Parent Teacher Association is serving lunch to us. I have a long list of things to do, but I don't want to miss this.

I decided to take the long way around the upper floor, turning to my left as I exited the room. At the end of this hallway, I saw an open classroom door and a teacher standing by her desk. A big boned, middle-aged woman wore a pleated, light green skirt and a white, long-sleeved blouse with a broad collar and soft bow at the neck. White high heels coordinated with the impeccable ensemble and her meticulously coiffed blonde hair.

She saw me coming and greeted me warmly, "Welcome to J.E.B. Stuart School. It's Jan, right? I'm Mrs. Carpenter, but you may call me Ann. I'm the sixth-grade level chairman. If you need anything, just let me know."

I surveyed her room from the doorway. My heart sank. *Her* desks were perfectly ordered in rows, a set of matched textbooks neatly placed in the center of each student desk. All the bulletin boards were covered with appropriate posters and lettering for the curriculum. Shelf sets appeared well stocked with books and additional supplies. Her teacher's desk, squarely centered at the front of the room, looked professional and neat; a red ceramic apple graced the corner.

The entire room looks perfect and ready for students.

"Come along to lunch now, and let me introduce you to the rest of the sixth-grade team," she commanded. I gaped in awe of her, the perfect teacher, ready for the perfect first day of school.

She took me into the lunchroom and held court over the sixth-grade team, introducing me as promised. Parents had provided us with a scrumptious spread of food, complete with decorations. The welcoming attitude warmed my heart. Most teachers seemed relaxed and enjoyed reconnecting with each other, catching up on summer vacation experiences. However, I felt uncomfortable, wanting to eat and get back to my classroom and all the work ahead of me. I noted Nancy hadn't come for lunch. Although Maria came in to eat with us, she left early. When it seemed appropriate, I too slipped out, almost running to get back upstairs.

The tarps were missing when I returned to my classroom, but I never saw the painters. I worked late into that evening. At last, my husband came to school to pick me up. He helped me move the desks, and then we stapled the bees onto the bulletin board. By that time, well familiar with each student's name, I felt eager to connect with the real live sixth graders.

"Maybe we should move those two bees a little more to the left," I directed for the umpteenth time.

"The bees are looking good, Jan. Maybe it's time to quit. We need to go home. You need to eat some dinner and get some sleep. You know, it will all work out okay tomorrow," my gentle husband urged.

"I just need to sharpen pencils and put one on each desk."

"I'll sharpen them. Why don't you get your things ready to go?"

I talked about school and what I planned to do with my students all the way home and through our late dinner. The details kept turning over in my head, until I finally fell asleep.

I'm quite certain Ann, "Mrs. Perfect Teacher," slept soundly and didn't have the nightmare I had that night.

The Nightmare

Desks in regimented rows.
Unsmiling faces staring at me.
Gray, everything gray.
Not ready.
Struggle to explain.
Useless assignments.
They're bored.
Won't follow directions.
Not paying attention.
Words dry up and stick in my throat.
Not enough planned to fill the whole day.
Can't think of anything to say.
Out of control.
Don't want to be here.
Caught in a trap.
Failing.

The dream repeated itself, with a few variations, every year of my entire career on the night before school started. The nightmare caused my habit of over-planning for those first days, making long lists of activities I didn't really need. It never mattered that I always came home exhausted, but thrilled by the way the real first day had gone. Unfailingly excited, hopeful, and confident for the year ahead, I remained in awe of my new students. I never ran out of words. And, I always had leftover activity plans I could use during the rest of the week. However, the annual nightmare persisted, keeping me humble in my quest to be the perfect teacher, prepared for the perfect first day of school.

Chapter 11
The Name Game

I wore my new polyester dress. It had short sleeves and an empire waist, white on the top and purple on the lower part, the conservative hem coming just above my knees. Nude-colored panty hose covered my legs. On my feet I sported stylish, black leather clogs. Long, straight hair hung past my shoulders. I pictured myself as an elegant young teacher, even in the era of miniskirts and hippies. I wanted to impress my new students.

We had been instructed to claim our students out in the yard after the bell rang. The P.E. teacher, Mr. Smith, would make all the kids line up on their classroom number. I arrived early.

When that first bell rang, the entire playground of loud, rowdy children stopped and froze silently in place. Those new to the school figured it out quickly. At the sound of Mr. Smith's whistle, they moved *en masse* to form lines behind the painted numbers on the asphalt. Such an impressive sight to watch!

When I stopped at number 25, smiles and delighted giggles greeted me from the girls at the front of the line, all dressed in their new clothes for the beginning of school. Most of the boys clustered at the back of the line, yet I could see their curious stares checking me out with a few nods of approval. Closer in age to them than the older, veteran teachers, I hoped my youth gave me an advantage in their eyes.

"Good morning, sixth graders! I'm Mrs. Wright. Please follow me."

I lead the chatty group into the building and up the stairway amidst a sea of students and their teachers heading in the same direction. The heightened energy that comes with the first day of the school year buzzed in the stairwell. Sixth graders, quite literally at the top of the elementary school pinnacle, had a swagger about them. Unwritten privileges came with the exalted position of being the oldest students in the building, and they knew it.

When we reached our classroom, I stood just inside the door, welcoming students.

"Where do we sit?" asked several of them.

"You may choose anywhere you'd like to sit today," I responded.

"Really?"

"Groovy!"

"Smells like new paint in here."

"Look, my name is on one of those bees!"

"Mine too!"

I hoped I could live up to their expectations . . . and my own. Starting over from the beginning, setting my own tone, maybe I'd be a better teacher.

The hallway emptied, and classroom doors began to shut. A straggling group of boys ambled down the hall toward my room. One older-looking boy lagged behind all the others. I'd have to work to win these students over as they reluctantly gave up their summer freedom to enter the structure of academia for the coming year.

The last boy took his time to walk to the back row and slumped into the far corner desk. I would take particular note of *his* name when I called attendance.

"I'm Mrs. Wright, and I'll be your teacher this year," I said with professional pride.

"By the end of this day, I will know your names," I promised. "I need to take attendance first. Please raise your hand and say 'Here' when I call your name. While I'm doing that, I'd like you to write your name inside the front cover of each of the textbooks on your desk. Okay, let's get started. Mayhew Albright . . ."

At last, I found him. William. I called the name three times. I followed the furtive glances of several students to locate him sitting in the far corner desk. Hunched down, staring at the stack of books in front of him on the graffiti-carved desk surface, he wore a clean, threadbare plaid shirt. My heart went out to him. He motioned ever-so-slightly with his hand, never giving me eye contact. I didn't know his story yet, but I knew I wanted to find the boy beneath the surface I could see. I moved on to the next name on the list.

Finished with attendance, I told them they could put their books away inside their desks. Noise filled the room. Desk lids squeaked, screeched, and groaned as they went up. Students talked to each other, and books clattered into the metal desks.

An announcement by the principal began on the loudspeaker. To my shock, many of the students did not stop to listen. They ignored the announcement and kept talking and putting their things away.

"It's time to shut the lid of your desk and listen," I said in a loud voice. The principal rambled on with his welcome speech. After a few more squeaks, bangs, and comments, the class settled down.

At last, the principal said, "Teachers, send a student with your attendance folder to the office now."

Hands shot up and several clamored for my attention, "Me! Can I do it?"

I handed the folder to the student closest to the door. He wore a buttoned-down, pale-yellow shirt that had a freshly ironed look to it. He had stuck a large black pick into the top of his impeccably shaped Afro. An infectious smile lit up his ebony face, and his eyes glinted with a hint of mischief.

"Tell me your name again," I said.

"Esaias"

"E-says?" I repeated.

"Yeah, Esaias. My mama named me after somebody in the Bible."

Snickers of laughter came from some of the boys in the back of the room. I searched my mind, but could find no name I knew like that from the Bible. Isaiah?

"All right, Esaias. Do you know where the office is?"

Someone said, just loud enough for me to hear, "He sure do know where the principal's office is!" Laughter erupted from the boys in the back of the room.

I gave them a stern look, and they quieted down.

"Esaias?" I asked.

"Yeah. Been going to this school since kindergarten. I know where to go."

"Please go straight there and come right back, so you won't miss the fun activity we're going to do next."

Esaias grinned back at the rest of the class. He loosened the pick in his hair, poked it in and out a couple of times, and nestled it back into place. He sauntered out of the room, attendance folder in hand.

I addressed the class. "We're going to play a game together. It goes like this. You say your name and then something you like that starts with the same letter. For example, 'Hello. My name is Jan, and I like jam.' Okay, now think of something you like that starts with the same first letter as your name, but don't say it out loud yet."

Several students nodded.

"I got mine!"

"Me too!"

"I'll start, I'll start!" clamored a boy in the back row. A muscular boy of unusual coloring, he had light brown complexion with dark, curly, blonde-tipped hair.

"All right, you may begin, and then I'll tell you the rest of the rules."

A boy from the other side of the room called out in a mocking, high-pitched voice, "My name is Mayhew, and I like marshmallows!"

"Mayhew likes marshmallows," teased another boy.

Hoots of laughter came from the back row.

"All right, all right. Let's let Mayhew do this. Stand up, please."

Clearly used to the attention, Mayhew jumped up with a big grin and began. "Hi, my name's Mayhew, and I like . . . motorcycles."

Mayhew sat down, and I could hear muffled motorcycle sound effects. I look around the room. "That's enough with the sound effects."

"You're next," I said to the girl sitting beside Mayhew. "After you say your part, you say, 'His name is Mayhew, and he likes motorcycles.' As each new person speaks, they have to repeat all the ones before, in order, until we get through the whole class."

Groans and mumbles ran through the room.

Betty stood up, raised her chin, and spoke distinctly, "Hello, my name is Betty, and I like bibliographies."

The boy in front of Mayhew rolled his eyes and groaned aloud. I looked at him and raised my eyebrows. He shrugged and got quiet.

Betty continued, "His name is Mayhew, and he likes motorcycles." She sat down and crossed her legs.

I said, "You've got it. Okay, the next person has to remember both of those."

The next boy rose up, leaning on his desk. "My name's Joe, and I like jelly beans." He paused and looked at the boys nearby, grinning. Then, he continued, "Her name's Betty, and she likes, um . . . " he frowned. "What did she say?"

The class tittered with laughter.

"Betty, please repeat what you said for Joe," I said.

"I like bibliographies," she enunciated.

With deliberation, Joe responded, "Okay, her name is Betty, and she likes bib-li-o-graph-ies." Then in a rush he finished, "His name's Mayhew, and he likes motorcycles." He sat down to applause.

"I got off easy! I don't have to remember any of these," interjected Mayhew, as he crossed his arms and lounged in his seat.

I looked at him and said, "Oh, I forgot to tell you. The first person, that's you, must name the whole list at the end of the game."

"Ughh, I didn't know that!" he responded to shouts of derision.

"You can do it, Mayhew! You know everybody!" said a girl.

The game continued. Some students didn't know what to say, but others supplied suggestions, often with lots of laughter.

Then, it was William's turn. He stared at his desk and mumbled, "My name's William. I like whistling."

"Yeah, he's a good whistler too," interjected Josh.

To my surprise, in a quiet voice, William rattled off the previous list of names and favorites without a problem. I realized he was a very good listener, even if he didn't *seem* to engage much with those around him.

The door to the classroom opened wide. With a big smile on his face, Esaias strutted into the classroom to hoots and hollers of, "Sure took you long enough!"

"What did I miss?"

"You'll figure it out!" Beatrice called out to him.

I said, "Thank you for taking the attendance folder, Esaias. I think you'll be able to catch on, if you pay attention."

He sat down, and the game continued until he was the last student left.

"This game's too long. It's boring, Miz Wright," interrupted Beatrice.

"We're almost done, Beatrice," I replied.

"Hey, you know my name!" she said with a delighted grin.

I gave her a wink and said, "Esaias, it's your turn. Do you think you can do this?"

"Sure, I got this!" he announced. Esaias zipped through the list with a few hesitations. His buddies jumped in to supply him with the correct answers. When he finished, the kids shouted their approval.

"Well done, Esaias," I said, nodding.

Then I turned to the first boy and said, "Okay, Mayhew it's your turn again."

"Hey, Miz Wright, you haven't had a turn. You said you would learn all our names. How about you go first?" he challenged.

"Fair enough," I replied with a smile. I started with, "Hello, my name is Jan, and I like jam."

Mayhew interjected with a twinkle in his eyes, "Can we call you Jan?"

"Jan is my first name. You may call me Jan for this game, but it's Mrs. Wright after that." I recited all the names, without missing a beat. My students cheered.

"Now it's your turn," I motioned to Mayhew.

"Darn. I'm gonna need some help," Mayhew warned. He stumbled through the list, and the group helped supply the answers he needed and shouted their approval when he finally finished.

I walked to the paper shelf and grabbed a stack of lined paper.

Esaias mumbled, "Oh no, we're gonna write."

"Yes, Esaias, it's time for a little writing."

I handed out stacks of paper to each row. "I'd like you to tell me a little about yourself to help me get to know you. You can write about what you like to do or what you don't like to do. You can tell me what you did this summer. Let's make it a letter."

I drew a picture of a piece of lined paper on the blackboard. On the top line I wrote: "Dear Mrs. Wright," in cursive handwriting.

"You may write until the bell rings for recess."

While they wrote, I walked through the class practicing their names in my head, memorizing. I sat down at my desk and made a quick sketch of the desk arrangement, a seating chart, and wrote each student's name in the appropriate square before I forgot.

Some students got busy writing right away. Some sat and stared at the paper for a while. Some wrote and wrote, while others seemed to struggle to get a single sentence down on paper before coming to a complete halt. William just put his head on the desk and seemed to fall asleep. Some students started chatting; I asked them to be quiet while others worked.

I'll need to separate some students who seem to distract each other. Maybe I'll redesign the arrangement of desks to make it easier for me to walk through the room. I'll give myself until the end of the week to figure out another seating plan.

By lunch time, I was relieved to take a break and go down to the staff room where the teachers ate together. I didn't have to supervise students while I ate lunch this year. I could sit down with Nancy and Maria and relax for a few minutes. I could ask for advice from the more experienced teachers. I looked around and thought about all the names I had yet to learn in this group of teachers. How easy it would be if they would just play the Name Game with me. But tedious, as I feared the game had been for my class.

I looked up at the big clock on the wall; the end of the day seemed to have arrived all of a sudden. I announced, "It's almost time for the bell to ring. I think I've learned all of your names. After you clear off your desk, we'll see if I can name each of you correctly."

I strode over to the bulletin board at the end of the room through the commotion of kids getting ready to go home. I picked up the yard stick and pointed to a "name-bee." The kids settled down. Finding her in the class, I said, "You are Beatrice."

"That's right, Miz Wright!" she answered with a little clap of her hands.

I successfully connected the names on each of the "name-bees" with each student in the class. They cheered when I finished the last one.

I walked to the door just as the bell rang. Perfect timing. Students filed out of the room in a rush as I said good-bye to each one.

At last, William shuffled toward me. I smiled at him and said, "See you tomorrow, William-who-likes-to-whistle."

He passed me slowly. Then he looked back with a slight grin on his face. "Goodnight, Miz Wright, Jan-who-likes-jam."

I heard a soft whistle as he disappeared down the hallway.

For a moment, I basked in the happy glow of being a teacher at the end of the first day of school, filled with energy, hope, and promise for the year ahead. Then my thoughts rushed back through the day.

Maybe I let my students get too talkative. Did I bore my students with the Name Game? What do I need to prepare for tomorrow?

Chapter 12
Schedules

Each day he shuffled down the hallway and into the classroom in well-worn shoes. He took his seat in the back corner of the room, folding his long limbs into the narrow space between the seat and its attached, flip-topped desk. Without speaking to the other students around him, he slouched down until the frayed knees of his too-short pants were wedged up against the metal bottom of the desk. His shoulders slumped.

William. Not Will, not Bill, and certainly not Billy or Willy. William, a dignified name that demanded respect, or so I'm sure his proud mother intended.

At the end of the first week of school, I received a list of six students who would be taken out of my class for an hour every day for extra help with reading. I didn't find William's name on the list. I knew, by that time, he was the one student who most needed help with reading.

After school, I walked to the small room at end of the hall, next to the stairway. I poked my head around the corner and asked, "Are you Mrs. Chapman, the reading specialist?"

She nodded.

"I'm Jan Wright, one of the new sixth-grade teachers. Could I talk to you about the list of students from my class you will be working with?"

"I'm getting ready to leave, but I can take a few minutes." Her voice came out like a whine, high pitched and grating.

"I didn't see William Cooper's name on your list," I said.

"I work with small groups. The sixth graders I see test at third grade level or high second grade."

"But what about those who fall below that? William, for example, really needs help with reading."

She held my eyes and said, "I know William. His reading level is too low for my class. I don't have time to work with everyone who needs help. I'm already taking more students than I should. I focus on the levels I can make the most progress with."

It sounded like she had given up on William. I simmered. *I'm not a reading specialist! How will I be able to make a difference for these kids she won't take?*

In as calm a voice as I could manage, I said, "What can I do to make sure William and the others get some help?"

"William is at pre-primer level," she replied.

I stood my ground, looking directly into her eyes.

"He's just not a reader," she said dismissively. She looked down at her desk and said in a quiet voice, "I'll see what materials I can find for your lower groups next week."

She continued to pack up her things and prepare to leave for the weekend.

"Thanks." I turned to leave, wondering just how much help I would get from her. At least she would work with some of the students who needed help.

I walked back down the hall toward my classroom. I'd seen the reading scores from the previous year for my students. Since Mrs. Chapman would work with five of my students, I would be responsible for teaching reading to the remaining students in all the other levels: sixth, fifth, fourth, mid to low second grade. And William. Five different levels would be hard to manage. *How can I work with William at his level and keep his dignity intact?*

I stopped at Nancy's room. Busy writing assignments on her blackboard for Monday morning, she paused and smiled at me when I walked in.

"Great week, huh?!" she said.

"I loved it. What a super bunch of kids we have! Boy, I'm tired."

"Yeah, I'm pleased with this first week, but I can hardly think at this point. I need to get a few more things ready for next week before I can leave, though."

"Nancy, do you have students on the list to go to remedial reading?"

"Yes, I have four going."

"Do you have any materials for kids who are even lower than that group?"

"Not yet. Do you?"

"Nope. I just talked with the reading specialist. It's great that some of my students will have her help, but I have more than the classic three reading groups to work with."

"Me too. How about you and I trade some students for reading instruction, so we won't have to teach all the levels by ourselves?"

"Oh, I like that idea, Nancy. We're both too pooped to do that now, but why don't we sit down next Monday after school with our class reading lists and divide our students into groups, see what we've got between us. Mrs. Chapman said she'd try to get some lower-level books for me."

"Sure, Monday's good. Hey, I bet we could talk with the primary teachers to get the extra books we need."

"You're full of good ideas, Nancy! Thanks. You have a great weekend!"

"You too, Jan."

I returned to my own classroom, still thinking about how to work with William. *I could group him with Curtis and Richard.*

I had placed Betty next to William in my new seating arrangement, which we had just accomplished that afternoon, ready for a fresh start on Monday.

Maybe I can use Betty as an occasional tutor for him. She's the only student at a sixth-grade reading level in my room. She's conscientious and works well independently. I'll watch to see how they interact before suggesting it.

My thoughts moved on to the other subjects I had to teach. All the textbooks we had were designed for students at a sixth-grade reading level, an obvious concern when only one student in my class had that level of competence. *How can I keep all my kids motivated and not too frustrated when the materials are difficult to read? I'll need to give them support to use those texts.*

Back to the puzzle of working out my teaching schedule, I remembered band classes would begin in another week. On Mondays, Wednesdays, and Fridays, more than half my class had signed up to leave for an hour of band in the midst of the most productive teaching time, the middle of the day. The rest of the class would remain with me. *What can I do with a handful of students? I can't teach something the band students also need. Too bad I won't have all my low readers for that period. Band might just be good for them anyway.*

I had an inspiration. *During that period, I can tackle my responsibility for teaching classroom music. We could all do music at the same time. Besides, music will require reading and maybe a little math.*

I had almost no experience with the subject of music. Three hours a week would be a lot, possibly too much.

Maybe I can schedule a study period, too. I could work with William, since he's not one of the band students. We could do some special projects and maybe a little art, too. Oh, I'll figure it out over the weekend.

Bone-tired on this Friday afternoon at the end of the first week, I still had work to do before going home, but my thinking jumped back to music. I decided to go look for that stack of music books I'd seen in a closet down the hall from my room.

Chapter 13
Figaro

I looked up and down the hallway and saw Mrs. Perfect's closed door. I knew she left school ten minutes after her students. In fact, none of the doors were open, except mine; I heard nothing in the late Friday stillness of the school. Feeling bold, I opened the unlocked door and began to search through the clutter in the closet. I found just what I needed, a stack of Level Six music books, complete with a teacher's manual and a coordinating set of record albums. A quick glance through the Table of Contents showed opera as a key concept addressed in the sixth-grade music curriculum. I had a sinking feeling this focus might not work so well with my students from inner-city Norfolk.

I don't know anything about opera. How will I ever be able to interest my kids in such "high-brow" music?

After a moment of hesitation, I carried the box of records back to my classroom along with the teacher's manual.

In the cloakroom, I found an old record player. I lugged it to the counter at the end of the classroom, plugged it in, and opened the lid. I slipped the first record out of its cardboard case and placed it on the turntable. Selecting the 33 1/3 RPM speed, I then twisted the knob to turn the record player on. It hummed to life, and the record spun around. Next, I picked up the arm and tested the needle with my finger. *Scritch. Scritch.* It worked. I set the needle on the vinyl record, trying hard not to scratch it.

A section from the opera, "The Marriage of Figaro," began to play as I found the corresponding lesson in the manual. I soon recognized a familiar melody and pictured the image of . . . Bugs Bunny? . . . Woody Woodpecker? . . . Or was that Tom and Jerry? Did I know this music from viewing cartoons? I listened to the record while I continued to clean up around the classroom. I found myself moving to the music. Drawn in by its passion, I abandoned my chores and sat down to listen. By the end of the first side of the record, I decided to introduce my students to this classic form of music. It would broaden their backgrounds and fill their ears with the mesmerizing beauty of a music they may never hear in any setting other than cartoons.

On the first day the band students left for their class, smiling and joking as they went, only nine students remained in my classroom. Not a single smile remained in the bunch. They had the look of those who were left out of a grand adventure. I glanced at the clock. We had an hour to wait for the return of those joyfully departing band students. My plan for these left-over kids better work, or it would be a long hour indeed.

Beatrice asked aloud, "What are we gonna do now, Miz Wright?"

"I have a surprise for you today," I announced, hiding my trepidation. "Since the rest of our class has left for music lessons, we will learn a little about music too." I stared out at the handful of students who seemed less than thrilled. Was I about to fall flat on my face in front of these tough critics?

"Beatrice, will you pass out these music books for me?"

"Sure thing, Miz Wright," she drawled, moving slowly to accomplish the task.

As she passed out the books, I walked to the counter where the record player sat. With a bit of a dramatic flourish, I opened it up and turned it on. Then I pulled the record out of its case and held it up above my head with my fingers on its edge. Curious eyes fastened on me.

"I'd like you to listen to some music you might not hear very often. Just keep an open mind about this and see how it makes you feel."

I set the record down on the turntable, aligning the central hole with the spindle, and placed the needle on it. I turned up the volume and music filled the classroom. Smiles lit their faces. Some students giggled. Some began to conduct the orchestra. Their unexpected joy delighted me and relieved some of my concern.

At the end of the first track, I turned off the music. Now for the hard part of the lesson, teaching a subject I had never been taught myself. It had taken me much longer to prepare for this lesson than it would take me to teach it.

"Keep playing it!" Joshua cried out.

I grinned and said, "Let's find out what this is all about, and then we can hear some more music. Please open your books to page 12."

I kept the lesson short. It seemed to go well. I had forgotten that these were the non-music kids. Even though I needed to learn the subject as I taught it, classroom music might just turn out to be fun for all of us. I finished by playing one more track of music from the same opera, and again, their joyous response surprised and pleased me.

With a sense of relief, I gave my students time to work on their reading assignments.

About five minutes before the end of the hour, I walked to the counter and turned the record player on again.

"Can we hear that opera song again, Miz Wright?" asked Beatrice.

I turned and asked the group, "Would you like that?"

"Yeah! That music is fun!" replied Joshua.

I put the needle on the record and played the first track again to a giggling, animated group of sixth graders. We would do all right with these opera lessons, at least for a while.

I turned the record player off when we heard a commotion in the hallway. The band students were returning. The classroom door flew open; talkative students streamed in.

"I'm gonna play the trombone!" announced Mayhew, strutting through the room, miming playing his instrument.

"I'm going to play the violin," said Betty, nodding her head with a broad smile.

Esaias shuffled in and grumbled, "We didn't get to play any instruments today."

"Well, we got to hear opera!" interjected Beatrice.

"What?! You did what?" asked Mayhew.

"It's from the cartoons! La, la, la, la, la, la, la, la, la," sang Beatrice in reply.

"You got to watch cartoons?"

"No, Silly. We heard the music. It's about a wedding and a hair dresser in some foreign country, right Miz Wright?"

"Yes, Beatrice. We listened to the 'Marriage of Figaro.' It comes from an opera called *The Barber of Seville*," I replied, feeling a sense of success.

"All we did was sit around in band. Boring," complained Esaias.

I felt the balance shift that day. I didn't know it at the time, but within a month, almost every student would drop out of band to rejoin my class. And, it all started with a little opera.

Chapter 14
Black Mollies

On the third week of school, just after the last band student left the room, Beatrice piped up, "Are we gonna hear some more music today, Miz Wright?"

"Yes, Beatrice, but first, I have a surprise for our class. I'd like your help to set it up."

A chant of "What is it? What is it?" followed.

"Wait here for just a minute while I go get something." I walked into the cloakroom and came back holding a large box.

"What's in the box, Miz Wright? Can we see it? Can we?" asked Beatrice.

I set the box on my desk and opened it while the nine non-band students watched. First, I pulled out a bag of colored gravel.

"What's that for, Miz Wright?" asked Curtis.

I smiled and reached into the box again. This time I revealed two ceramic figures, a treasure chest and a miniature diver.

"I know, I know!" clamored George and Kara at the same time.

I put my finger to my lips to keep them quiet and brought out a plastic bag of fresh water plants, a small net, and then a box of fish food.

George could not contain himself any longer. "Fish! We're gonna get some fish!"

I reached into the big box once again and brought out another plastic bag, this one containing water and five small black fish.

"Yay!"

"Come on up here and take a good look at them," I said.

The kids rushed out of their seats and surrounded me.

"Ooooooo!"

"They're so pretty!"

"What kind of fish are they?"

I replied, "They're called black mollies. If we're lucky, they may give us some babies so we can watch them grow. But first, we have to set up the aquarium. Who wants to help?"

"Me! Me! Me!"

"William and Curtis, I'd like you to be responsible for the water. Would you go get the two buckets in the closet?"

"Yes, ma'am," they chorused.

I sent them down the hall to the restrooms to get the water while Harold moved a vacant desk to the wall between the classroom door and the closet door. "Place the desk right next to the electrical outlet," I directed him.

I asked Richard and Beatrice to get the aquarium from the closet and set it on the desk.

When the last of the water filled the tank, Kara plugged in the filter. The bubbles began to purr in the water. Richard positioned the diver, and Beatrice selected her perfect spot for the treasure chest.

I held up the bag of fresh water plants. "These are called elodea." I wrote the word on the blackboard and pronounced it slowly. "EL ... O ... D E ... A. Now you say it."

"Elodea," they responded. "Elodea."

"Harold, you can take the elodea and place some in the bottom of the aquarium, using a little gravel to anchor a few where you want them. The others can float on the top."

Finally, Kara lowered the heater in the water and plugged it in.

The group stood back and admired the aquarium.

"Can we put the fish in now?" asked Joshua.

"Not yet." I went back to my desk and reached into the big box once more. I pulled out a small aquarium thermometer and handed it to Joshua.

"The water should be between 70 and 80 degrees Fahrenheit. Joshua, would you look to see where those numbers are?"

"In the green zone."

"Show it to Gail to check."

When Gail nodded her head, I said, "Good. Now please show the thermometer to each of the others, so we'll all know what to look for when we check the water temperature. When everyone has seen it, Joshua, you can put it in the fish tank."

I walked back into the cloakroom and brought out one more small box. I pulled out a small plastic container. "If our black mollies have babies, we need to keep them separated from the other fish. Does anyone know why?"

"The big fish will eat 'em!" cried Beatrice.

"You're right Beatrice. So, we will keep the babies in this nursery container until they are big enough to fend for themselves. We don't need it now, but I have it for when we do."

"Okay, now can we hear some more opera?" asked Joshua.

I smiled, remembering how worried I'd been to introduce this style of music to these inner-city kids.

"We're going to listen to a part of another opera. This first section is being sung by a clown who is very sad, maybe he's even crying. While you listen, try to imagine something that has made you feel sad and see if the music fits."

I walked over to the record player and selected the right track for this day's lesson. The classroom filled with music from *Pagliacci*. I turned around to see all nine of the non-band member students listening intently. Joshua even had his eyes closed as he listened. Heads nodded with the rhythm, not a single interruption or look of disinterest. A proud moment for me.

"Miz Wright, why's the clown so sad?" asked Beatrice.

"Let's find out what our music book has to tell us about this opera," I said, leading them into my lesson.

When the noise from the hallway let us know our band students were returning to class, I said, "Let's sit and watch as the band students come in and see if they notice our new aquarium. Don't say anything until they discover it on their own. Okay?"

"Hide the fish, Miz Wright!" said Harold.

I did as he suggested and set the bag of fish and the nursery container under my desk, on my chair.

They all grinned as the door opened and Ayesha came in with Joan followed by Sam and Tom. Busy talking with each other, they walked past the aquarium without a glance.

Then Tom noticed the quiet in the room and looked around. "What?" he said as he scanned the smiling faces that awaited him. "What?!"

"Hey, look here! Where'd this come from?" said Mayhew. He came through the door and walked straight to the aquarium. "We got fish?"

"No dummy, the fish aren't in there yet!" replied Beatrice. "The water ain't hot enough."

"Beatrice, what did I tell you about that word?" I interjected.

"Sorry, Miz Wright. The water *isn't* hot enough."

At least she had paid attention to the grammar usage, if not the name calling.

The rest of the band students streamed through the door, some stopping at the aquarium before taking a seat, everyone talking at once about the new addition to our classroom.

I got them all settled down and then began to let the non-band students explain what we had done. To my surprise, William raised his hand. "Yes, William . . ."

"It's 11:45."

"Very good. How about explaining to the class what you need to do?"

After a pause, he said, "We're waiting for the temperature to get up between 70 and 80 degrees so's we can put the black mollies in the water."

"Good job. You and Curtis may go take a look."

We watched in silence while William checked the thermometer first and then showed it to Curtis, who nodded his head. William turned to me and said, "It's ready, Miz Wright."

"Thank you, boys." I walked to my desk and retrieved the bag of fish.

"Ooooo . . ." Eyes alight, the group's attention riveted on the fish.

"These are black mollies," I told the band students. "Beatrice, would you like to place the bag of fish in the tank? Don't open it, just set it in the water. After a few minutes, when they have adjusted to the temperature, we'll open the bag and let the fish swim out into the aquarium."

Beatrice sashayed her way up to the front of the room and took the fish from me. Holding the bag in both hands, her gait calmed to a prim walk until she placed the fish into the tank.

Spontaneous applause followed. Beatrice turned and bowed to the class.

When the tittering laughter died down, I said, "Band students, how about telling the rest of us what *you* did in class today?"

Betty raised her hand, "Yes, Betty?"

"We're learning to play 'Mary Had a Little Lamb.'"

A few students giggled, and then Kara bragged, "We're studying opera while you're gone!"

"Well, I'm working on more difficult pieces at home," Betty said, sounding defensive.

"We don't get to play our instruments very much in band. It's just a lot of waiting around and kids talking," said Mayhew.

"Yeah. We never do anything fun like you're doin' in here. All the teacher does is yell at us. I wanna quit band," complained Esaias once again.

Just before the lunch bell rang, we released the fish into the tank. They scattered, free at last. Students clustered around the tank to see them, taking their time to leave for lunch. William ambled up to me, last in line.

"Some of those fish are hiding in the elodea, Miz Wright," he said.

"Yes, it gives them a safe place to be when all of us are staring at them. Good job remembering the name of the fresh water plants, William."

The following day, Esaias brought in a note from his mother giving permission for him to drop out of band. The harried, over-worked band teacher seemed only too happy to agree.

Esaias became the tenth student in my music, study, and miscellaneous projects class. I didn't mind his switch to my class, but I began to worry how I would manage my customized plans for small group lessons if others followed his lead. In fact, I realized I expected more to follow him. I wondered how many and how soon.

Chapter 15
The Math Lesson

"Hi, Mom! It's good to hear your voice. How're you feeling?" I tucked the phone between my cheek and my shoulder while I continued to sort 3 x 5 cards into piles.

"I'm doing just fine, Jan. I went back to work part time last week, a little tiring, but I'm planning on going back full time next week."

"That hysterectomy took quite a toll on you, didn't it? Wish I could be there for you, Mom."

"I'll be just fine. How are *you* doing, dear?"

"Jerry's at the base on duty for the weekend. I've been grading papers and working on creating a math game for my class. I've been writing cards with math problems on them. I'm sorting them while we talk."

"You're always so busy, Jan."

"I know Mom, but I discovered some of my students don't even know their addition and subtraction facts, things like 6 + 5 = 11 or 14 - 7 = 7. How can I teach sixth-grade level math if they can't even do that?"

"Aren't you supposed to take a couple of college classes this year, too?"

"Yeah, my master's degree wasn't good enough for the Norfolk School District. They've got me taking undergrad classes in economics and US history," I complained.

"You'll do all right," my mother said.

"It's just such an irony that I'm forced to study college economics while I'm trying to teach such simple math."

Holding the phone in the crook of my neck got uncomfortable, so I set down the stack of cards, grabbed the phone in my hand, and sat down at the kitchen table to have a nice long chat with my mother.

When math period began, I announced, "I have a game for you, but I need your help moving our desks."

Cheers erupted. Students jumped up to follow my directions. Within minutes, we rearranged the room. We clustered most of the desks at one end of the room. Then we lined up five desks for the starter line and five desks on the opposite side of the room as a finish line, with an empty gap in the center of the room. I set up my decorated answer bags on top of the goal line desks.

"I assigned each of you to teams that match the pictures on these bags. We have the apple team, the orange team, the grapes, the pineapples, and the bananas."

"I wanna be a banana!" shouted Esaias through fits of laughter.

"Pineapple, I want to be a pineapple from Hawaii," said Mayhew, doing a little hula dance.

"Okay, okay, settle down. I've already picked your teams, but we can switch team names the next time we play." I held up a stack of fruit-decorated envelopes. "Each one of these envelopes contains identical problems. I shuffled them though, so they will not appear in the same order as any other team. Some problems are simple, some are harder. Some have words, some don't." I set an envelope on each of the starting desks.

I read the team names from my list to hoots and laughter. I did an example of the problem-solving process, and we were ready to begin.

All the students joined in with enthusiasm. They stayed focused on the math, working out sums and differences with loud, happy chatter. They cheered for each other when problems got solved and then ran to place their answers in the goal line bags.

In the middle of this constructive, noisy chaos, a voice boomed over the loudspeaker in the classroom, "What are you kids doing? WHERE

IS YOUR TEACHER?" It was the principal, Mr. Green, on what I now understood to be an intercom. I had no idea the principal had been listening in on my classes.

The entire class froze in stunned silence. Their heads turned; their eyes sought me. Feeling like I had been caught doing something wrong, I answered, "I'm right here, Mr. Green." After an uncomfortable pause I said, "We're playing a math game."

"Come see me after school, Mrs. Wright," he demanded.

"Yes, Mr. Green."

It sounded like he had just reprimanded me in front of my students, but I knew the math game was working better than any textbook pages I could have assigned. I faced my class and said, "I'm glad you're excited, but I think we need to be a little quieter. Can we do that?'

"Yes, Miz Wright," they grinned in unanimous reply. We began again, this time in more subdued voices. However, the excitement built until I called a stop.

"Sorry, kids. It's getting a bit noisy again. I guess we'd better stop for today."

"But which team won?" cried Beatrice.

"I'll figure that out while you move the desks back. And, take out your math texts."

Grumbling, they began to return the desks to their normal places.

"Can we play the game again, tomorrow?" asked Esaias.

"We'll see," I said. "We have some work to do in our books first."

⧉⧉⧉

After my students had gone home for the day, I walked downstairs. Dreading my summons to see the principal, I entered the office. The school secretary sat at her desk, typing. I waited for her to stop and look up at me. "Well?" she said.

Feeling nervous, I asked in a quiet voice, "May I see Mr. Green, please?"

"Nope, he's left for the day," she replied and went back to her typing.

Dumbfounded, I raised my voice to be heard, "Would you please tell Mr. Green I came in to see him, as he requested?"

The secretary grunted in reply and kept typing.

"I'm Mrs. Wright."

No response.

I turned around and walked out, feeling confused. Did he forget? Had I just dodged a bullet? Would he lower the boom on me tomorrow?

I went back upstairs to my classroom to finish up a few more things. Then I grabbed some papers to grade and got ready to head home for a quick dinner before going to my economics class.

The following morning, just before the first bell rang, Mr. Green walked through the open door into my classroom. "Mrs. Wright, you'll be having a helping teacher work with you for a couple of weeks, starting on Monday."

"A helping teacher?"

"It's a district program."

"What will this teacher do?" I asked.

"Oh, you'll work that out with him."

With that, he turned and left, leaving me standing alone, feeling bewildered. After spying on me through the intercom, he decided I needed help with my teaching? Did he think I wasn't doing a good job? He didn't even mention missing his "appointment" with me.

RING!

The bell to start the school day stopped my thoughts about Mr. Green and the helping teacher. I shifted gears to greet my students.

Chapter 16
The Helping Teacher

Her laughter caught my attention as I entered the staff room. Easy to spot, I could see Mrs. Parker dressed in a bright floral print. I made my way across the room with my bag lunch and sat down in the empty seat next to her at the table. A big-boned black woman with dark hair neatly shellacked into tight waves and just a touch of gray showing at the temples, she had been teaching for many years. I liked her stories, her sense of humor, and her comments that revealed the depth of her connection with her students. I liked her.

Mrs. Parker had what I supposed Mr. Green pictured as near perfect student behavior management. Whenever I saw her on the playground or in the halls with her students, they followed her like ducklings trailing behind their mother, a straight line through a mass of unruly kids. She could turn and give a wordless look at a student that would wither a stone. The student in question would lose all his bravado and hang his head, staring at the floor until she released him with a turn of her head, the chastened student not daring to return to whatever behavior had caused her to set her sights on him in the first place.

Opening my lunch bag, I pulled out a napkin, an apple, a bag of corn chips, and my sandwich. "Mrs. Parker," I began.

"Just call me Cora Lee, darlin'," she interrupted, turning her jubilant face to me.

It was still hard for me to think of teachers as my peers. Until recently, I had been on the other side of the divide, an ever-so-respectful student. "Cora Lee, I've been thinking about my classroom management. My students talk a lot." I took a bite of my tuna sandwich. "Whenever I pass your classroom, it's very quiet. How do you establish such extraordinary control over your students?"

"Be mean from the first day. Scare the bejesus out of them from the get-go," she laughed. "When you start off stern, you can let up later. You're the boss, not the students."

Being "mean" didn't much suit my nature, as I had discovered during the spanking incident the previous year. I knew many people considered a silent classroom the gold standard for behavior control. However, I just couldn't seem to inspire silence to that extent, and I couldn't bear to strike fear in a child's heart. My passion for teaching spilled out of me in a great big smile and a lot of interaction between me and my students which then created interaction between students. Years later, I would learn just how important "verbal processing" is for many students in their learning; however, I had no knowledge of that in those early days of teaching. Most of the time, pure instinct guided me to what seemed to work.

The other new teachers, Maria and Nancy, joined us at the lunch table, setting down lunch trays from the cafeteria. "Good morning, Mrs. Parker. Hi Jan," Maria said.

"Cora Lee, call me Cora Lee," Mrs. Parker insisted.

"Yes, ma'am."

Picking up her empty plate and utensils, Cora Lee said, "Gotta go. I've got the painters coming to my classroom next, so we're moving into the library this afternoon."

"It wasn't as bad as I expected when I had to do that last week," said Maria. "But it's not easy. There are a lot of distractions in there."

"We'll do just fine," replied Cora Lee, as she walked away.

I had no doubt about that. Her class would be focused on their lessons . . . or else.

Nancy took a bite of her meatloaf and then looked at me and said, "How's your day going, Jan? You look like something is bothering you."

"I'm a little upset," I said. I told them about the math game and how I discovered Mr. Green had been listening to my class through the intercom followed by his ominous command to come see him after school. "He came into my room this morning and told me the district is sending me a helping teacher next week," I confided.

"Maybe that's not such a bad thing, Jan," said Nancy. "As new teachers, we can use all the help we can get, right?"

"Yes, lucky you," Maria added. "I wish he'd give me a helping teacher. I heard this is a new program. They're supposed to be the best of the best, and they share some great ideas. Besides, they can help take a load off for a few weeks."

"That's a better attitude than I had about it. Thanks."

He was standing in my classroom, looking around, when I arrived on Monday morning. The helping teacher. My arms encircled large grocery bags filled with graded student papers and teaching manuals, my purse, and my lunch bag. "Hello," I said.

The tall, sandy-haired man turned around, rushed to help me unload, all the while talking at breakneck speed.

"You must be Mrs. Wright. I'm Charles Raynor Dewitt the Third. I know, that's a pretentious sounding name, isn't it? I was named after my father, who was named after his father, my grandfather. Obviously. My students call me Mr. Dewitt. My close friends call me Raynor. I know that's an odd sounding name too. Raynor. Most people call me Chuck or Charles; it's easier. You can choose what you'd like to call me, just don't call me late for supper."

I laughed out loud. "My grandmother used to say that!"

My arms now empty, he took my hand in his to shake it. Looking straight into my eyes with disarming warmth, he finished, "I have the honor of being your helping teacher." He impressed me as the most friendly, welcoming person I had met since I became a teacher.

I chuckled as he held my gaze, then I said, "You can call me Jan, just Jan. Not Janet or Janice, just Jan. Welcome to my classroom, Raynor."

He went on, "I'm here to support you in any way I can. You've got me for two full weeks. Together we'll stir things up and create your vision of a masterful learning environment for each and every one of your students." He pulled me right into in his infectious enthusiasm.

"For this first day, I'll greet the students with you. Then I'll just sit in the back of the room and take a few notes, gathering ideas for what I might offer to do for you." He rushed on, without pausing, "Your room appears so clean and welcoming, Jan. I just love the bulletin board and those bees with all your students' names. Did you make those all yourself? And the fish tank here by the door. Are those black mollies? Have the students seen them give birth to little ones yet?"

Since had I prepared my students for his arrival, they were eager to meet him that first morning. He stood at the door when they entered the classroom, high-fiving the biggest of the boys and making several of the girls giggle at his nonstop commentary. We were off and running.

He watched me teach, sometimes sitting in a chair at the back of the room, sometimes wandering around the edges. When students were working at their desks, he walked throughout the class, stopping to assist or encourage as he went. We exchanged brief comments throughout the morning.

By the time lunch break arrived, Raynor knew all their names and was brimming with ideas he wanted to share with me. We ate lunch in the classroom and talked through the entire period.

"You've got quite a range of student abilities in this class," he started.

"You're right about that. Betty is the one student on grade level in reading. They range all the way to William who's in a pre-primer."

"What are you doing to manage all those levels?" he asked, taking a bite out of his banana.

"A reading specialist takes six of my students in the afternoon. That's when I trade students with the teacher next door. I work with fourth-grade reading level and those at the very lowest levels. Nancy takes the fifth and sixth-grade levels. I try to add extra support during the band period, too." I paused to pour some milk from my thermos into the cup.

"How do you manage the other subjects? You have textbooks that are written for sixth-grade readers, right?"

"Yeah, it's a challenge. When we use texts, I make sure it's all read aloud, either by me or by students." I thought for a minute. "My kids also struggle in a wide range of math abilities. I've created some games to help them practice math facts."

"Ever used learning centers?" he asked me.

"I learned about them at the University of West Florida, liked the idea, and tried using them with my first class." My experiences with sixth graders in my previous teaching position tumbled out in a long discourse, along with my feelings of disappointment and self-recrimination.

"Wow! Talk about a challenging start to a career. I'm glad you're still teaching."

With a tight smile, I shrugged my shoulders, feeling a touch vulnerable for having shared so much with him.

"I don't believe it's as bad as you may think. I can see in the way you interact with your students that they like you, and that's more than half the battle."

"I want to do a better job of reaching all my students at their various levels and moving them along."

We sat in silence, thinking.

"Are you willing to have another go with learning centers?" he asked.

"Sure," I said.

"I think I have an idea that might work, Jan. We could use large boxes to make stand-alone centers with self-directed learning in both math and reading." He grabbed a piece of paper. As he talked, he began to sketch boxes and then a series of small squares on the sides of each.

"Kids could use them any time they have a few moments, like during that band period or when they finish an assignment early. Let me show you what I mean."

He pointed to the squares in his drawing and said, "We could put pockets on each of the sides, like this, to hold activity cards or math problems and place the answer keys in the pockets on another side so students could check their own work. They could put their completed work on that side, too. See, in this big pocket here. I know where I can get some refrigerator boxes to set these up. What do you think? Is this something you think might work for you?"

"Worth trying, but it'll take a lot of time to set up."

"That's why I'm here. I can work on the cards while you teach your normal lessons. We can put the boxes together after school. I could also teach lessons for you while you work on parts of the centers. Or, I could teach while you go to observe another teacher in her classroom, if you'd like. I'll also take a look at William and the others who struggle with reading and see if I can give you some extra tips to help them. Anything you need, Jan, I'm here to support you as you teach."

I gushed, "That's far out!" I blushed realizing I had just used a typical 70's phrase, not the professional teacher talk I'd normally use with a colleague. I felt comfortable with Raynor. "Could I really go see another teacher at work?"

He grinned in response. "Sure, that's a groovy way to learn new techniques and get a sense of how someone else does what you do, teach. You know this helping teacher program is new. We're just beginning to figure out how to best use our time. You're my second assignment. I think we can just do whatever you find helpful."

I grinned. We were going to get along very well.

Chapter 17
Extension

Raynor exuded confidence, full of fun and energy. He had been teaching for twelve years and freely gave me tips, made suggestions, and dispensed encouragement. We planned and taught a few lessons together as a team. At the end of each day, we evaluated what worked well and what I could do to improve. It thrilled me to have a confidant with whom to share my work and passion for teaching. The days together sped by.

The middle of the second week arrived. We were well into creating the learning centers, but not yet finished. At the end of the day, we watched the last of the students leave.

"I wish you could stay longer," I blurted.

At the same time, he said, "I wish I could stay longer."

We laughed. We both enjoyed our shared teaching adventure.

"Let me see what I can do to extend my time with you," Raynor responded.

The next day, he came in late to lunch and sat down next to me. "Guess what?" he grinned. "I managed to talk them into letting me stay for another week. My next assignment doesn't begin until after that, so it worked out."

"Wonderful. Now we can finish those learning centers, and maybe we'll have enough time for me to do those observations of other teachers you suggested."

"Super! Who would you like to observe? I'll set it all up for you and teach while you're out watching them."

"I'd like to see our sixth-grade chairman, Mrs. Carpenter. I'm in awe of her and her perfect classroom set up."

"Good. Is there anyone else?"

"Mrs. Parker teaches fifth grade. She has extraordinary control over her students, from what I've seen."

"Excellent. Now don't you worry about a thing. I'll get the observations all set up and then you can let me know what I can teach while you're gone."

Before I had time to say anything more on the subject, Raynor, as usual, took off on another topic. "I have an idea. You're studying Japan, right? How about doing some cooking with the students?"

"Great idea! And, we can reinforce the use of fractions to measure ingredients."

"We could get chopsticks and serve tea," Raynor added.

We talked about the logistics of setting up a menu of Japanese food and doing the cooking in the classroom as we left the lunchroom together. We would use the band period to get it organized and let the non-band students put all the ingredients together on our cooking day.

The next morning, Raynor showed me a recipe for Teriyaki Chicken with rice. We agreed on it and decided to surprise the class with our plans. He set off to work in the staff room to create a large poster of the recipe with directions for the students to follow. By the end of the day, he had finished it, so we decided to present it to the kids.

Curious students watched us walk to the back counter. We picked up the Teriyaki poster with the back side facing the class.

"Mr. Dewitt and I are planning a very special lesson for you to experience a little of the culture of Japan," I began. "How would you like to cook a Japanese meal in our classroom?"

With a flourish we flipped over the poster together, so students could see it.

Cheers went up from the excited students.

We carried the poster to the front of the room and set it into the chalk tray, leaning it on the blackboard.

"We get to do the cooking?" asked Pearl.

"Do we get to eat it?" interjected Esaias.

"Yes, of course," I answered to both.

Raynor continued, "We'll have to figure out who can bring each of the ingredients and the cooking utensils like measuring cups and spoons."

Hands rose into the air, vying for attention.

"I want to bring something," cried Beatrice.

I explained each of the parts of the meal and asked who wanted to bring each item on the list. Raynor added their names to the board.

"Can we use chopsticks, Mrs. Wright?" asked George.

"Yes, indeed."

"We going to do this tomorrow?" asked Mayhew.

"Heavens, no! It'll take a while to get it all together. I'll have a letter ready for you tomorrow to explain to parents what we're going to do and what you have each volunteered to bring. How about we have our meal next Friday? We can make this a Japanese going away party for Mr. Dewitt."

"Does he have to go? It's fun having him in our room," said Josh.

"I wish I could stay," said Raynor. "I'll be working with another teacher at another school, but I'll have a fantastic celebration with you next week. How about if I bring a surprise Japanese food for you to try?"

"What is it?" Beatrice asked, clapping her hands together.

"Oh, I can't tell you now. That's what a surprise is," he smiled.

The following week, Raynor and I worked to finish the new learning centers and completed our plans to set up our cooking class. Raynor also scheduled me to observe the veteran teachers.

After Raynor had gone for the day, I began to pack up things to take home with me. Maria walked into my room, wearing her suede jacket with the fringes. She set her purse and a stack of papers down on the desk closest to the door.

"Love your jacket, Maria! What brings you to this end of the hallway?"

"Just wanted to check on your progress with those learning centers you've been talking about."

Rounding the corner of the doorway to join us, Nancy said, "Me too." Also dressed in a jacket, purse in hand.

"Come on in and see what we've done." I motioned to them. We made our way through the room and circled the transformed free-standing boxes, the new learning centers.

"Wow! They're so neat! This is going to be wonderful for your students," Maria admired.

"And I hear you're going to do some cooking on Friday," said Nancy.

"Yes, we are." I pointed to the Chicken Teriyaki poster I had hung on the wall next to the door. "It's also our farewell party for Mr. Dewitt."

I walked back to my desk and finished shoving a stack of papers into my bag. Maria picked up her things, and I met them at the doorway, turning out the lights as we left. We walked down the empty hallway together.

"We're always the last three to leave the building, aren't we?" Nancy noted.

"And the first to get here in the morning, too," added Maria.

"It's been a lot of work, but you two were sure right about being lucky to have a helping teacher. He's inspiring to work with, and he's so encouraging." I continued in a conspiratorial, stage whisper, "Not at all like our principal." I rolled my eyes.

Maria said, "Did you know I went in to see Mr. Green to ask if I could have a helping teacher too?"

"You did? What did he say?" I asked.

"He told me he'd already put in a request for me and Nancy to have our own helping teachers. Looks like you've led the way for us. I can't wait!"

Chapter 18
Observations

The appointed day arrived for me to observe the two teachers I had chosen to watch. In an attempt to look professional, I took special care with my appearance. I brushed and brushed my freshly shampooed hair. I opened a new package of panty hose and carefully pulled them up my legs, making sure there were no runs. Then I put on my favorite teacher dress, the white with black polka dots, and a matching black belt. I slipped my feet into my new black patent leather shoes. As a final touch, I grabbed the blue bottle of Heaven Scent and dabbed a bit of the perfume behind each ear. I checked myself out in the mirror. Ready.

At school that morning, toward the end of recess, I found a notebook and a pen to take with me. With mixed feelings of anticipation and trepidation, I walked down the short hallway from my room to Mrs. Carpenter's room. Anxious to learn the keys to excellence in teaching reading from the best of the best, I still worried. I feared her judgment, concerned she would question my competence as a teacher, and I didn't want her to think I *needed* help.

I knew my own students were in good hands with Mr. Dewitt and his math lesson for the day. He'd sent me off with, "Go! Have a good time! Take notes, learn what you can learn, and we'll talk all about it at the end of the day."

I reached the doorway and consciously straightened my posture a bit. Mrs. Perfect, not a hair out of place, sat at her classic teacher's desk at the front of the quiet room, facing straight rows of desks. Perfect. She looked up at me.

"Do come in, Mrs. Wright. I have set up a chair for you at the back of the room. Go ahead and have a seat," she commanded.

"Thank you, I appreciate you allowing me to watch you teach reading, Mrs. Carpenter."

"I've told my students you will be here this period." Her focus returned to the paper in front of her, as if to dismiss me.

I walked to the back of the room, my shoes clacking on the wooden floor with each step I made in the silent room. I sat down in my assigned chair and set the notebook and pen on my lap. Mrs. Carpenter continued to write. I looked around at the crisp clean edges, paper piles, books, supplies, everything in its proper place. I admired the posters and precise lettering on each of the bulletin boards. Then, I noticed the reading books on top of all the student desks. *Wait a minute. They're all the same, all level six readers. How can that be?* I dared not voice my questions aloud.

The students arrived from recess, walking in with very little talking, quickly taking a seat. Some glanced at me, but not one student spoke to me. Mrs. Carpenter, still seated at her desk, continued writing. At last, she set her pen down and looked up. She reached for the teacher's manual on top of her desk, opened to the page she wanted and then rose from her chair. All eyes followed her, as if she had cast a spell upon us.

"Open your books to page 44," she said with authority. Together, they opened their books.

How did they get to page 44 in the book already?

"Sonia, read the first paragraph aloud for us."

Sonia read, perfectly, of course.

Mrs. Carpenter consulted her manual. "Belinda, read the sentence that is the main idea in this paragraph."

Belinda read aloud the correct sentence.

Mrs. Carpenter continued to follow the directions from the teacher's manual, telling students to read from the text and then asking them guided questions which she read from the manual. She called on various students who responded with little correction needed. Then she told students to open their workbooks to page 14. She read the directions aloud to that page and the next page. She sat down at her desk. Quiet settled on the room.

Dumbfounded, I opened my notebook wondering what to write about what I had just witnessed. *Mrs. Carpenter read word-for-word from the teachers' manual. That's all she did! Besides that, she used that one teacher's manual for her entire class.*

With a start, I realized she had all the top level sixth-grade readers. *This has to be a hand-picked group of the "best" students. I'll never be able to teach my students this way.* My heart sank with disappointment.

I sat quietly, watching the minutes tick by on the clock, waiting for the reading period to end, frustrated I would not learn anything useful to improve my teaching for my own wonderful, varied students. More disappointing than that to me, the shiny aura of excellence I had constructed around "Mrs. Perfect" began to look a bit tarnished. She hadn't done anything to address the gifts of these students.

I sat patiently while she read the answers to the workbook pages aloud. Students diligently checked their own work. When she told her students to put the reading books away and take out their math texts, I stood up and walked to the front of the classroom. I whispered a polite "Thank you" to Mrs. Carpenter and made my escape.

I closed the door to her classroom and let out a big sigh. Turning to the left, I continued down the long hallway into the fifth-grade wing. Mrs. Parker, Cora Lee, was next. I wondered what I would observe in this classroom. As I approached, I could see the open door; she expected my visit. I smoothed out the sides of my dress and stepped through the opening.

Mrs. Parker stood up from a chair at the back of the room, her face warm with welcome. "Class, please say 'hello' to our guest, Miz Wright."

"Hello, Miz Wright," they chorused in unison, cheery smiles on their faces.

"Hello fifth graders," I nodded, smiling back at them.

"Miz Wright will be walking around the room and checking to see if you're doing your work correctly, so you be on your best behavior for her."

"Yes, ma'am," they chorused.

Mrs. Parker walked to the front of the room and shut the classroom door. She took me aside and said in a loud whisper, "We are in the middle of a math lesson. You just feel free to stop and work with any student who needs help. Okay now?"

"Yes, that sounds great," I said, relieved I would not be relegated to an assigned chair in the back of this room for the period.

"Group 2, meet me at the circle," she announced. Six students made their way to a small circle of chairs set up in front of the side blackboard where Mrs. Parker met them, sitting in the large chair at the far side of the group.

I watched the students work for a while, set my notebook and pen on a bookcase near the door, and then started to walk through the room, stopping at student desks.

The first girl I approached looked up at me and said, "Hi, Miz Wright. Could you help me with this problem?"

"Sure," I said, squatting beside her desk. "What's your name?"

"Delila, but you can call me Lila."

"All right, Lila. Where are you stuck?"

"I'm working on this problem right here," she pointed.

I nodded my head. "It looks like you're on the right track. What's your next step?" I asked.

"I got to add 7 plus 8," she said counting on her fingers to get to 15. "Now I put down the 5 and carry the 1."

"That's right," I smiled. "Keep going."

I straightened up and walked to the next student.

Like Lila, instead of any actual help, most students just wanted my attention. I saw many counting on their fingers as they worked. Several also had multiplication charts to consult. Apparently, most of these students did not know their basic math facts.

I could hear Mrs. Parker working with her small group of students. They would stand up one-by-one and work through a multiplication problem on the blackboard. She encouraged them, corrected mistakes, and told the group to repeat aloud each step to take.

I began to scan the pages of math problems at each desk where I stopped. Some students were nearly done and others had written only a few problems. I searched each page for a mistake and then I asked the student to recheck the work on that problem, helping each one work through to the correct answer.

After a while, I could also observe students a little farther away from me. I saw one girl playing with a small pink eraser, poking her pencil through a hole in the middle of it and using it to drum quietly on the desk surface. Another girl was writing on a small scrap of paper. I watched her fold it up into a tiny wad and surreptitiously pass it to the girl across the aisle from her, who then looked around before opening the note. The two girls grinned at each other over the shared secret message.

In the front corner across the room from me, two boys lifted their desk lids and rummaged around aimlessly inside, whispering to each other. They jumped when Mrs. Parker yelled, "Josiah and Tony! You two are just fooling around, up to no good. Go put your names on the front blackboard!" All eyes turned toward them, watching the mini-drama play out. Sheepishly, they each got up and trudged to the board.

The first boy picked up the chalk and wrote his name, Josiah, in small, barely readable print. He looked toward Mrs. Parker whose attention had returned to her group. Then he handed the chalk to the second boy, made a face at him, and turned to go back to his seat. The second boy, Tony, took the chalk and signed his name with a big flourish, glancing at the girls in the front row, who giggled at him. Setting the chalk down a little too hard in the tray, it broke in half. His head snapped in Mrs. Parker's direction, but she seemed absorbed with the small group. Tony grinned at the girls again and headed back to his seat, giving the first boy a bit of a shove along the way.

"Now you two, get back to work!" yelled Mrs. Parker.

They startled again, dutifully picked up their pencils, and bent their heads into their math assignment.

By the time I worked my way to their corner of the room, I could see Tony had accomplished very little. Mistakes filled the problems he had already finished.

I leaned down to Tony and said, "Let's work the next problem together, okay?"

Before I knew it, the lunch recess bell rang and the math period was over. The class put away their books and gathered their lunch things. Mrs. Parker approached me while her students lined up. She said, "I'm so glad you came to visit our room."

"Thank you for letting me share this time with you." I gathered up my notebook and pen and walked toward the door.

She turned to the line of students and said, "Class, say 'Good-bye' and 'Thank you' to Miz Wright."

"Good-bye and thank you, Miz Wright!"

With that, Mrs. Parker walked out of the classroom, her students following in a line, straight through the maelstrom of students in the hallway. I followed them out, allowing Josiah to shut the door behind us. I paused for a moment in the hallway, watching Mrs. Parker and her students retreat and marveling that the line retained its integrity amidst the chaos of students swirling around them.

I backtracked toward Mrs. Carpenter's room, rounded the corner and walked to my own classroom, lost in thought. I entered the now silent room and stood still for a moment holding my blank notebook, thinking about the two teachers I had observed. I couldn't teach like Mrs. Carpenter; I'd be bored silly after half an hour in her perfectly arranged classroom. More comfortable with Mrs. Parker, I doubted I would ever have the force of personality she had with her students. I also knew I did not have the non-stop ebullience of Mr. Dewitt. My classroom control might never be perfect, but I knew I could make improvements.

I looked at the "name-bees" on the bulletin board and scanned the desks in the room, envisioning each one of my students. Glad to be their teacher, I vowed to continue to hone my own personal style of teaching, so I could do my best for each one of them.

Chapter 19
Celery

After lunch, students flooded through the door in animated conversations and energy left over from free play. Esaias darted into the room and ran past Mayhew, giving him a jab on the arm, then veered off in the opposite direction. Mayhew sprinted after him for a retaliatory sock, both boys laughing and giving each other back talk.

"Boys, recess is over. You need to settle down and have a seat," I said over the din. I sighed.

Mr. Dewitt arrived with the last of the students, exchanging spirited banter about basketball. Within seconds, everyone found a seat and the class began to calm. I stood at the front blackboard ready to start our grammar lesson for the day and smiled at my wonderful mix of students who looked at me to begin the lesson.

Toward the end of the school day, Mr. Dewitt and I reminded students of the list of items they had agreed to bring to class on Friday for our Japanese cooking lesson.

When the final bell of the day rang, students left the classroom filled with chatter about our plans. Mr. Dewitt walked out with the group, telling me he needed to grab some sheets of colored paper and would be back in a few minutes.

William lingered behind until everyone else left. He made his way to the door where I waited for him and stopped with head hung low, staring at the floor.

"William, everything all right?" I asked, bending my head down toward him with concern.

"Yes, ma'am."

He continued to stand at the doorway. In a quiet voice he said, "I signed up to bring celery." His head dropped just a bit lower.

"You can tell me, William. Is there a problem?"

I waited through the long pause.

"My mama doesn't know what celery is," he confided.

I tried not to let the surprise show on my face. Then I searched my brain for a way to explain celery to this young man.

"Come over to my desk, William. Let me explain while I draw a picture for you."

He followed me. I took out a piece of paper and a box of crayons from my desk drawer. I selected the green and yellow-green crayons. "Celery is a light green vegetable. It grows in a grouping, like this." I sketched while William watched. "You might find it with some of the leaves at the tops, but sometimes these get cut off at the grocery store."

Looking at William's face, I knew I had to continue. His silence compelled me to fill in the empty space with talk.

"You pull off one piece at a time. It always needs to be washed because it grows in the dirt." I drew a single stalk of celery and continued. "Celery is very crunchy and light in flavor. People eat it just plain or sometimes with a scoop of peanut butter or cheese in the groove. Often, it's cut into smaller pieces and cooked with many different ingredients like our Japanese Teriyaki. Once it's cooked, it's no longer crunchy."

Unsure my explanation helped, I continued, "William, would you like me to talk with your mother about the celery? Or . . . I could bring the celery instead."

William shifted from one foot to the other, then stood a little taller.

"No, ma'am, I think I can explain it to her now. Can I take your pictures?" he said looking directly into my eyes.

"Yes, of course, William." I handed the sketches to him. "Please let me know if there is anything I can do to help."

He walked toward the door, my sketches in hand, and glanced back at me, a slight smile on his face. Just before he disappeared into the hallway, I heard a quiet, "Thanks, Miz Wright." And then he was gone. *How could William and his mother have no knowledge of celery?* I had forgotten the lessons from my teacher preparation classes about the disadvantaged child. I had made assumptions based on my own comfortable, well-educated background, instead of looking at the child in front of me. I felt awful.

My thoughts about William were interrupted when Raynor returned to the room carrying huge rolls of red and yellow paper. "We'll spread these on the counter tops on Friday morning, like table cloths," he enthused. "Let's put them in the back of the cloakroom for now."

We cleaned up from the day and talked about the lessons I had observed. Raynor listened while I unloaded my disappointment and frustrations without fear of judgment from him.

"How do they decide which teachers get which students? It's just not right to dump all the 'low kids' and the 'behavior problems' on the new teachers. It's not fair to these kids to get the least experienced teachers. It's not fair to the new teachers, either. And, those top-level students? They deserve a more creative teacher who would challenge them and push them to reach their potentials.

"Why do administrators think a quiet class is so important? Walking kids in a line or keeping them silent in the classroom is not the same as giving them a good education."

When I ran out of steam, Raynor sat me down for a piece of advice.

"Things aren't always fair. Sometimes it's just the embedded culture at a particular school. Put your self-doubts aside. You just need to continue teaching with your infectious enthusiasm. The compassion and respect you have for your students are obvious. You can't help but inspire them. Just be yourself, Jan."

His positive words encouraged me.

"Thanks for listening, Raynor. Guess it's time to get back to work."

We walked over to the completed learning centers and got down to business figuring out how to introduce them to students. They would need to try out the activities, be shown how to use the answer cards, and learn where to put their completed work. Excited about the centers, I also worried about finding time to replenish the activity cards and keep up with the work students would generate on all the various independent levels. I'd just have to figure it out.

I needed to go over my preparations for the next school day and get home in time for a quick dinner before my economics class that night. Raynor grabbed his coat and told me he was off to a specialty store to get his surprise Japanese food.

On the ride home, I thought about how I would manage to thank him, my encouraging guide and supporting teacher, for the three weeks he had spent with me and my class. What a gift Raynor had been to all of us!

The day of our Japanese feast came too soon. Raynor and I spread out the colorful paper on the counter tops, set up the cooking utensils, and plugged in the hotplates. I had already stored the chicken in the staff room refrigerator.

"Did you find enough chopsticks?" I asked.

"Sure did," Raynor replied. "My wife and I had dinner at Mr. Soto's restaurant, and I talked him into donating a whole box of them. He also gave me some wonderful pictures we can use."

"You're amazing!" I said.

Raynor brought out a bag filled with pictures of Japanese scenes: Mt. Fuji, cherry trees in blossom, a pagoda, a girl in a kimono, and others. We tacked them up around the room.

I looked around the room, all decked out and ready for cooking with the completed learning centers standing in the corners. The big finale promised to be a doozy.

"I've got one more thing to get," said Raynor. "I'll be back in a few minutes."

I sat down at my desk to review the day ahead of us. In a few minutes, I heard slow limping footsteps in the hallway coming in the direction of my classroom. When I looked up from my desk, William waited in the doorway, smiling at me. He held a large bunch of celery in his left hand. A stout, gray-haired black woman in a faded housedress clung to his other arm. I walked over to greet them.

"Miz Wright, this is my mama," said William.

"I'm so pleased to meet you, Mrs. Cooper," I said, holding out my hand to her.

She took my hand in both of hers. Her hands felt warm and strong, despite fingers gnarled with arthritis. "William has been talking 'bout this cookin' party for days. Give her that celery, son."

I took the celery he held out to me.

"Thank you so much for bringing the celery into the classroom this morning," I said to his mother.

"I just want to thank you for all you doin' for my William. I know he's not the best student, but he sure do enjoy being in your class. He's trying real hard to learn how to read now that you workin' with him. He's a good boy, my William."

"I'm sure of that, Mrs. Cooper. He's always well behaved and dependable, and I know he's working hard. We can both be proud of his effort. I'm glad to hear he tells you about what's going on at school."

She beamed with motherly pride.

"Well, I's got to go now. You have a good day, Miz Wright. William, you just get me down those stairs afore all those hooligans come chargin' in."

"You have a wonderful day, too, Mrs. Cooper. You go now, William, the bell's about to ring. Take care of your mother."

"Yes, ma'am," he replied. He held onto her arm while they made their way back down the hall.

I watched their slow, limping progress for a minute, realizing what an effort this visit must have been for William's mother. I walked over to the counter and laid down the precious bunch of celery. I would make sure William got a taste of it raw and cooked.

Chapter 20
Farewell Feast

Esaias bounded into the classroom before the others. His running always heralded an escape from pursuit, having provoked someone into chasing him.

"Esaias, slow down," I admonished, yet again.

George dashed in behind him, barely putting on the brakes when he saw me standing at the doorway. "Esaias, I'm gonna get you for that!" he yelled.

Esaias laughed at him, eyes twinkling. He darted out of George's path, headed toward the center of the room and held up a bag of rice. "Where do I put the rice, Miz Wright?"

George zigzagged between desks, stalking Esaias, who evaded him.

"Esaias, please walk. You can put the rice on the counter next to the celery. George, let him be and sit down."

From the doorway, Beatrice hollered down the hall to a friend, "We gonna cook Japanese food and eat in the classroom." Holding onto the neck of a small dark bottle of soy sauce, she trounced through the door, Joshua on her heels.

"Give it back!" Joshua demanded.

"I will, I will," Beatrice teased, moving farther into the room. She held the bottle just high enough to be out of his reach.

Joshua jumped, trying to grab the soy sauce. "Give it back!"

"Beatrice . . ." I called to her, trying to intervene.

She lowered the bottle. Joshua grabbed it and tore past her.

A flood of students streamed into the classroom in high spirits. The room filled with the excited buzz of adolescent energy. I anticipated a long, busy Friday for us, ending with a touch of sadness over the imminent departure of my new friend and treasured colleague, Mr.

Dewitt, the helping teacher.

By mid-morning, we were all anxious to get on with the cooking. I planned to do most of the work with the group of students who did not go out for band. I counted seventeen non-band students, eight having dropped out of band since it started three weeks before.

Mayhew, the first out the door, sighed, "Awww, I don't want to go to band anymore. You always do the good stuff while we're gone."

"Yeah, I'd rather be here, too," said Mary.

I smiled at their comments. Maybe I was doing something right.

I explained the work stations and who would be in each group: vegetable choppers, sauce makers, chicken fryers, and rice cooks. At each station I had placed an instruction sheet along with measuring spoons and cups. I had purposely included fractions in the ingredient measurements for each group, posing problems of doubling, tripling, subtracting, and adding.

"Each group must agree to the measurement accuracy, and then you must have it checked by either me or Mr. Dewitt before going on to the next step on the direction card. Be sure to take turns, so everyone in the group has a chance to participate," I instructed.

"Oh, good. Here he is with the chicken, just in time," I said as Mr. Dewitt walked through the door into the room, carrying a big paper bag.

He stopped and held up the bag. With his deep dimpled grin, he teased, "Were you waiting for me?"

"Yeah!" chorused eager sixth graders, smiles of anticipation on their faces.

"Are you ready to cook some teriyaki chicken?" he yelled.

"YEAH! YEAH! YEAH!" they cheered.

I thought of all we had done together in the past three weeks and knew we would miss his presence in our midst.

"Hey, Mr. Dewitt, when do we get to see your surprise?" asked Beatrice.

"I have it tucked away for now. I'll bring it out just before we sit down for our meal. After Mrs. Wright says it's time to eat, you can remind me, Beatrice. Okay?"

"Okay!"

"Before we begin to cook, we all need to wash hands," I said. "I'll go with the girls to the restroom, and Mr. Dewitt will go with the boys. Be sure to walk quietly through the hallway. We don't want to disturb other classes."

The cooking adventure began. Mr. Dewitt took responsibility for the sauce makers and the chicken fryers. They moved to the far corner of the room on the counter under the "name-bees" bulletin board.

I took my groups to the other end of the counter. I told the rice cookers to read their directions and to work out the measurements. Then I moved to the vegetable chopper group: Kara, Curtis, Joshua, and William. I placed an onion on the wooden cutting board and picked up the knife I had brought from home. Next, I cut the onion in half, and then I sliced off one end. I showed them how to peel away the stiff outer skin. I cut the second onion the same way and handed a piece to Curtis and one to Kara.

"Now, you two peel the outer skin off the rest of the onions," I instructed.

"Joshua and William, you can pull the celery stalks apart, so each one can be washed."

I moved back to the rice cooks. While I listened to these students discuss the measurements, I watched Joshua showing William how to pull off the celery stalks, telling him to make sure to get the whole stalk and explaining where they would find the most dirt inside.

"Ooooo, my eyes are stinging from these onions," whined Kara.

"That's just normal," responded Curtis. "You just have to breathe through your mouth instead of your nose." He demonstrated.

Curtis and William began to wash their celery stalks in a bowl of water, while I helped Kara and Curtis chop the onions. When the time came for cutting the celery, we stopped to let each student take a small piece of celery to eat. I watched William, knowing this was a new experience for him. He looked up at me and gave a slight nod of his head, a shy grin creeping into the corners of his mouth. I smiled in return.

When teams completed their tasks, we began to combine the ingredients. Mr. Dewitt monitored the hotplates making sure students took turns and worked safely.

I put those who were finished to work moving the desks into groups of four, like dining tables. Students covered each desk with a red or yellow sheet of construction paper, like place mats. Then they distributed napkins, cups, and chopsticks.

By the time the period ended, the smell of chicken teriyaki wafted down the hallway, drawing the band students back at a run. Mayhew burst into the room waving a familiar pink piece of paper in his hand. "I've got my drop slip from band," he announced triumphantly.

"Me too," followed Sara close behind him. "Gee, it smells yummy! When do we get to eat?"

"That means there's only seven students left in band from our class," said Esaias.

Betty arrived and said, "Golly, it smells so good, and it looks beautiful in here!"

After the commotion of finding their desks in the new arrangement, the class settled down and turned to me for directions to start the meal. I waited for silence. Before I could speak, however, Beatrice's patience ran out, and her hand shot up.

"Beatrice, do you have a question for Mr. Dewitt?" I said slowly, drawing out the tension.

"What's our surprise?!"

"Oh, that. Did I forget?" he said with a sly grin. "Are you ready for a very special treat?"

"Yes, yes, yes!"

"Okay, I'll be right back." He walked into the cloakroom, all eyes following him. We could hear him make exaggerated shuffling sounds, as if searching for something. "Now where did I put that?"

"Come on Mr. Dewitt, we know you have it!" Beatrice called to him.

"Hmmm, all right, all right. Here it comes." He stepped out of the closet holding a lunch bag. "Inside this bag is something Japanese boys and girls eat for lunch," he began. "It comes from the sea. Can you guess what it is?"

"Dried fish? What is it? What is it?"

"No, it's not fish, but that's a good guess. Here's another clue: it's often an ingredient in ice cream."

"What? Show us, Mr. Dewitt. Show us!"

"I'll show you, but first I want to see how many of you will be willing to try eating it."

A few hands went up.

"Not enough. You need to be willing to try something new. I promise it's good for you. Remember they eat it in Japan."

Several more hands went up.

"Just a sample bite?" he cajoled the last of them to raise their hands.

"All right. Here it is . . ." With a flourish, he put his hand into the bag and pulled out a square package about the size of a piece of bread. Japanese writing covered the plastic wrap, obscuring the contents.

"That's awful small. What is it? Open it!" cried Beatrice.

He made a big show of opening the package. Teasingly slow, he pulled out a single, thin green sheet.

"Seaweed!" he said gleefully.

"EWWWWW," they yelled in unison.

"I ain't eatin' that!"

"Me neither."

"Hey, Mr. Dewitt, you said it's an ingredient in ice cream. There ain't no seaweed in ice cream!" challenged Esaias.

"Ah, believe it or not, there is. Another word we might use for seaweed is algae." He pulled out an empty, vanilla ice cream carton he had stashed in the cloakroom. "Here," he said, handing it to Esaias. "Read the ingredient list. Look for a word like algae."

"It's not there," Esaias replied after scanning the carton.

"Look again. Is there any word that comes close?"

"Well, there is agar-agar."

"Right. Good. That's the Japanese word for red algae. A very long time ago, in 1658, a Japanese innkeeper supposedly left some seaweed soup outside overnight. It froze in the winter cold, but when it thawed out, it became a gel-like substance. Today agar, or agar-agar, is used to thicken ice cream. Pretty neat, right?"

"Weird! Seaweed in ice cream," said Joshua, scrunching up his face.

Mr. Dewitt walked over to the cooked food, took a spoonful of rice and plopped it onto the seaweed he held in the palm of his hand. Tucking in the ends and folding it over, he held up a tube of rice-stuffed seaweed. "Japanese boys and girls take their rice to school like this. It's their kind of sandwich."

He took a big bite and announced, "Mmmmm, GOOD! Now, who would like to try it?"

"Me! Me!"

"I'd rather eat seaweed in ice cream," said Beatrice.

"I tell you what. If you'll try a seaweed sandwich, we'll give you ice cream for dessert," I smiled.

"Okay, okay," Beatrice grumbled.

"But first, it's time to eat our chicken teriyaki . . . and seaweed sandwiches!"

And so, we feasted farewell with Mr. Dewitt.

Chapter 21
Smile

I sat at my desk looking at the list, finding my name at the 11:30 slot. One thing I knew, the times on this schedule were just an estimate. We had a noisy, draining day ahead. Not for the first time, I missed Mr. Dewitt, and he'd only been gone for a week.

The bell rang. Time to start this day. I walked to the classroom door, ready to greet my students.

Dressed in a suit and tie, Esaias arrived first with George hot on his tail, as usual. They raced down the hallway. Mrs. Wallace yelled at them as they passed her room, "You boys stop that running!"

They slid to a slower pace and yelled back toward her, "Yes, ma'am."

When they reached our classroom, I said, "Esaias, George, you've got to slow down. Especially now that I can see how dressed up you are this morning."

Esaias slipped around the corner of the desks. He wore shiny black shoes with slick soles. I could see how sliding across the wooden floor would be a temptation for him.

"Esaias . . ." I gave him my stern look.

He shrugged. "Okay, okay, Miz Wright. My mama would have a fit if I got my Sunday clothes all messed up before I had my picture taken," he muttered. He scooted into his seat at the same time he took a swipe at George passing by him.

George batted back at Esaias.

I sighed. I knew these skirmishes were friendly play, but I wished I didn't have to keep telling them to stop fooling around.

Students filled the hallway in high spirits. Girls wore colorful, fancy, frilly dresses, and black patent leather Mary Jane shoes. Boys arrived in ironed shirts, dress pants, and shined shoes. I wondered how we would ever keep them all clean and looking sharp for their school photos.

"Good morning, Kara. What a pretty dress!" I admired.

Kara brushed down the sides of her pink ruffled dress, her charm bracelet tinkling. Her cheeks blushed, and a shy smile crossed her face. "Good morning, Miz Wright."

"Mayhew, don't you look nice this morning!" I continued as he approached.

"Did you see Esaias? He's wearing a tie!" he laughed.

"Look at me, Miz Wright. I got to wear my new dress for the pictures today," announced Linda, twirling in front of me.

"Beautiful, Linda."

Beatrice trudged down the hallway, a frown on her face. She wore the same dress she had worn yesterday, the same one she wore most days.

"Good morning, Beatrice. What's the matter?"

"Nothin's the matter. Don't want no stinkin' pictures, that's all."

"Well, *I* would like to have a picture of you," I replied.

"I forgot it was picture day, Miz Wright. Everyone else is all dressed up."

"You're perfect, just the way you are, Beatrice," I smiled at her, knowing she had not forgotten about picture day. She acted like a tough kid, because she lived in a group home. I doubted anyone there would purchase her photos.

I took a deep breath and closed the classroom door.

Before I could finish with attendance, the intercom crackled to life. Mr. Green boomed, "Good morning, boys and girls. Today is picture day."

A flurry of comments erupted from my students.

"Is he for real?"

"We *know* it's picture day."

"He's told us that every day for the last week."

I shushed them with a finger to my lips.

Mr. Green continued through the clamor, "Classes will be called to the auditorium throughout the morning. You will be instructed which camera to go to when you get there. And, try to be quiet in the hallways. Teachers, send your attendance folders right away."

We began the day with math as usual, but there would be no special reading classes or band. With the normal schedule suspended, I still wanted to fill the day productively. I planned to spend extra time on language arts, a subject I never had enough time to teach well. We worked on through the morning.

At the recess bell, I reminded my students to take care of their good clothes, but several students came back with scuffed shoes, shirt tails out, and sweat running down their faces. So much for being careful. I gave them a moment to settle down, and then we started on our social studies lesson about Japan. I began to read aloud about the processing of seaweed.

"Too bad we don't have some seaweed for lunch today," interrupted Mayhew.

"Yeah, like in that ice cream Mr. Dewitt gave us after our feast," Beatrice interjected.

"Let's stay focused on the lesson," I encouraged.

My students and I glanced at the clock several times during the next hour, waiting for 11:30 to arrive. At last, we began to hear other classes at the end of our hallway. The clock read 11:25.

"Must be the fifth graders going for photos," said Beatrice.

"It will be a while before it's our turn, so you need to pay attention and not let them distract us," I replied without much conviction. Spirits were high, attention low.

"Take out your language arts books," I said. "Turn to page 37."

We kept trying to work. Twenty agonizing minutes passed.

"We also use a comma after an introductory word. I'll show you two examples," I said.

I wrote on the blackboard:

Mayhew, will you take the folder?

Yes, our photos come next week.

"Who can give me another example?" I waited. Eyes averted, no one responded.

A strident voice on the intercom broke the silence. "Mrs. Wright, bring your class to the auditorium for photos now."

"Yay!" yelled my class.

I gave my students a few parting directions. "Pay attention to me when we get there, so you'll know where to go. Try to walk in a single file line. No talking in the hallway. Okay, let's go." I led my sixth graders out the door and into the hallway already buzzing with noise from other classes.

By the time we reached the auditorium, the buzz became a roar with noisy kids everywhere. Two boys from another class raced toward the doorway, almost running into me. A couple of girls followed, yelling at them and shoving each other. I tensed in anticipation of the struggle to manage my own class amidst this commotion.

A young woman, wearing a light blue smock with a picture of a camera on the front pocket, walked over to me.

"Mrs. Wright?" she inquired over the din.

"Yes, I'm Mrs. Wright," I nodded.

"Follow me to camera number two." She turned and walked through a sea of students, never glancing behind her to see if I followed.

Several classes milled around the auditorium, waiting. I looked back at my class and motioned for them to move with me into the room. Animated faces turned to watch the goings-on around us. Three more students darted in front of me.

The camera girl took us to a harried-looking gentleman. He stood by a large camera and two sets of lights in front of white umbrellas. Across from the camera, a student sat on a stool in front of a scene of mottled blue brush strokes. The photographer stepped in to reposition the student's head at a tilt. "Hold it there," he demanded.

Five more students milled around, waiting for their turn to have their photos taken. On the other side of the photo area, the rest of that class swarmed in a disorderly horde. They were chasing, teasing, poking each other, and playing tag. Robbie, their teacher, lounged in a chair, seemingly oblivious of the mass of adolescents cavorting in front of him.

"Stay behind the line, right here," the photographer's assistant directed us.

I motioned to George and Esaias to tuck in their shirts, helped straighten Richard's bow tie, and tucked an errant curl behind Linda's ear.

"I need to comb my hair. Where's the mirror?" Beatrice asked above the ruckus.

"You can ask the photographer's assistant, Beatrice," I said.

I watched the attendant hold up a smudge-covered, rectangular mirror for her. Mayhew, Richard, and Mike clustered around the mirror with Beatrice, making faces.

"Get outta here!" Beatrice whirled around and swatted at them.

"But I need to use the mirror, too," shot back Mayhew.

"Nah, uh . . . " teased Beatrice. "Here, Betty and Kara, you can use the mirror with me. They're my friends," she said with a saucy lilt, blocking the boys and holding up the mirror for the girls.

"Beatrice, share the mirror with the boys when you're done," I said. "And, Esaias, you need to put that pick in your pocket instead of in your hair."

"Do I have to?"

"Yes. Your mother had you dress up for this picture, so let's not disappoint her."

When the last of Robbie's students finished having their pictures taken, the photographer paused and fiddled with his camera for several minutes. My students fidgeted, waiting in a squirming line. I began to understand why Robbie checked out, ignoring his class and their playful behavior. Not me. I vowed to keep my students in order.

Shaking me out of my thoughts, the photographer announced, "Mrs. Wright, you're first. Please have a seat on the stool."

"Smile, Miz Wright," shouted Esaias.

I smoothed down my shoulder length straight hair, took a seat, and attempted to smile through my tension.

Students had nothing to do but stand around, waiting. They teased and annoyed each other. I moved from one end of the group to the other, settling squabbles, reinforcing boundaries, encouraging positive comments. Exhausting for me, my effort seemed minimally effective.

Once we were through with the individual photos, the girl with the blue smock led us to the area for our group photo. By that time, patience ran in short supply.

Kara sniped at George, "Stop fooling around. You stepped on my good shoes."

"Put that pick away, like Miz Wright said," Beatrice scolded Esaias.

"Get out of my way," complained Curtis when Mayhew stepped in front of him.

"Linda, I know you want to stand beside Kara, but the photographer asked you to move because you're too tall to be in the front row."

I addressed the group in the loudest voice I could manage, "Stop the shoving; it's not safe. Give each other a little room, and be patient with each other. Let's have a good class picture taken . . . please."

When they settled, I stepped in front of the group and said, "Now, all we need is your eyes on the photographer and a big smile from each of you. And, Mayhew, put your hand down, we don't want bunny ears in the picture."

"Mrs. Wright, you need to get in the picture, too," said Esaias, grinning at me.

I moved to the edge of my class and tried to remove the strain from my face. I thought about my class, frozen for an instant in time, and of the relief I would feel when this ordeal ended.

October 20, 1972

Chapter 22
Autumn Bounty

William noticed it first. He stopped beside me on his way out to lunch. I turned to him. "Yes, William. Do you need something?"

"Miz Wright, I think it's time for you to get out that plastic nursery you showed us." He pointed at the aquarium.

We leaned over to look at it. Sure enough, one of the black mollies looked wider, shaped a bit squarer, than the others.

"Thank you, William. You're very observant. I'll get that container. Would you like to help me put the mama fish into it?"

He nodded and waited while I went into the cloakroom to get it.

"Here it is. Why don't you put it into the tank?" I suggested to William.

He took it from me and submerged it, slowly allowing water to fill in. Then he gently scooped up the enlarged fish along with a couple of strands of elodea. "That will make her feel safer when she has her babies," he said. We watched the fat fish swim around her new enclosure.

"You did a good job with that, William. Let's see how long it takes for the others to notice what we added to the tank."

He looked at me and the corners of his mouth turned up into a conspiratorial grin.

After lunch, we started our language arts lesson. In the middle of giving the writing assignment directions, Curtis spotted the addition to our aquarium. "Miz Wright, are we going to have babies soon?" he interrupted.

All eyes turned to the aquarium. William and I exchanged glances.

"Yes, Curtis. It looks like she's pregnant. We needed to separate her from the other fish. We might just see them being born if you keep an eye out for it. It may take a few days, though."

Mid-October weather had begun to turn the leaves on the trees outside our windows into a colorful pallet of yellows, oranges, reds, and browns. Pumpkins and signs of Halloween heralded the changes. To perk up the corner of the blackboard where I wrote the date and reminders, I found some colored chalk and drew a pumpkin and a vine with a few leaves.

Later that morning, on her way to recess, Betty stopped to say, "I really like your cool drawings, Mrs. Wright."

"Thank you, Betty. I enjoy drawing. And, thank *you* for helping William this morning. You're a very good tutor."

"Reading is hard for him, Mrs. Wright, but I know he tries."

"How do you feel about going to Mrs. Smith for reading? Is that working out okay for you? Is it challenging enough?"

"Yeah. It's fine. I like reading anyway, and I already knew Samantha and Jill from Mrs. Smith's class, so we get to sit and read together."

Knowing she had other students at her level, at least a portion of the day, pleased me. When we followed the regular schedule, the coordinated switch for reading groups seemed to work well for all of us, including the students who went to the reading specialist.

"Mrs. Chapman lets her kids out too early. We hear them when they come back. Mrs. Smith always takes too long, and the kids in the hallway are distracting when we need to finish an assignment," said Betty, sounding a bit more like an adult than a sixth grader.

"Yes, I understand, Betty. Timing can be hard to coordinate." The noise in the hall annoyed me too, a small price to pay in order to manage the huge range of reading abilities both Nancy and I managed.

Betty continued on her way out to recess. I stood for a few moments thinking about reading and teaching. Mrs. Chapman had never followed through to help with our lowest reading groups, but Nancy and I had gathered materials from a couple of the second-grade teachers. I hoped our librarian would help point out books on easy reading levels that might interest our older students when we were finally allowed to go to the library. We always looked for ways to motivate these struggling readers, to keep them from giving up on the effort to learn.

The partner system I set up seemed to support the rest of the curriculum; my struggling readers had someone to help with directions or reading passages in other subjects. Of course, some pairs worked better than others. Betty and William were complete opposites in reading skills, but they got along well and had become a strong duo. I felt proud of both of them.

The next morning, William and Betty walked into the room together. William carried a giant pumpkin. "Look what William brought us, Mrs. Wright!" said Betty. She held out her hands to showcase the autumn bounty.

"My mama said I should bring this to you for our class," said William.

"How wonderful, William! It's gorgeous, and it looks very heavy. Why don't you set it down on that back counter?" I walked ahead of him to clear a spot.

"Is it for us to carve for Halloween?" I asked him.

"My mama usually makes pies and breads. She roasts the seeds too."

"Really? She uses fresh pumpkin? Not canned?"

"Yes, ma'am."

*Does his family depend on this pumpkin for food? William's mother
intends this as a special gift for our class, maybe for me in particular. I feel
humbled by her generosity.*

"I don't know much about fresh pumpkins, William. Do you think
she could still make a pie and use the seeds if we keep it just like it is
and then sent it back to her in a week or so?"

"Yeah, I think so. She's a good cook," he said with pride. "I think
she'd like that, Miz Wright."

"Wonderful! Please thank her for us. Let her know I'll send it
home, so she can use it for cooking."

Later that day, during the band period, we were into a music lesson
when Richard called out, "Miz Wright, Miz Wright! I think we're
havin' babies!"

Indeed, we were. Without hesitation, I motioned for the kids to
come over to the tank. We clustered around to watch. "Don't tap on
the tank to disturb the mother. Just watch what happens."

"Ooooo, Miz Wright, there's one coming out . . . and another one!"
Joshua whispered loudly.

In awe, we watched. In all, we counted twelve baby black mollies.

Two weeks later, right after Halloween, I sent the pumpkin and a
thank-you note home with William. I didn't know if it would still be
good for cooking, but it looked okay. I wanted the family to be able to
use it for food, rather than let it rot in our classroom.

The next Monday morning, William arrived at our classroom door
with a home baked pumpkin pie in each hand.

"My goodness, William."

Did his mother think I asked her to make the pies for the class?

*No use dwelling on this guilty feeling. I'll just show them how much I
appreciate their very generous gift.*

"What a wonderful surprise!" I gushed.

"She sent a jar of roasted pumpkin seeds for us, too," he answered. He nodded to Curtis who held up the jar he'd been carrying for William.

Kids gathered around as the boys placed the goodies on the back counter.

"Cool, William!"

"Yummy!"

"We get to eat 'em, right, Miz Wright?" Beatrice looked expectantly at me.

"Yes, of course," I answered. "Then we'll make a great big thank-you card for Mrs. Cooper during band period. William can take it home to his mother."

William beamed with pride. He took his seat next to Betty, and she nodded at him with a gentle smile.

The following week, only two students from our class remained in band.

Chapter 23
The Pedestal

Bare trees stood outside our classroom windows in the grey cold, stark reminders of the changing season; colorful autumn had turned into bleak winter. The final exam for my economics class loomed ahead of me. A flurry of preparations for the holiday season piled on top of my studies and teaching work.

I sat down next to Nancy at lunch and stifled a yawn. "Sorry. There's so much to do these days! I can't even remember what it's like to sleep in and not worry that I've got to finish something."

"I hear you," she answered. "I love the Christmas season, but with teaching, it just adds to the pressure. Too bad we don't each have a helping teacher to take some of the load off."

"Yeah. You know those learning centers in my classroom? I just can't get to them anymore, and my students have lost interest."

"I don't think I could take care of that set up either, Jan." She bit into her carrot and then said, "Your kids told me about the opera lessons. Are you still doing that?"

"Not really. Most of my students dropped band and are back in class now. I teach music once in a while, because they ask about it. Even though it's supposed to be in our curriculum, none of the teachers do any music."

"There's too much to teach in the other subject areas. Besides, I don't know much about teaching music," said Nancy.

"I didn't either. You're right, it took a lot of extra time to prepare."

I took a big gulp of milk, enjoying its icy cold taste. Then I said, "Now we've got Christmas to distract us. I'm trying to work the holidays into writing assignments and add a few art projects into the mix. I found a great Hanukah song I think I'll teach my class, too."

"I wish I could do that," said Nancy sounding wistful.

"We could combine our classes and do a little singing together the week just before Christmas, Nancy."

"Cool. I know my students would like it. They'll be antsy for vacation by then. Thanks, Jan."

We sat for a moment, eating lunch, lost in thought, hearing the hum of other conversations around us in the staff room.

"Hey, speaking of Christmas, did you get the invitation to Ann's party?" Nancy asked.

"Yes," I paused. "My final exam in economics comes earlier that week. It'll be nice to take a break from all the studying I've done for that class." I took a bite of my apple and folded up the waxed paper from my sandwich.

"I might have to skip Ann's party. We have a family gathering the next day," said Nancy.

"You've got a lot going on." I looked around and added in a whisper, "Aren't you curious about Ann's place? I wonder if it's as perfect as her classroom."

Nancy grinned.

Florence, one of the older fifth-grade teachers, set her lunch tray down on the table next to me and eased herself into the seat. "Ah, it's good to rest for a few moments, isn't it?"

"Sure is," I sighed.

"Jan, do you plan to go to the dinner theater outing and Ann's after-party?" she asked me.

"Yes, I think so."

"You said you live out by the Beach Streets, right? Would you mind giving me a ride? It would be right on your way," she said.

"My husband and I would be happy to pick you up," I answered, feeling a bit of awe that I had been selected to escort this grand old teacher to an evening out.

"Good. These parties are not to be missed," she said with a gleeful tone.

I exchanged glances with Nancy, eyebrows raised.

Winter cold settled on Norfolk, but our spirits were bright that Friday party night.

We parked in front of her red brick, cottage-like house. Florence stood outside waiting for us at her front door, dressed in a warm winter coat. My husband and I walked up to her porch together.

"Mrs. Weins, this is my husband, Jerry," I offered.

"Hello, Mrs. Weins. Nice to meet you," said Jerry.

"Oh dearie, just call me Florence," she responded.

Jerry offered his arm to help her maneuver down the steps and across the frosty sidewalk.

"Oh, that's one of those car/trucks, isn't it?" she said to him, hanging on tight to his arm.

"Yes, it's an El Camino. It's built like a car, but has a truck bed in the back. We added the camper top before we left California."

At the theater, Jerry dropped us off close to the door, and I walked with Florence into the lobby while he parked. Several other teachers from school and their spouses had already arrived; a flood of introductions followed.

The evening settled into a pleasant dinner theater experience, filled with the holiday spirit. During dinner, Florence ordered a glass of wine, and then another. I enjoyed hearing the sound of her giggles, seeing her relaxed like this.

After the theater, we drove to Ann's apartment building for the after-party. Florence held onto Jerry's arm, as he led her into the elevator.

When the elevator doors reopened, loud music and laughter assaulted us. A smokey haze poured into the hallway from an open door.

We entered a party in full swing. The crowd yelling out welcomes to Florence. Robbie, hollered, "Hey, Florence, ready for your usual gin and tonic? We saved a seat for you at the bar."

Looking over the packed room, I realized why I had not seen some of the other teachers at the theater. They were already partying at Ann's along with several people I did not recognize. Robbie whisked Florence away to the bar to get her drink. Jerry and I made our way over to our hostess who was talking with Tom Barry, our vice principal. In good spirits, Ann held a drink in one hand and a cigarette in the other. She sloshed her drink, as she spun around to greet me.

"Oh, there you are, darlin'," she said in an exaggerated southern drawl. "Make yourself at home. Take your coats off and put them in the bedroom over there."

"Ann, this is my husband, Jerry," I said in a voice loud enough to be heard over the crowd.

She slung an arm around his shoulder. "Ah, he's a handsome devil. Jan, go get a drink for you and your guy."

"Leave the poor man alone, Ann," admonished Tom.

"Oh, he's a big boy, Tom," she replied with a sultry look as she relinquished the hold on my husband.

We made our way through the crowded room, deposited our coats, and headed back into the living room.

"I'll just grab us a seat over there," Jerry said.

"Okay, I'll get us something to drink."

"Make mine a soda," he answered.

I had never been to a party with a group of teachers before. At the tender age of twenty-five, I had never been to a cocktail party. Oh, Jerry and I had tried some Boone's Farm apple wine with friends, and we were no strangers to beer parties with Navy guys, but the scene at this party awed me. In my mind, teachers were held on a pedestal, sage and revered. I had not yet come to the realization that they were regular people who partied, smoked, and drank alcohol.

I sat near my husband watching the raucous evening progress. Florence looked settled and happy, telling stories to a group at the bar. Drinks and more drinks were poured. Laughter grew louder. Someone started to play the piano and the group joined in singing a few Christmas carols. Then the jokes began. "Did you hear the one about the man and the blonde? . . ."

Then Ann, cheeks flushed, told risqué jokes to loud applause and hoots of laughter. Not sure how to respond in this crowd, I kept quiet, trying to keep a smile on my face. It might have been the wine I was drinking, but I could feel my cheeks blushing.

Robbie yelled to her from across the room, "Ann, you're embarrassing yourself in front of our young newbie teacher!"

With that she, staggered to her feet, put one hand on a hip while hoisting her martini glass in the air, and slurred, "It's about time she lost some of her innocence! Hey, I'm hot." With that, she put her hand on her head, whipped off her blond wig and threw it across the room to Robbie. She swayed there in wispy haired, drunken reveal while the crowd erupted in loud guffaws and the wig flew back and forth across the room.

Yikes! Ann just fell off her perfect-teacher pedestal.

My husband and I sat in flabbergasted silence. I stared at Ann in disbelief. At last, Robbie snagged the wig and took Ann by her arm out of the room.

I turned to my husband and whispered, "Maybe it's time for us to go home."

Chapter 24
Radiator

Carrying a stack of papers I had graded at home the night before, I could hear the radiators in the hallway creaking to life as I climbed the stairs to the second floor of the ancient school. I remembered seeing the outdated heating system when I first arrived here, wondering then if they worked at all. On cold days like this one, I was thankful they did. I never saw it, but I imagined a huge boiler room, somewhere in the bowels of the school where some poor soul arrived earlier than I to stoke the fire, so I could be warm.

In early March, the news filled with hope for peace in Vietnam; troops started coming home. Jerry, assigned to the maintenance of jets at Virginia Beach Naval Air Station, had gone out for a three-week trial cruise on the aircraft carrier, Independence. Meanwhile, I slogged through a semester of United States history at Old Dominion University to complete my credential requirements for the state of Virginia.

With months of dreary weather behind us, we awaited spring warmth. When I arrived at my classroom, I decided to liven up the announcements on the blackboard with a few drawings, like I had done at the start of the school year when my energy seemed boundless. These days, I had too much to do, just to keep up, so I seldom drew anything. A few spring flowers might cheer us up.

As I sketched, somehow a picture of our new van began to appear in the middle of my drawing. The kids would like the van, and I could tell them how Jerry and I were paneling the interior and would lay bright orange shag carpet in it. Being with these students, like a daytime family, I got to know them well. I thought about all sorts of details they told me about their lives.

Before I knew it, I'd spent too much time thinking and drawing, so I had to rush to prepare for the rest of the academic day. Although I felt pressured, it seemed satisfying to spend those few moments in artistic distraction.

Later that morning, the wind picked up and rain seemed imminent. My students were restless and less attentive, unfocused. I sent my small group to the reading specialist and switched students with Nancy.

When we had almost finished the reading period, I heard the familiar commotion of students returning in the hallway.

"They're back early, again," said William to me, as I bent over his desk using my finger to track the words for him to read.

"Why don't you finish up this paragraph, and we'll be done for the day," I said.

Just then, the classroom door flew open. Esaias ran into the room, "Miz Wright, Miz Wright. Come quick. Mayhew's been hurt . . . bad!" The class came to a hushed standstill. I rushed out into the hallway with Esaias, calling over my shoulder, "Stay in your seats!"

Just outside my classroom, on the floor next to the metal radiator, sat Mayhew, encircled by a stunned group of students. He held his head in his hands; blood dripped through his fingers.

"Get the first aid kit. It's hanging on the wall, right there inside the door," I ordered Esaias, squatting down in front of Mayhew.

"Mayhew, I'm right here. Let me see what's going on underneath your hands," I said with a calmness I did not feel. I took ahold of his hands and pulled them gently away.

The surrounding students gasped. The skin on his forehead was split open in a vertical line above his left eye. I could see the white of the underlying skull. Blood dripped down that side of Mayhew's face from the bottom of the cut, but not much came from the rest of the wound. He seemed alert, but a bit dazed. I checked his eyes and noted that his pupils seemed normal, both the same size.

Seconds seemed like minutes. Esaias handed me the first aid kit. "Thank you, Esaias. Now go to the office and get help, quick." He took off running down the hall.

"Let's see what we've got in here for you, Mayhew," I said opening the kit. I grabbed a package of 4 x 4 gauze. "This will work perfectly. I'm just going to put this sterile gauze pad on your forehead."

I tore the package open, took out the gauze square, and pressed it over the wound. The bleeding had already begun to stop. I noticed how quiet the normally talkative Mayhew had become.

I held the gauze on his forehead, still squatting in front of him. "You're going to be all right, Mayhew. Let's just get some of this old blood cleaned up. Joshua, go to the boys' bathroom and get us some wet paper towels." Joshua took off down the hall.

"Mayhew, tell me what happened." I kept my eyes on his and my reactions measured and calm.

The students inside my classroom crept up to the open door to see the drama in the hallway.

The small group of students who had come with Mayhew from the reading specialist's class clustered around me, eager to tell the story.

"We were coming back from reading . . ."

"Mayhew was running, and he slipped . . ."

"He hit his head on the radiator . . ."

I interrupted them, "Mayhew's going to be all right. Let *him* tell me what happened. In fact, why don't all of you go back into the classroom now?"

Just then, Nancy's classroom door opened and my students who went to her for reading poured into the hallway. Seeing Mayhew sitting on the floor, with me holding the gauze in place and blood on his face, they crowded toward us. I spoke over my shoulder to them, "Okay, everyone go into our classroom. Mayhew's going to be fine."

In the commotion, I could hear Nancy. She began directing the children to get them all settled, my students into my room and all of her students back in her room. She remained at her doorway keeping an eye on us in the hall.

Meanwhile, Joshua arrived with wet paper towels. "Thank you, Joshua. Now you go into the classroom too."

He left us and the hallway settled into quiet.

Leaving one hand on the gauze, I used the other hand to clean off Mayhew's face and shirt. "Well, Mayhew, tell me how you managed to hit your head like this," I said to him.

"I was runnin', Miz Wright," he started. "I just skidded when I got to our room." He shrugged. "I lost my balance, stubbed my toe, tripped, and fell head first into the radiator. Not such a smart move, I guess."

By the time he finished talking, I had his face cleaned up. "Here," I said handing him the wet paper towels, "Clean up your hands now." He took the towels from me and cleaned the dried blood from each finger.

Esaias came marching down the hallway toward us with the vice principal in tow. "I got him, Miz Wright. Mr. Barry's right here!" he yelled to me. "I told him Mayhew hit his head on the radiator."

Tom Barry, a tall, lanky, well-dressed black man, had a lot of swagger, the perfect complement for the principal, Lou Green, a portly, bald-headed, rumpled-looking white man. Tom started talking as he approached us. "Aw come on now, what's all the fuss. You again, Mayhew? No big deal. Get off the floor and get back into the classroom."

"Um, no, I don't think so, Mr. Barry," I said, still squatting in front of Mayhew. I lifted my head to look at Tom and said, "He needs to see a doctor."

Not even glancing at me, Tom replied, "Just put a little bandage on it. Mayhew, come on, get up." He bent down to take the boy's arm.

Trying not to sound alarmed, for Mayhew's sake, I put my free hand on Tom's arm to stop him and said in a quiet, but firm, voice, "No, I think he's going to need stitches."

Tom looked at me, "Aw, he's a tough kid. He'll be fine."

I held his eyes with mine and said more insistently, "Take a look at this."

I pulled the gauze away to reveal the wound; the white of Mayhew's skull gleamed at us. Tom blanched. He gulped. For a moment, I thought he might faint.

"Oh." It took him a moment to gather himself together. "Ahhhh ... let's get him down to the office. Mayhew do you think you can walk? Esaias, help me get him up."

Before I could stop them, they pulled him up and took off down the hall. Nancy and I exchanged glances and then walked into our respective classrooms and closed our doors. Each of us would give the unnecessary talk to a subdued group of students about the importance of not running in the hallway.

At the end of that day, just as the final bell rang, Mayhew returned with his parents, a big white bandage encircling his head. The kids greeted them, all talking at once, wanting to know all the gory details. Mayhew grinned as he told them the doctor put ten stitches in his forehead. The smile and the banter with the other kids relieved me of worry over him. However, my concern shifted to his parents' reaction. I felt terribly guilty that Mayhew had been hurt just outside my classroom.

Mayhew's dad, dressed in his Navy uniform, had a serious look on his face. "Mayhew, get in here, and you apologize to Miz Wright right now," he commanded.

I tried not to let the surprise show on my face. An apology?

The kids disappeared down the hall. Flanked by his mother and father, Mayhew bowed his head and cleared his throat. "I'm sorry I got hurt."

"Son, you know what we talked about, . . . " prompted his dad.

Mayhew looked up at me and spoke more distinctly. "Sorry I was fooling around, running in the hallway. I won't do it anymore."

"I'm pleased to hear that from you Mayhew, and I'm glad to see you're okay. You gave us all a bit of a scare," I said, placing my hand on his shoulder.

"Yes, ma'am," he grinned up at me.

His father stretched up a bit taller, as if ready to salute me, and said in a stern tone of voice, "It won't happen again, Miz Wright. You just give me a call if you have any more trouble with my son."

I smiled at Mayhew, knowing he would indeed be fooling around again, but also knowing I now had an ace up my sleeve. His dad.

Chapter 25
Gifts

On May 19, 1973, President Richard Nixon gave a speech in Norfolk, Virginia on the *USS Constitution*. Jerry and hundreds of other young Navy men spent days preparing for the President's visit aboard ship. That evening, Jerry slammed through the front door of our apartment grumbling to me, "What a waste! We painted the entire path Nixon walked through. Nothing else. Just the rooms and hallways he would see. Not the places that needed to be painted. All just for show."

Looking up from my lesson plans, I asked, "Why did Nixon travel all the way here to give a speech? What did he talk about?"

"Something about Armed Forces Day. He said we need to keep the spending high for the military. What sense does that make? The last of our ships are expected home from 'Nam as soon as they finish sweeping for mines in the harbors."

He plopped down on the couch next to me with a sigh.

"Oh, and my fleet will be shipping out next month," he added, treating the news almost as an afterthought.

"Jerry, your fleet's leaving? Does that mean you, too?" my voice rising in pitch.

"Calm down. I won't know anything until I get my new orders. I could get my discharge; my four years in the Navy are up in September."

"Oh, I hope you don't have to ship out, Jerry. Why would they bother, for such a short period of time? They'd have to turn around and send you all the way back here."

"The Navy's priority is not logic," he said shaking his head.

"Well, let's have dinner," I said with resignation, setting aside my worry. "I made your sister's recipe for hamburger pie."

I put my papers down, and we both got up to get dinner on the table. Jerry set out the silverware while I poured a glass of milk for me and a cup of coffee for him. Then I grabbed the hot pads and took the casserole out of the oven.

Changing to more comforting thoughts I said, "When we do go home to California, let's travel across the northern states this time." I used the serving spoon to dish out steaming hot portions onto each of our plates. "I want to stop and see Niagara Falls, Mount Rushmore, the great Salt Lake, and a place I saw as a little kid, the Corn Palace."

We sat down at the kitchen table to eat dinner. I took a bite of hamburger pie. It burned my tongue, and I took a swallow of my cold milk. "Watch out! It's hot," I warned Jerry.

I speared a green bean and blew on it before putting it into my mouth.

"Jerry, you know what I don't like about the end of the school year?" We ate in silence for a few seconds. Then I set down my fork and looked up at Jerry. "Leaving these kids. They're a part of my life. You know, I spend more time with them than their parents do. Heck, I spend more awake time with them than I do with you!"

"You wouldn't see them if we stayed here anyway. They go on to another school next year, right?" he said in his always practical manner.

"Yeah, you're right. But, it's just so hard to think of losing all my kids like this." I stood up to get the saltshaker from the stove. "I guess I just have to think about what comes next. We get to go home."

I sat back down at the table, salt in hand. Almost in a whisper, I said, "Still, I'm going to miss my kids."

The end of the year came all in a rush, a blur of frantic activities. I fussed over final grades, report cards, student records, and endless lesson plans.

The night before school let out, I worked late. Jerry stood at the stove, stirring a saucepan full of rice when I walked through the front door.

"Sorry I'm so late, Jerry. There's just so much to do to be ready for tomorrow." I wrestled an armload of papers. "I've got to finish writing the comments on all these report cards tonight and get them into the envelopes."

He glanced at me. "Dinner's ready. I'll put it on the table." He looked glum.

"What's up? What happened today?" I said, putting my papers down on the coffee table and walking into the kitchen to stand beside him at the stove. He took his time to respond.

"Orders came out today," Jerry said, serving the dinner onto our plates at the stove.

"Well, what *are* they?"

Jerry picked up our plates and set them on the table. "The *Independence* is going to the Mediterranean." He looked at me. "I've got to go."

I let out the breath I didn't know I'd been holding, "Darn, I thought they might let you out early."

"Yeah, me too."

We sat down at the table, neither one of us starting to eat. I looked over at Jerry and grabbed his hand, "So, when do you leave?"

"We ship out on June 21st."

"A week from tomorrow. Shoot!"

Already feeling the sadness of separation, he said to me, "I don't want to leave you, Jan."

Putting on a brave face, I said, "We just need to think about being together when you return, Jerry. Three months will go by fast, and then we can go home."

We talked throughout dinner, making plans for the big changes to come. Although the few other wives I knew were leaving to go home, I'd stay in our apartment, alone, until Jerry came back. Then we would load up the van together and drive home, taking a few days to see the sights in the northern states along the way.

After dinner, with reluctance, I refocused on the report cards, searching for just the right words to write about each one of my students.

The next morning, the bell rang to start my last day of teaching at J.E.B. Stuart Elementary School. Positioned at my classroom door, I momentarily shut my eyes, and breathed in the familiar sound of excited students coming up the stairs and down the hallway. I glanced at the radiator across the hall from my room, remembering the day Mayhew got his stitches. I knew he would always have this reminder of our year together, the faded scar on his forehead.

Esaias sprinted down the hallway and came to an abrupt halt in front of me. "I know, I know, slow down!" A giant grin spread from ear to ear and his eyes sparkled with pure joy as he held up a small, gift-wrapped box with a card and announced, "I got a present for you, Miz Wright. Open it! Open it!"

I had not expected gifts on the last day of school. Before I could respond to Esaias, other students swarmed into the room.

"Got you some candy, Miz Wright," announced Linda, displaying a box of sweets.

"Me too," said Kara, grinning at me, holding out a sucker with a bow on it.

George came through the doorway with a handful of flowers that looked like he had picked them on his way to school.

"Thank you," I managed to squeeze out, feeling a bit flustered. "Why don't you put everything on my desk?"

"Hey, Miz Wright. I'se goin' to the beach next week!" shouted Beatrice as she bounded into the room.

"Open the presents now!" repeated Esaias.

"Esaias, thank you. I'll open them later. We have to get settled, so I can take role. The announcements are about to start."

By noon we had cleaned up and turned in all the books and supplies. I handed out the "name bees" I had saved from the first days of school. Then, I faced my class and said, "Think for a few minutes about what you have learned this year. Remember all the things we've done together."

"I'm thinking about summer vacation!" said Mayhew. The kids laughed.

"Open your presents," demanded Esaias.

"It's . . . it's not . . . not very polite for me to open gifts in front of you. I'll . . . I'll do it later," I stammered, trying to keep a smile on my face for him. Something in me questioned my thinking, but I remained firm in the thought that it didn't seem right for me to open gifts when *they* had nothing to open. Besides, I worried about how those who didn't bring gifts might feel. So, I pressed on and moved to the next activity I had planned.

Then came the time to give my students their final report cards.

"You need to take these home. They're confidential. Do not share them with anyone except your parents." I called the names and handed out the report cards. Some of the students opened the envelopes to look at their grades and started talking with each other.

"Put those report cards away until you get home," I said without much response from my students. I should have known it would be too tempting not to look and discuss grades.

Before I knew it, the final bell rang. A shout of "Yay!" went up from a thrilled group of kids released from the last day of school for this year.

At the doorway, I offered a hug or a hand shake to each of my students as they left the room.

"Go! Have a wonderful summer. I'll miss you!" I said as they departed.

At last, William paused beside me, the final one to leave, as usual.

"Would you like a hug, William?"

Without saying a word, he stepped up and gave me hug.

"Good bye, William. Keep up the good work. I'll miss you." He smiled at me and turned to leave. I listened to him whistle down the hallway as I watched him stroll out of sight.

147

My footsteps echoed in the silence of the emptied room. I returned to my desk. A few cards and notes, a small basket of candy, a handful of flowers, and the wrapped gift from Esaias still covered the surface. I sat down, my eyes a little damp, but I held back the tears. I opened the cards, smiled at the hand-written notes from the students and their parents, and finally picked up the package from Esaias. The tag on it read: "Dear Mrs. Wright, I'm going to miss you. From Esaias." The tears began.

I pulled off the ribbon, picked at the tape, and peeled back the paper. I opened the box and pulled out a little gold-colored trophy seated on a small block of wood. The plastic plaque on the front read: World's Greatest Teacher.

I pulled in a ragged breath, the turmoil of emotions coming to full force.

After all the nagging I had done to keep Esaias quiet and on task, *this* boy had given me *this* gift? Why hadn't I opened it before he left? Now I would never be able to look at him and tell him how much his gift meant to me. Heartbroken, I felt ever-so-proud of having become "the world's greatest teacher."

Forty-six years later, his gift still sits on my book shelf.

DECADES IN THE MIDDLE

Jerry and I moved back to California and raised two sons, David and Brian.

I became an active volunteer where my sons attended school.

As they grew up, I took on part-time teaching roles.

In 1986, I returned to full-time classroom teaching.

PART TWO
The Seasoned Teacher

Transitions

Mountain View, California

1999
2000

Chapter 26
Moving

O n an early spring day in 1999, Damon sat in his wheelchair, second in line, waiting for his turn to play four square and yelled, "Great shot, Aaron!" He reached for the red rubber ball, but it bounced out of bounds, over his head.

"I'll get it," yelled Ryan. He sprinted after the errant ball.

The next kid in line moved into the beginning square and Damon wheeled himself one step closer.

I smiled as I watched the game proceed.

Damon's turn. He raised himself up to a standing position on wobbly legs. Then he shuffled forward to the starting spot in the square while Ryan moved the wheelchair out of range. With a huge grin on his face, Damon maneuvered his body into position, knees slightly bent. He clapped the back of his droopy hand with his good hand, eager to play. Cerebral Palsy did not keep this boy from joining in the fun.

Eric set up the ball. He launched the first easy serve across the diagonal, directly to Damon, just as I had taught them. With glee in his eyes, Damon batted the ball to his left, catching Tony off guard and making him dash into the corner to send the ball back to Eric.

The sound of jackhammers started up, adding to the constant *tap, tap, tap* of hammers and the *zing* of electric saws. Seeming unfazed by the cacophony of sounds, the kids dialed up their own volume and continued to play.

I sighed, thinking about the huge changes ahead of us as we reshuffled our work spaces around the remodeling and construction projects.

"Sorry I'm late," Mira projected her voice to be heard above the din. She had come out to yard duty halfway through recess, as usual, and stood next to me instead of taking her assigned duty spot across the playground. From bitter experience, I knew not to call her on it again. I continued to stare out at the students playing four square on the asphalt in front of our classrooms, feeling annoyed.

"When we hired you, did you imagine we'd be right in the middle of all this remodeling reconstruction?" she yelled.

I shook my head. Due to increased enrollment, the district had moved all fifth graders to Crittenden Middle School on a temporary basis so the closest elementary school, Theuerkauf, could be remodeled and expanded. No one told me a remodeling project would be scheduled for Crittenden at the same time.

The jackhammering paused. I said to Mira, "I thought fifth grade would be settled back in the elementary schools before work began here."

"This old building needs to be torn down," she gestured toward our classrooms. "It was designed in the days when the 'open school' concept was all the rage. I didn't mind teaching in the open space, but the whole thing was a complete disaster. It just didn't work, and we got stuck with those horrible accordion walls to separate our classrooms when they finally gave up on the idea." Both of us in our mid-50s, I too knew about the "open school" concept, but I didn't bother to share my own experience with her.

"Mira, speaking of that, could you turn up the heater? Some of my kids complained about being cold," I said. She controlled the thermostat for both rooms in this ancient open pod configuration.

"We've been so busy packing I got overheated." She leaned in to speak in a loud whisper, "And I'm having those damned hot flashes. I had to take off my sweater and work in my sleeveless blouse."

I knew we would not likely get any increase in heat. I stepped back a pace and looked her in the eye.

"Packing? You're packing already? Do we have a date for our move across campus?" I asked.

"Not yet. But I copied off packets of busy work for my students to do and put my best kids to work packing up the classroom. The district doesn't pay me enough to do all that packing myself."

I'd better start organizing for this move. I certainly won't be using teaching time for packing.

She paused, and I sensed she was about to tell me the real reason she had come to talk with me.

"We need to stop switching classes for social studies and science. I'll just keep my own kids from now on, and you can keep yours." She turned to look out at the field.

"I haven't quite finished the science unit with your students yet," I replied. "To give grades for your kids, I need to keep them until Friday, as we agreed."

She faced me straight on. "Okay. I'll just keep your kids busy. I've got some coloring pages of Revolutionary soldiers they can do."

Coloring pages for fifth graders? Defying copyright laws again?

I simply nodded, keeping my well-known concerns to myself this time.

The jackhammer started up again.

Damon, who had made his way into the second square, yelled, "Come on, Aaron, shoot it to me!" He clapped his hands in anticipation, grinning.

"Here it comes," yelled Aaron. He served the ball just in front of Damon.

Damon gave a big swipe with his strong arm and sent the ball flying to Leah in the third square. She propelled the ball back to Aaron, the server. He just managed to tip the ball with one hand to send it out of bounds beside Damon. The group cheered as Damon made his way into the next square. Just then, the bell rang, ending recess.

Students walked back to form lines in front of their respective classrooms, waiting for their teachers to claim them while the sound of jackhammers continued to pound in our ears. I watched Mira walk directly into her own classroom, leaving her kids to follow.

After each of the other four, much younger teachers arrived and claimed their students, I gave the signal to release my own students.

On the way into the classroom, Damon stopped beside me to ask, "Mrs. Wright, will we still get to play four square when we move?"

"I don't know yet." I looked at him and had a sudden inspiration.

"Would you all like to go take a look at what they're building and where we'll be moving?" I said to the class.

"Yeah, that'd be cool," answered Kendra aloud as the rest of the kids murmured agreement, all smiles.

"We could walk past the construction site for the new science building. Then we could walk over to the dirt lot at the other end of campus where they'll place our fifth-grade portable classrooms. We'd be closer to the lunchroom by then. We might be a little early for lunch."

A cheer went up from the group.

Hmmm, I wonder how I can incorporate a bit of math with our little trek.

How could I have foreseen the disaster that was to come with the move just a few days later?

"How could you THINK THAT WAS TRASH?" I screamed at the custodian standing beside me. In a fit of anger, I waved at the mound of papers on the floor of the recycling bin.

"Do you know how many years of teaching that represents? Do you realize what you've done?" My voice shook while I ranted. I paced back and forth in front of the surly man who didn't seem the least bit apologetic.

"WHEN did you do this? I was just here packing on Saturday, on . . . my . . . day . . . off!" My eyes brimmed with the tears I struggled to keep at bay.

"I went around picking up trash early this morning. Lots of teachers put boxes of garbage out to be thrown away," he said in a defiant tone of voice.

"These boxes were stacked neatly in my office space, not tossed outside like garbage. And why in the world did you have to DUMP OUT those boxes? WHY?"

"It was just old papers," he replied with one eyebrow raised.

"Did you not notice they were all filed . . . in alphabetical order?" I was running out of steam and control on imminent tears.

Dave, the vice principal, had heard the commotion and came sprinting toward us.

"What's going on here?" he asked, slowing down to catch his breath.

"He threw out all my teaching files," I sniveled. Tears began to stream down my face. I felt thoroughly embarrassed at having lost control of myself.

"We'll take care of this. You go, Mrs. Wright. The bell's about to ring."

Dave retrieved a box and started filling it with handfuls of my precious files. The custodian grabbed another box and slammed a handful of papers into it.

Heartbroken, I headed back to start my teaching day. "It would take years to unscramble this mess now," I muttered to myself, feeling utterly defeated.

A white paneled truck sat on the asphalt on top of the four squares. From my open classroom door, wheeling a large platform loaded with my teacher desk and chair, came two men dressed in paint-stained white coveralls. I watched as they maneuvered the load onto the lift and then raised it to the level of the truck bed. The men shoved my desk into the truck stacking it next to the shelf sets and other school furniture already filling the space.

"Are you moving the student desks next?" I asked.

"Nope," responded the burly guy with the heavy eyebrows. "This is our last load. You'll have to manage the rest of it on your own."

I stood with my mouth agape, speechless at his casual edict. This was nothing like the moves I'd made in any of my previous schools where everything had been moved and set up for us during non-school hours.

Is he being serious?

Before I could question him further, a stream of students carrying boxes erupted from Mira's room. Mira appeared with her purse and a tote bag in one hand, locked her door, and stopped long enough to yell up to the movers.

"Hey, Joe, you guys take good care of my desk now; it's getting to be an antique, just like this ol' gal." They chuckled with her.

"Sure thing, Ms. Smith. Anything for you, darlin'," the one called Joe responded.

"And leave me one of those wheeled carts for my kids to use in the morning. Pretty please," she batted her eyes at them.

"Sure. I'll see what else we can round up for you, Mira."

"Mira, are you aware that we're expected to move our student desks?" I asked her.

"Oh, yeah. The kids can move their own desks. We'll use the wheeled cart from Joe to move the really heavy stuff." She looked at me and added, "You can use it when I'm done, Jan."

"Umm, thanks, Mira."

"Good night," she yelled as she departed in pursuit of her little group of students. Her skirt swished as she deliberately swayed her backside.

Joe let out a loud wolf whistle.

Mira threw a saucy look over her shoulder. "Now Joe, you be a gentleman."

I had nothing to say. Nothing. I retreated to my classroom to stand in the midst of half-emptiness.

What should I do next? How can I prepare lessons for tomorrow, moving day . . . with students?

Like ants carrying food to the anthill, fifth graders made their way to the far end of campus toting all sorts of books, boxes, buckets, and student desks. My class followed me to Portable #3. We marched down the newly laid asphalt path and up the ramp into our new home, setting the books in piles around the edges of the room as I had instructed them.

At the end of the room sat the battered old teacher's desk and the two mismatched, dented file cabinets looking out of place in our new portable classroom. Stacked in the corner I saw the boxes of rescued files, raising my blood pressure even higher.

How can I manage to teach without these resources? I'll have to sort these files in my "spare" time. What "spare" time? I'll never get it all done.

I can't think about it right now.

Excited kids milled around, some spinning in the middle of the open space we would soon fill with desks.

"Hey, Mrs. Wright, look what we've got here," Samantha shouted above the noise as she pointed to the thermostat on the wall. "We can control our own heat and air conditioning now!"

"Yay!" rose a chorus from those who had heard her.

I flipped off the lights and within seconds the movement and chatter stopped while kids froze in place. "Have a seat on the floor," I said as I turned the lights back on.

"Oooo, new carpets," said Kendra, sprawling on the floor. "Nice."

I smiled at my students. "I need you to partner up. Each pair of students will bring back one student desk together. If any of you feel that's too heavy for you, you can carry lighter things. Above all, I need you to be safe."

The headache lurking behind my eyes told me how high my concern level had risen after seeing the lack of control and supervision with the other classes.

I hope we can get through the day without injury to anyone, including me.

I leaned down and said, "Damon, would you and Leah be responsible for the buckets of math manipulatives?

"Sure thing, Mrs. Wright. I can carry a lot on my wheelchair, you know," he said.

"Thanks, Damon."

I took a deep breath before we headed out into the moving chaos and announced, "Okay, kids, let's go!"

Somehow, we managed to survive the move and settle into school life in Portable #3. The year ended and a new one began; old buildings disappeared and new ones rose throughout the fall and winter of 2000.

Chapter 27
Portables

"Mrs. Wright, one of our red balls is missing. It's not in our bucket," Alma yelled from the door.

"I'll be right there," I answered. "I wrote our class number on all those new balls. Take a look to see if anyone else is playing with it."

I grabbed my whistle and sunglasses from the top of the pile of boxes still filled with unsorted files, a year after the crazy, cross campus move. By the spring of 2000, I had managed to salvage enough to teach a year of fifth grade out of those jumbled files, but the irritation of wanting to use something I couldn't find continued to plague me.

The clean, separate classroom space did have its advantages, but the outside area we shared with a group of alternative school students left much to be desired. The recess yard was nothing more than an asphalt pathway running through the middle of our cluster of seven portables. But, worse than that, the district had relegated us to use portable toilets at this distant end of the campus. Our fifth graders solidly rejected what they called "those nasty potties." Teachers waited until lunch break to hike across campus to use the staff bathrooms.

I stood on the corner of the ramp scanning the milling sea of students. From the porch I had the advantage of height, but I could not see our ball. Steven stood beside me. I turned to look at him, sensing he had lingered to tell me something.

"I know where that ball is, Mrs. Wright," he said in his quiet voice.

"You do? Where is it?"

"I saw one of the older kids from #7 playing with it while we were in class," he said.

"Okay, Steven, remind me to go talk with the alternative teacher,

Ms. Duval. She'll make sure we get that ball back." Steven almost never spoke up in class, but I had learned to trust the observations he shared with me in private.

I walked down our ramp and out into the crowd of students to patrol the space at the far end while Cheryl, who had taken Mira's place while she was out on extended leave, stood watch at the end closest to the rest of the school.

I stopped to watch a crowded four square game in progress. The asphalt strip was barely wide enough to play the game. A familiar argument started up.

"The ball went out of bounds."

"No, it didn't."

I interjected, "It's getting hard to tell the boundaries. Robert, you can go get a piece of chalk from the basket just inside our door to re-mark the lines."

A louder than usual buzz started up at the opposite end of the portables. I couldn't see the source through the throngs of kids who began to gravitate in that direction.

Doug raced back toward me, yelling, "Mrs. Wright, Mrs. Wright, Booker pushed Cody into one of those nasty potties! They're fighting."

I strode through the crowd to the scene of the commotion. Cheryl held two sputtering boys by the backs of their collars. She leaned down and said something to them I couldn't hear. The two red-faced boys dropped their eyes to the ground, shoulders slumped.

When I reached her, she said, "I'm taking these two to the office. Back in a few minutes. Watch my class for me?"

"Will do. Thanks for taking care of this, Cheryl."

I watched her lead them away.

How terrific is that? This new, young teacher took charge and diffused a volatile confrontation without any assistance from me. She's a keeper.

I checked my watch.

I blew my whistle as loud as I could manage, ending recess. Deep into rehashing the events of the "nasty potty fight," the witnessing mob dispersed.

I'd better write myself a note about our missing ball and go talk to Bonnie Duval. I need to figure out what's going on with that group of alternative high school students. What are they doing here with us, anyway? Thank goodness the fifth grades are moving to the elementary schools in the fall.

I sat in the principal's glass-fronted office in the new office building. Elaine Vogel had come to Crittenden as our new principal at the beginning of the school year, just as the remodeling project began to wind down.

"I know you're preparing to move with the fifth grades to an elementary school next year, but I have a proposal for you, Jan." Elaine held me in suspense, pausing way too long for comfort.

"Our seventh-grade science teacher, Charlene, is pregnant and has decided not to come back next year," she finally said. "I'd like you to take her place."

Did I hear her correctly? Did she just offer me the seventh-grade science position?

"Me?" I croaked out. "I don't have a single subject credential in science."

"I've seen enough of your work to know you have strong teaching skills. I'd rather hire a really good teacher than someone with a strong subject background. You can learn the science you'll need, but it's much harder to teach someone how to be a good teacher."

My mind raced from thrilled excitement to shear panic. *I haven't done any science at that level since I was in college! Besides, how could I ever follow in the footsteps of a revered teacher like Charlene?*

Elaine studied my reaction with a smile on her face. "You think about it. You fit in well with these middle school teachers, Jan. If you decide to stay with us next year, we'll figure out how to get you qualified."

Still reeling from my conversation with Elaine, I inched my car up tight to the rear bumper of the car in front of mine, keeping a sharp eye on my side mirror. A bright red Trans Am zipped past me, close enough to make me flinch. Two cars ahead, it angled into the slight space left by a distracted driver. I fumed over the bold line-jumper; the rest of us had been inching toward the highway exit for the past thirty minutes.

Who does he think he is?

I renewed my grip on the steering wheel and watched as the formerly distracted driver moved his car up, getting within a hair's breadth of the front end of the Trans Am, squeezing him out. Within seconds, tires screeched as the Trans Am driver blasted his horn and peeled off, heading up the freeway, unsuccessful at bullying his way into our tight line of determined commuters. I wondered if the so-called "dot com bubble" could make my drive out of Silicon Valley any worse.

Once I'd made my way off the exit and crept through the stop lights in East Palo Alto, the bumper-to-bumper tension eased. I picked up speed to cross the Dumbarton Bridge on my way home to Newark at the south end of the East Bay. In the relief of open sky space, my mind returned to the career choice ahead of me.

Maybe I should get a job on my own side of the Bay. I could end the long commute and stop fighting jerks like that Trans Am driver.

Or, do I want to stay at Crittenden and teach seventh graders? I wouldn't have to deal with Mira when she returns, and I'd be able to let go of my frustration about those messed up fifth-grade files.

What am I thinking? I haven't dissected anything in well over thirty years, and I never did a frog like Charlene does with those seventh graders.

Ahhh, but do I have the courage to try?

Shifting Focus

Mountain View, California
August 2001 – June 2002

Chapter 28
Past and Present

Buzzzzz. Buzzzz. Buzzzz.

I jammed my hand down to silence my alarm and lay back in bed thinking about having to get up an hour earlier, at 5:30 AM, in less than a week. With a groan, I pushed myself upright, slung my legs out of bed and made my way into the bathroom. Summer vacation had not quite ended, but eager to get a head start, I made the choice to go in several days early.

I dressed in cotton pants and a t-shirt, ready for a steady day of work in my classroom. There would be time later for reconnecting with the other teachers, but this day would be for me to begin to set things in order for the school year to come, my second year as a seventh-grade science teacher.

Ten minutes into my forty-minute commute across the Dumbarton Bridge to Mountain View, I cranked up the radio in my little green Honda Accord. Feeling the rhythm and singing aloud to "Lady Marmalade," I gazed at the blues and greens of open sky and vast expanse of the San Francisco Bay, marveling at the glorious August day.

Before I knew it, I turned onto the exit from Highway 101, across from NASA and Moffett Field. Traffic was light, nothing like the days just before the "dot com burst" a couple of years earlier, when it took an hour or more to get to work. I pulled into the parking lot in front of Crittenden Middle School and noticed only two other cars. Carol, our school secretary, sat at her desk, visible through the huge wall of windows in the contemporary-styled building.

Entering the sunny office, I rounded the counter, set down my lunch bag and purse, saying, "Good morning, Carol! You're here bright and early."

"Hi, Jan. You're early too! Welcome back," she said, standing up for a hug.

I twirled around in the middle of the room with arms outspread. "This office is so much nicer than that dingy, old office we used to have. I love the space. Don't you?"

"Yeah, I do. All these windows make it a lot cheerier, especially on the dreary days. See the new fabric panels hanging from the ceiling?" I looked up to see sound baffles filling the tall space above.

"Hey, aren't those the same designs from the papers that were taped on the door over there?"

"Yup, Deborah Sanz's art class made them last year. Those high paid art consultants the district hired transferred the designs into fabric. They hung the banners a couple of weeks ago. Sure seems to cut down on the awful echo we had in here."

"They're colorful, too. Too bad Deborah had to quit; she did some wonderful art projects with the kids," I said.

"Want the key to your room, Jan?" asked Carol.

"Yes, and the key for the art room, too."

"Oh, that's right, you're teaching the art elective this year, aren't you?"

"I'm looking forward to it, although I don't think I can fill Deborah's shoes," I said. "I'll spend time in the art room tomorrow, but I'm dedicating today to science."

Carol pulled open a desk drawer and found the envelope labeled "Room 210," opened it, and poured out the key into my hand. Next, she found "Room 302," the art room key. She picked up the first one she had given me, slipped them together on the same ring, and then handed them back to me. She pulled out her key list and wrote my name next to the two room numbers.

"Thanks, Carol. I'll take good care of my keys."

We grinned at each other, both of us knowing how often she had dealt with key issues last year. I wondered if she'd ever trust me to keep my key through a summer.

I walked over to the counter and picked up my lunch bag and purse where I had left them. Then, I turned and headed toward the back door. "See you later, Carol."

"Enjoy the quiet while we have it, Jan."

As I passed through the mail room, I grabbed the stack of summer mail, mostly catalogues and ads, and pushed open the back door. I breathed in the fresh morning air. The day would get much warmer, but I had no worries. This year I knew I had a dependably air-conditioned classroom to work in; no wishing for the PTA to outfit my room with one, no fussing with the teacher on the other side of the wall to manage the controls to my room, no pleading with those maintenance guys when my classroom thermometer reached a daily 92 degrees. I could smile at the memories now, thankful to work in the comfort of this beautiful, newly remodeled school.

So much money had been poured into the school renewal project we even had a fancy new art construction. In the middle of the open area between the buildings rose a thirty-foot wide, circular, art plaza named "Circle of the Muse." The unfinished structure had caused conversation and controversy at the end of last year concerning the obvious expense, as well as the design. On top of a series of three, wide, concentric, concrete steps stood four rusted-metal frames, each one facing a different direction. A brushed-steel panel, filled with the cut-out letters of a student-written poem translated into different languages, hung within each frame. I liked the poems and the shiny metal, but their combination with the old-looking, rusty frames didn't pair well, in my opinion. Some folks complained about the tripping hazard of the four, half-height, pointed steps jutting out between the frames. We expected to see the completion and dedication of the commissioned art piece sometime this year. The "muse" had already given us a lot to think about. I wondered if I'd like the finished piece.

I headed toward the science building at the north end of the campus. My room, the farthest room from the office, required an energetic series of walks to and from it each day. Across from the door to my classroom, the athletic field spread out in green grass splendor, bordered by a row of redwood trees and then a currently empty parking lot where I usually left my car. I savored the blissful solitude and quiet of the early morning.

My precious key slipped easily into the lock, and I opened the door to my science classroom. Sunlight spilled through the lone, multipaned window in the back of the room, dimly illuminating four long rows of desks and, deeper into the room, the set of black-topped lab tables. My eyes scanned the unadorned light beige walls and birch cabinetry. I'd cover some of the walls with bright backgrounds to display this year's student work. Above the door, I'd hang up the poster of my three class rules framed as questions: Is it safe? Is it polite? Is it your best?

When I flipped on the lights, I could see how the polished floor shined and the spotless whiteboards gleamed. I took a strong whiff to savor the clean scent, such a joy for me after all my years of teaching in musty, over-used, and under-cleaned rooms.

I walked in and stopped for a moment at the demonstration counter, facing the desks. I felt grateful to be among the first to work here. I had watched the designing and construction of this new building. Charlene, the previous seventh-grade science teacher, had done all the moving in and setting up. She had only taught in this room for a year and a half.

I glanced down at the class lists I held in my hand and thought about the students who would sit here with me in a few days. Many of these kids had been in my last fifth-grade class, two years before, in those portable buildings. Come to think of it, I would know most of these students because of all the combined grade-level activities we had done in those days.

Ready to get to work, I walked to the far end of the classroom, past the lab tables, through the door leading into the shared science supply room. I glanced to the right, to the stack of dusty boxes filled with partially sorted fifth-grade teaching materials.

Maybe I should get rid of that mess. But maybe I'll need them again someday. They're really not in anyone's way, stacked there. I'll just leave them for now. You never know.

My work area to the left filled the corner, bordered by a tall file cabinet jammed with science lesson plans collected by decades of previous science teachers. We had no textbook to follow, so we gathered lesson ideas from workshops, classes, and other teachers.

I set my hand on the old file cabinet.

See. These old files can be mined for treasures, and ancient trash can be ignored; no one ever throws anything out. Here live the ghosts of past teachers.

I looked over at the center of the room. Four tall rows of open shelf sets filled most of the space. They were packed with supplies, also a legacy from past science teachers.

Too much to worry about now. I need to get started with this year.

I put my purse, the summer mail, and the class lists on the counter next to the computer I had positioned to fit deep into the corner. I loved the royal blue, plastic, see-through sides of my iMac G3. Stacey, the eighth-grade teacher had the red one in her corner on the other side of the room. I pushed the power button and heard the familiar "thung" as it powered up. I grinned, remembering the first Apple II computer donated to each school when I worked across the San Francisco Bay in Fremont. My mind traveled back through the years of work I'd done to bring computer technology to schools I'd worked in, the computer labs I'd set up, the advances I'd championed. Here, at last, I had my own personal tool to help me do some of the clerical work that went with teaching. We'd come a long way from hand-written grade books and ditto machines.

Today science; tomorrow the elective art class. My two favorite subjects. The school year ahead, 2001 – 2002, looked promising.

My second year of teaching science should be easy.

A hint of doubt crossed my mind.

Nothing in teaching ever goes quite as smoothly as I expect.

Chapter 29
The Art Room

When my alarm rang the next day, I managed to get out of bed with a little less reluctance than the day before. Again, I parked in front of the school and passed through the office. I felt pulled to MY room, the science room, but this morning I planned to prepare for teaching the art elective, so I turned in the opposite direction. I headed to the art room, conscious of an uncomfortable sensation, like feeling guilty for trespassing.

I'd offered to teach the art elective, a subject I enjoyed, even though I'd never seen the inside of the art room at this school. It seemed a waste of resources to have a whole room dedicated to only one period a day, and I expected it wouldn't take long before Katherine, our new principal, figured out a way to make greater use of this asset. For now, however, I could claim it as mine, in the way teachers tend to get possessive. I reveled in knowing I could prepare art materials before school and clean up later without concerns about sharing the space with anyone else, like I did with my science materials. I smiled at the fleeting, rare richness of classroom spaces.

When I opened the door, I felt like I had ascended to art-teacher heaven. Sunlight streamed through the huge bank of windows, emphasizing the contrast of the bold, black and white, checkerboard floor pattern. How extraordinary and fun! Perfect lighting for doing artwork, so different from the subtle beige and solitary window in the science room. I hesitated at the door, caught in a moment of doubt.

Do I really belong here?

Too late for that thought. Carol already gave me the key. I stepped inside and the door slammed shut behind me.

Large tables surrounded by plastic chairs filled the main space. I walked to the center of the room and set down my lunch bag and purse. Above me, cheery clothes pins dotted the wires that crossed the room, ready to hang drying pieces of student art.

I took my time and wandered around to survey the room.

Wow. Look what that "part-time" art teacher did. I can't imagine all the time it must have taken to set up this room. Now I really have to make this gem shine with artwork we'll produce this year.

I tamped down the turmoil I felt building and took a calming breath.

Drying racks and a multi-hued myriad of supplies in plastic bins covered one whole wall, opposite the windows. Here I saw glitter, paste, stickers, pipe cleaners. I found an overwhelming bounty of beans, buttons, and baubles. Looking at the countless odds and ends, I couldn't think of anything else I would ever need to teach this subject.

My attention turned to the stacks of unopened boxes on one of the tables. Someone had ordered replenishment supplies, but no one had been there to put them away. The yoke of responsibility settled onto my shoulders.

Grrr. I only expected to spend a couple of hours in this room, planning the first few art lessons, but now I have the sinking feeling this day will take more time than I want it to.

In the silence, I began to open the boxes and figure out where the materials belonged. When I took packages of construction paper to place them in the drawers of the storage cabinet, I discovered a mishmash of paper.

Gosh. I need to reorganize the drawers. My mother always said, "If a thing is worth doing, it's worth doing well." Might as well get started.

I cleared out the top drawer and moved the large colored construction paper there, where I would be more likely to use it. I arranged the paper according to the hues of the rainbow, overlapping them by about an inch. At one glance I would be able to see any color I needed and would know when to reorder any specific hue. Then I organized the poster board followed by the various sized whiteboards and types of drawing papers.

Ah, now that feels complete, like placing the last piece into a jigsaw puzzle.

On a shelf nearby, I recognized two boxes of art prints, the same Art in Action series I'd used during my days of teaching in Placerville. I opened one of the boxes to find the Great Wave by Japanese artist Kasagawa on the top of the stack. I skimmed through the treasured prints of famous artwork, the prehistoric cave painting, the medieval tapestry called the Unicorn in Captivity, and then, Escher's print of the unending staircases, entitled "Relativity." I let my mind's eye follow along the impossible paths, lost in appreciation of this stunning piece. I knew his work with tessellations would interest our middle schoolers.

I moved on to unpack the rest of the supplies on the table, starting with containers of glue. I found the glue bin and realized many of the old bottles needed to be thrown out. Most had dried-on crusty tops; some were empty, and some had been left open to harden. No way to avoid the task, I sorted through them.

When I opened the watercolor trays, some appeared almost new. Then I came across several in desperate need of cleaning. Others contained brushes with bristles bent over and splayed out like static-filled hair. I shook my head in dismay for this unnecessary neglect of easy-to-care-for materials; I could imagine my mother, who had been a painter, cringing. To be useable, I needed to sort and clean the watercolor supplies. The feeling of being in heaven had worn off; my feet were now firmly grounded in earthly reality.

I continued to work through the room, unpacking, discarding, reorganizing, cleaning. By lunchtime, I'd made significant progress in making this space feel more useable, more like my own. I tried to squelch resentment for the extra effort and not let it tarnish the feeling of accomplishment.

I decided to wash my hands in one of the large, deep sinks at the back of the room before eating my lunch.

Oh, look at that! The water can be turned on without using my hands.

I stepped on the foot pedals to operate the faucets. I chuckled out loud. *Students will love this, just as I do.*

Finally, I sat down at a table with one of the art textbooks, the job I had planned on doing before I got sucked into managing supplies.

I munched on a peanut butter and jelly sandwich. Not used to being alone and quiet for so long, I began to talk to myself. "Look at this, the elements of design. Of course! I can use this to guide my planning."

The sound of my own voice made me smile. Often apparent in a teachers' workroom, talking to ourselves seemed to be an occupational hazard.

I continued, "Let's see, what do we have here?"

Then I read aloud, savoring each word, "Line . . . shape . . . color . . . value . . . form . . . texture . . . space. Yeah, I know these." I flipped through the pages and stopped to delight in the visual examples.

The next section shifted into the seven principles of art and design. Again, I read aloud to myself, "Balance, contrast, emphasis, movement, pattern, rhythm, unity/variety." Depth and nuances of these principles could keep us busy for quite some time. My mind combined what I saw in front of me with lessons I had learned from my own art classes and those I'd previously taught. I grabbed a piece of scratch paper and began to jot down ideas. Creative thoughts consumed me, and the minutes ticked by unnoticed. Lost in a whirlwind of imagined art lessons, I realized with a start, how late it had become. Pulling out of the rabbit hole of artistic possibilities, I forced myself back to the clipboard list of things I needed to accomplish before going home on this still-summer-vacation day.

I retrieved the related teacher's manual, read the first couple of sections and took notes while I ate my apple. Although I liked teaching art, I began to sense I was drowning.

What have I gotten myself into? Will one period of art steal too much time and energy from my main job, teaching science for the other five periods of the day?

I needed to get back to the science room.

The art room is set up for a still life drawing lesson.

Chapter 30
A Scientist

A small cluster of students waited outside. I opened the classroom door, just as the bell rang before first period at the end of our first week of classes. Sunshine and warmth heralded a balmy day ahead.

"Good morning. Buenos días!" I greeted them.

Heads bent, eyes down, mumbled responses, they rushed to go inside. I stepped just outside the door and watched the scattering of backpack-carrying students hurrying to classes. Moving past the other rooms, my first period seventh graders scurried toward me.

"Good morning, Maria," I said to one of my new students. *Now what's her last name?*

"Good morning," she murmured in a shy voice, heavily laced with a Spanish accent. She tilted her head to give me a quizzical look, as if to affirm her pronunciation. I smiled and nodded as she walked past me into the classroom without stopping. I was pleased with her attempt to greet me in English. I knew she would remain silent during class until she felt more comfortable with her English, at first relying heavily on Sabrina, the partner I had assigned her for translation support.

Then I turned my attention to the next arrivals.

"Good morning, Jose, Isaac."

"Whazzup? Ms. Wright," Jose said, adding a little swagger to his walk and giving a tug to pull up his sagging pants.

They kept coming. Many were second language learners in this period, a class of slightly fewer students than all the rest of my classes, designed so they could be grouped for additional support in English.

The last one scooted past me, "Good morning, Malik."

"Mornin', Mrs. Wright," he said, out of breath from the dash to the classroom. He zipped in to take a seat as the final bell rang. I shut the door.

I walked over to stand behind the demonstration counter at the front of the room and smiled at the class in anticipation of the surprise lesson I had waiting for them. Behind me, on a huge wall cabinet covered by large white-board sliding doors, I had written today's date at the upper right-hand corner. Beneath that I had written, "What is science?"

Mindful of the two newest English language learners, Maria and Fernando, I pointed at the writing and said, "Today we're going to talk a little about science and what scientists do."

I held up a piece of lined binder paper and a yellow #2 pencil. "Please take out a piece of paper and put your name and the date on the upper right corner." I pointed to the spot.

A soft rustle began as students dug into backpacks and binders snapped open. They took out paper and started writing. Jose leaned over to Isaac and whispered something to him. Isaac shook his head. Jose looked at him pleading with his hands in a prayer position, his eyes fluttering. Isaac rolled his eyes, shrugged, and took out another piece of paper to hand to Jose.

I set down my paper and pencil, then flipped open the attendance folder. As they wrote, I called aloud each name, reinforcing my memory and learning the few I still needed. *Maria Gonzales. Got it.*

I sketched a large rectangle in the middle of the whiteboard and said, "Write the title, 'A Scientist,' at the top of your paper, centered like this." I added the title to my drawing.

"You know a lot about science already." I paused. "On your paper, please write a few ideas about what you think scientists *must* do."

I hesitated, watching as they started on the assignment, letting the partners I had assigned help with translations when needed.

Then, with a bit of a grin, I said, "Oh, and stay seated. I'll be back in just a moment." Startled looks followed me as I made my way across the room. They knew teachers didn't just leave the classroom. I walked past the lab tables and through the doorway to the supply room. I turned around the corner to the right, just out of sight, and donned a white lab coat over my navy-blue slacks and yellow blouse. Grabbing a clipboard and a red pen, I returned to the classroom.

A few students giggled when they saw me, others grinned, some shook their heads, and others kept their eyes on their papers.

I crossed the room back to the demo counter, a six-foot long cabinet with a countertop that had a small stainless-steel sink at one end. Using a step stool I had placed on my side of the cabinet, I climbed up and stood on top of the demo counter. I struck a pose with my left arm straight down and held the pen in my left hand at my side. With my right arm bent at the elbow, I held the clipboard close to my chest. My feet were planted on top of the counter, shoulder-width apart.

Students gaped up at me.

"Without talking, take a good look at me and all the details you can see," I said. I nodded at the translators who understood they could explain any needed directions, in whispers.

I counted to thirty in my head. Students stared. "Okay, now sketch a picture of me, draw what you see. You have three minutes." I set the timer on my watch and returned to my statue position.

"I can't draw," complained Jose. The boys behind him laughed.

"Me neither," said Felipe from across the room.

"That's okay. It's not a drawing contest. Just do the best you can. You can use labels to help explain what you're drawing," I said, trying to stand still. "You only have three minutes to draw everything you see about me. Get started or you will run out of time."

"Really? We have to do this? What does it have to do with science?" asked Jose.

"Good question, Jose. Yes, you do have to do it, so get busy," I said, trying not to smile. "A couple of tips: use the rest of the page for the drawing so it's not too small. Don't spend much time drawing my face. Be sure to get the whole picture, from my feet to the top of my head."

I heard a few exaggerated sounds of erasures and some groans, a snicker or two, some whispered translations, but for the most part they worked without talking until the alarm on my watch went off.

At that point, I climbed down, saying as I did, "You may finish your drawing and labels while I leave the room again." I began walking to the supply room.

"Ha, ha, look at your picture," Isaac said to Jose.

I turned and gave Isaac a look, "No talking, please." I continued to walk away. "And, do not share your work yet. We're not finished."

I turned the corner, set the pen and clipboard down, and unbuttoned the lab coat. I rebuttoned it, mismatched by one snap, leaving the hem uneven. I slipped one of my yellow hoop earrings into my pants pocket, stepped out of my navy-blue shoes and shoved my feet into a black pair, picked up a blue pen and put it in the chest pocket. Then I tucked my bleached blond hair behind my ears. I grabbed the clipboard and held it facing out this time.

Students had started whispering but stopped the minute I came into the classroom.

I said nothing, walked straight to the step stool, and climbed up on the demo counter once again, taking a pose in the same spot as before. This time, I placed my feet right next to each other.

"You probably notice a few changes. You have one minute to look at me and find as many differences as you can. Circle your drawing where you see changes and make a list of them. Do not talk to each other as you do this. Ready? One minute. Go!" I set my watch alarm and then remained still.

They worked: circling, writing, sneaking an occasional glance at each other. I saw a few kids surreptitiously point at a pertinent detail or two.

Beep. Beep. Beep.

"Okay, stop drawing, please. Number each of the changes you observed, then put your pencil down."

I stepped down from the counter and waited.

Showing them four fingers, I said, "Raise your hand if you got four or more changes." All hands shot up. "That's a good success rate," I said, smiling at them.

I raised my thumb, adding it to the four fingers, "Keep your hand up if you got five or more." A few hands went down.

Adding another finger from the other hand, I asked, "Six or more?" Several students dropped out.

"All right, let's see what you observed."

After confirming the seven differences I had intended, Jose raised his hand.

"Yes, Jose. Do you want to ask your question again?"

"Yeah. What does all this have to do with science?"

"Thank you for your excellent question, Jose. What do you think this lesson is all about?"

I led them in discussion for a while, then summarized, speaking slowly and distinctly, "Yes, science is about observing and recording, with accuracy, what you observe, what you see. It's about noticing changes, both big and small. Speaking of small . . . one of the first topics we'll study is cells, the tiny building blocks of all living things. They're so small we'll need to use microscopes to see them, and you'll need to record what you see, as accurately as you can, by drawing and labeling, just as you did today."

I turned around and slid open a whiteboard to reveal a set of microscopes on shelves. I set one on the demo counter. All eyes watched me. "I will teach you how to use a microscope by yourself. You must follow directions and be careful around them because microscopes are expensive." I thought about my language learners and repeated in other words for them, "They cost much money, and they aren't easy to replace."

Then I looked at my students with a slight grin and a tilt of my head. "Did you notice your picture of a scientist was a woman?" I paused, raised my eyebrows, and let the corners of my mouth stretch up into a wide smile. "What do you think about that?"

"A real scientist would be a man," said Isaac. Several boys snickered.

"Nuh unh," piped up Sabrina. "Girls can do science, too."

Maria leaned across the aisle and high-fived with Sabrina.

I knew it was vitally important for me to encourage girls' interest in science and math at their age, and I planned to address the issue many times during the school year.

"In fact, each one of you can be a scientist," I said. "You can ask important questions, do experiments, observe results, draw conclusions, and tell others what you learn. Every one of you."

The lesson continued with an introduction to the parts and use of microscopes.

When the seventh period of the day began, I again met students by the door as they entered the classroom.

"Good afternoon, Doug."

"Hi, Mrs. Wright."

"How you doin', Tanya?"

"Fine."

"Hey, Mrs. Wright, I heard what you're going to do. I already know all the changes you're going to make," smirked Aaron.

"Maybe not. Who did you talk with? Did you know I made different changes for each class? I've saved the toughest ones just for you." I grinned, happy to know students were talking about my lesson.

This period of thirty-two students filled the eight columns of four desks. For larger classes I had to seat some students on the stools at the lab tables. The last period of the day had been designed to combine the most advanced students into a group for more challenging verbal interaction.

After taking attendance for the period, I said, "I'm wondering how astute you can be as science students today. Are you skilled at observation?" I could see the reaction on their faces, grins with eyes alert, attention focused; they were ready to play my game.

They worked conscientiously on their drawings and labels; some wrote paragraphs of description.

This time I made more subtle changes. I parted my hair on a different side. The pens I exchanged were black and navy. I switched earrings to similar yellow hoops, but different in size. I slipped my wedding ring into my pocket. Instead of flipping over the clipboard, I held it three inches lower.

Discussion about science and microscopes was rich with details from these kids who had facility with language and backgrounds abundant in resources. Five students responded when I said, "Raise your hand if you have a microscope at home."

"Do any of you have sets of slides you might be willing to bring to class to share with us?" I asked them.

"I could bring some of mine to school," offered Simone. "One of my favorite sets is the parts of a fly."

"Gross!" interjected Raymond. Several students tittered.

"How many of you would like to see the parts of a fly?" I asked. Hands shot up.

"Thank you for raising your hands to respond," I said, giving them a broad smile as I reinforced this behavior management technique.

All hands lowered except one. Harry kept his up, waving at me to call on him.

"Yes, Harry?"

"My mom uses an electron microscope for her biotech job. She looks at things that are way smaller than parts of a fly."

"Sounds like she might be a good source for some additional information as we study about cells," I said, making a mental note of this asset.

At the end of the lesson, the bell rang, releasing us from the constraints of the classroom. Most students shouldered backpacks and dashed out the door. Others dawdled, slow to put away their things, conversing with each other as they went. I waited at the door, watching the room empty.

"Not bad, Mrs. Wright," said Aaron as he paused on his way out. "Of course, I got all twelve changes you made," he gloated.

"You were one of only three students who spotted the missing wedding ring. Excellent observations, Aaron. I'm looking forward to seeing your work this year."

As Tran approached the door, I smiled at him. "You know you inspired this lesson today, Tran."

"Me?"

"Yes, you. Remember the picture you drew of me in fifth grade? The one they put in the yearbook?"

"I remember, Mrs. Wright." Tran beamed with pride.

"I think you'll like all the drawing we'll do in science this year," I said.

His face lit with pleasure.

Great start to the year. So much fun to see my dear students again!

However, outcomes in science are not always predictable; life can change in an instant.

Chapter 31
A Day Like No Other

The day started like a typical day for me. Out of bed at 5:30 AM, I showered, ate my bowl of cereal for breakfast, whisked out of the house, and hit the road by 6:10. Jerry had already left for his job at United Airlines in South San Francisco. An ordinary morning at the beginning of the school year.

As I drove, my mind sorted through the list of things I needed to do at school. While ascending the east side slope of the Dumbarton Bridge, in the rear-view mirror I caught sight of a line of California Highway Patrol and police vehicles speeding toward me, lights flashing. I crossed over to the far right-hand lane. I counted ten vehicles racing past me. Then I noticed how few other cars were on the bridge. Come to think of it, I had seen almost no other cars since leaving home and could see none ahead of me on the normally crowded commute.

My cell phone rang. With my right hand, I dug around in my purse, pulled out my new flip phone, opened it, and held it up to my ear.

"Hello?"

"Jan, have you listened to the news yet?" my husband asked, his voice laced with urgency.

"No, but something's going on here," I answered thinking of the CHP and police vehicles.

"You've got to turn on your radio. An American Airlines jet crashed into one of the World Trade Center buildings in New York half an hour ago . . ."

"That's terrible," I interrupted, thinking of the airplane crashes we had discussed since Jerry started working for United Airlines long ago. I rushed on, "We ate at the top of one of those buildings, on the 106th floor, when we visited New York with Dennis and Martha."

Jerry continued, sounding impatient, "At first, they thought it was a freak accident, but another jet just made a sharp turn and hit the second tower ten minutes ago."

I gripped the steering wheel. A million questions stuck in my thoughts.

He went on, "Both planes originated in Boston, headed for Los Angeles, full of fuel. Both towers are on fire, huge explosions. No accident, Jan. Those planes were deliberately flown into the building. They were hijacked."

My breath caught. I trusted his analysis, but my mind reeled at the conclusion he had come to.

Then he said, "The second plane was United Flight 175." He let that hang between us.

"Was that one of your planes, Jerry?" I asked. It was all I could do to maintain a controlled, quiet voice.

"Yes, I worked on it with the mechanics just two weeks ago. Jan, we checked the passenger list; a couple of our United guys are listed on that flight." We held the silence for long seconds.

"This is bad, Jerry." I knew that didn't begin to describe it, but I didn't know what else to say.

"We're watching the news on a TV some guy brought in. They're evacuating both towers, but no one could have survived on those planes, carrying all that jet fuel. As soon as they crashed, they became infernos."

We paused again. Listening to each other breathe.

At last, I said, "I'm nearly at Highway 101. There's almost no one on the road with me. I'll be at school soon."

"Turn on the radio. Got to go, Jan. I love you."

"I love you, too, Jerry. Talk to you later." I hung up, not wanting to lose the connection with him, but knowing he would be in the thick of this catastrophe, and I would have students to care for.

Just as I arrived at school, the announcer on the radio repeated the description, "The North Tower's upper floors are engulfed in smoke, flames lapping from its gaping gash . . . oh my gosh, look at that!"

He took a loud inhale. After a pause, in a deep and sorrowful voice he continued, "I . . . I . . . We've been telling you there's debris coming down." Another pause. "Some, some of that is bodies. People are falling or . . . jumping from the building."

This human portrait of terror seared desperate, fiery images in my mind and held me in its grip, paralyzing me. I sat in stunned disbelief. Tears pooled in my eyes.

Then, as if I was angry, I jammed on the parking brake with my foot and yanked on the key to switch off my car; the radio died. I reached for my purse and lunch bag, hugged them close to my chest, and hurried to the mail room to grab my attendance folder, clinging to routine to settle my mind.

On my way out, Gretchen came toward me across the quad and yelled, "Did you hear the news? Two jets flew into the World Trade Center buildings in New York!"

"Yeah, I know. Have you heard anything else?" I said, wondering if, or how, the west coast might be involved and wondering how this could even be happening.

"Looks like hijackers," she replied as she veered off to go into the staff room.

I hastened across campus to my classroom.

Within minutes, Stacey came racing in from her side of the building. "Jan, they think terrorists hijacked some planes. One was a United flight." We held each other's eyes. We shared a connection; Stacey's dad and my husband both worked for United.

She ran to the counter near the sink and turned on her radio.

We listened together, unable to do the simplest steps in our normal routines. Speculations and revelations kept us in suspense, grasping to understand as reporters made statements and then retractions. Fear hung in the air.

Then the announcer told us another jet seemed to be circling downtown Washington D.C. Fighter jets had been scrambled, sent to intercept. Everyone tried to make sense of what was going on.

The reporter's voice got louder, "This just coming in . . ." His pause increased our tension. "Unbelievable! The jet has crashed into the Pentagon. There's been a massive explosion."

Gasping, we looked at each other. The reporter went on, revealing what little he knew.

We switched channels to hear other reporters. Each one seemed to have different pieces of the stories.

I could hear the sixth-grade science teacher, Scott Doren, arriving in his room. I dashed to the door leading out of the storage room into his classroom. He carried a small, portable TV set into his room. "Scott, did you know another jet just flew into the Pentagon?"

He responded, "Yeah. Let me get this TV working, so we can see what's going on."

"Stacey," I yelled. "Scott has a TV. Come see."

He fussed with the TV until he got the antenna oriented. The pictures brought the grim reality to life, the Towers on fire, billowing smoke, piercing sirens, firefighters running into the buildings as panicked people escaped out into the streets.

The scene changed to an aerial view of the Pentagon building on fire. A collapsed, charred section looked as if it had been bombed. We watched and listened, exchanging questions, bits and pieces of information, and worries.

The reporters, still trying to unravel the story of the hijackers, switched back to the burning Towers. We stared at the shocking pictures when the unimaginable happened, live, in front of our very eyes. The South Tower collapsed. We remained rooted to the spot in stunned silence. I felt as if the breath had been sucked right out of me. The reporter could barely speak. Then his words came in a rush. A gigantic cloud of dust billowed toward him, screaming people coated in gray, helping each other, raced past. The reporter and the camera man backpedaled, joining them in flight, away from the still collapsing building. Images burned into my mind.

At almost 7:00 AM our time, 10:00 in New York, we could do nothing more than watch, feeling helpless, unable to get our fill of the news. Scott changed the TV channel. At this hour, every station covered the tragic events. Each of the news crews, in different locations, gave us varying perspectives.

After a while, local reporters broke into network coverage and informed us of heightened security at key locations around San Francisco, including the Golden Gate Bridge. Now I understood why I had seen the speeding police vehicles on my way to work. They were racing to protect us against attacks on places near me, near my home. *Are we in danger here?*

Incredibly, the next news event broke only minutes later. Another flight crashed in a field in Pennsylvania. Information on the incident appeared sketchy. It all seemed so impossible, and yet so real.

After a while I could no longer stand there watching the sights and sounds of disaster, the unfolding catastrophic events, the heart-wrenching interviews, the endless speculations. Stacey and I walked back into our own classrooms to prepare for students. We knew they would come. I tried to take a look at my lesson plans for the day.

At about 7:30, Scott came rushing into my room.

Breathless, he said, "Oh my God, the north tower just collapsed, too. This wasn't supposed to happen to those buildings."

I called to Stacey as I ran to see the TV.

A few sixth-grade students wandered into Scott's room and came to see what we were watching.

"My dad works at Moffett Field. Is he in danger?" asked one of the boys. "Is America under attack?"

"We don't really know what's going on yet. All planes in the United States have just been grounded," Scott told him soberly.

"I'm sure everyone is on high alert at your dad's military base," I said, trying to soothe his worries. "They will make sure it's secure."

As more kids arrived, I realized the staff needed to deal with the trauma the kids would be feeling. This day would be like no other.

I raced to the office. Carol was busy answering phones, her face pinched. Although her voice revealed some tension, she sounded in control. I dashed around the corner and into Katherine's office. She sat at her desk, watching a small TV.

"Katherine, are you going to call a staff meeting?"

"Now? Before school?" she answered, her face scrunched, as if she was struggling to decide just what to do.

"Yes. I think it's important to talk about what's going on. The kids are going to be scared. Heck, *we're* scared. We need to figure out how to handle this day with our students. I think you need to call the staff together," I encouraged.

"But . . ." She paused. "I'm not very good with touchy-feely stuff. I don't know what to say to them, Jan."

"Just call a staff meeting, Katherine. You'll figure it out."

"I guess you're right."

Within minutes, Katherine announced on the intercom system. "All staff, there will be a brief meeting in the staff room in five minutes, five minutes."

Everyone buzzed with the news. We merged together in the staff room sharing what we had heard and seen on the news, trying to fill in the gaps, to make sense of the disasters and emerging tragedies.

"I can't believe it. How could this be happening to us?"

"They're afraid there'll be more attacks."

"I've been talking to my family in New York. They're keeping me updated. All the kids are coming into my room to see what's going on."

"Moffett Field has gone to DEFCON 3. I've never seen the defense alert that high there. Some of the kids are worried about their parents."

The principal, Katherine Murphy, who had been a sixth-grade teacher at this school, and vice principal, Bonnie Duval, who had been the alternative class teacher when we were in portables, walked into the room. We hushed and turned to them.

"By now you've all heard the news," Katherine said. "Apparently there have been a series of hijackings. The World Trade Center in New York and the Pentagon were targeted. It appears the White House may have been a target, too. Another plane has crashed into a corn field in Pennsylvania."

We all took a breath, no one daring to wonder what might be next.

"Jan, I'm turning this over to you."

Surprised and a bit flustered, I had a sudden moment of clarity; I knew what to do. I said, "Let's stand in a circle for a moment."

Solemnly, about thirty of us formed a circle. Without saying another word, some grabbed the hand of the person next to them until we all linked together, holding hands.

I began, "The news events are devastating, shocking. We're all scared today, but we know we have a responsibility to our students. School needs to be their safe place, as much as we can make it. I suggest we give the first period kids a few minutes to talk about the events and then try to keep the rest of the day at school as normal as possible. Routine will give us all a sense of normalcy, something familiar to help us feel safe."

I saw several teachers nodding in agreement.

"I think we'll find hope in our togetherness. If anyone would like to say something to give us strength for this day, please do," I said.

Several teachers spoke. Some prayed. All offered comfort to the group.

Finally, I said, "Look around our circle. We are an extraordinary team of adults, caring for our students." I paused. We held on to each other for a moment.

"Go, make it the best day you can for those children who are waiting for us." We squeezed hands and then let go.

Five minutes later, the bell rang to start the school day.

Several seats were empty in my first period science class. Late students kept coming in the door. The intercom came to life and Katherine said, "Teachers, please hold your attendance folders until I let you know when to send them. We have two late buses. There are so many late kids in the office, we're just going to send them all to class without tardy slips this morning."

The news seemed to be taking its toll on our families, but the kids kept coming to school. In fact, many kids came to school not knowing what had happened at all while others teetered on the verge of tears.

By third period, the early, anxious energy of the day had turned into the draining tension of worry. None of us really wanted to be at school, but we pressed on, reconnecting with each other and the latest news during our break between classes and at the early recess.

I saw Carrie, as I came out of the restroom, and asked, "How did the morning session go with your language arts class?"

"Oh dear, you know we did a lot of talking and writing about it. Several of my students didn't know what was going on, and then one of my students asked me if we were all going to die!"

I looked into her empathetic eyes and said, "Carrie, I'm glad our students have you to help them cope with this horrendous day."

"I just want to send them all home to their families," she replied. "*I* want to be with *my* family!"

"I know, Carrie, but I'm thinking some of our kids wouldn't have anyone to go home to. This would be a terrible day to send them home to be alone."

Side by side, we put our arms around each other's waist and squeezed in mumbled agreement and then turned and went on our separate ways.

Several students saw me coming and followed me into the art room. "I've just had an idea," I said to them. "What do you think about making red, white, and blue windsocks to hang around the campus as a sign of strength and support for our country?"

"I like it, Mrs. Wright," said Kelsey.

"Good idea," agreed Kevin. "It shows our American spirit.

I opened the construction paper drawer and pulled out all the red, white, and blue paper I could find. We placed the paper on the table closest to the door. Then I sent students to get the bins of glue, string, staplers, hole punchers, rulers, and scissors and set them on the table, too. I moved the paper cutter to another table. Kids filtered into the room, needing to talk and to have the comfort of being near each other.

The news pervaded all their conversations.

When the bell rang, the last of the students came into the room. They seemed subdued, quieter than usual. They looked to me for direction.

"We're all feeling upset by the events happening in our country, but many people in the world are sending us messages of sympathy and support. I think it might be a good idea for us to create something that gives us hope, something that unites us and reminds us how strong we are," I said.

"We're going to make patriotic windsocks to hang around the school. Think about designs you can make with stars and stripes." I continued with directions for the activity. Students started to work, gathering supplies, designing shapes, gluing the shapes onto the base paper. I chopped paper into strips to be hung from the basic windsock tube or used in their designs.

Close to the end of the period, I helped those who had finished their windsocks punch holes around the top and pulled a length of string through them. We moved outside the classroom, making our way to the Circle of the Muse in the middle of the campus. Some kids threaded the string through the rusted metal frames, tying the red, white, and blue windsocks to them. Other students found downspouts, doorknobs, and other protrusions from which to hang their windsocks.

"This looks really cool," said one of the kids.

"Can I make another one?"

"Yes, we can continue this project tomorrow," I said.

We admired our colorful creations until the bell to change classes rang.

We hurried back to gather up book bags, leaving the art materials all over the tables. I shooed the students out and locked the door, then dashed back across the campus to my science room, where my class waited for me.

"You're late Mrs. Wright," said Felix, grinning at me, a twinkle in his eyes.

"I'm sorry. Can you forgive me?" I grinned back at him.

"I guess so, but just for today there's no tardy slips," he replied, chuckling.

"Yes, just for today," I mused.

That night most of America watched unrelenting TV news coverage. We could not get enough. September 11, 2001 changed us forever.

A windsock hangs on my science classroom door.

Chapter 32
Welcome Back, Steven

He lumbered into the science classroom, joining in seamlessly with all the other students. I smiled when I saw him and gave him a slight nod to acknowledge his presence without drawing attention to him. He did the same in return and found an empty desk toward the back of the room, tucked his muscular frame into the seat, then slouched down.

I was pleased to have his familiar face with that signature crew cut in my class again. I knew not to expect much in the way of academic performance, but he would be aware of everything said and done in my classroom. Back in fifth grade, Steven had been my protector, my personal snitch.

Judy Costello, his Special Day Class teacher, came to see me after school that day. "Well, how did he do?" she said, standing in the doorway.

"Hi, Judy. Steven did just fine," I said. I finished erasing the last few words on the whiteboard, set the eraser in the tray, and turned to face her as she walked into the room and squeezed into a student's desk.

"He was pretty excited about coming to see you today," she said.

I walked around the demo counter to take a seat across from her. "It was good to have him in my class again. He didn't write much, but he'll get there."

"How did he do with the other kids?" she asked, pushing her glasses farther up on top of her head.

"He was quiet. The other kids didn't take much notice of him."

"Good. You know he was the one who asked me if he could start coming to your science class," she said with a smile.

"I'm glad. I think he needs to spend some time in regular classrooms, and I'm pleased he chose mine. I've always liked him. Steven had a rough time in fifth grade when his mother left them," I said, remembering this moody young man. "I'm sure it was painful when his sister took off with his mother last year, and he got left alone with his dad. We'll just do the best we can for Steven while we have him, Judy." I smiled into her eyes.

She nodded. "You're right, Jan. Just like we did with the kids I sent to you when our classrooms were in the old building."

After a pause, I said, "I'll keep you informed about assignments coming up so you're aware of what we're working on. Any help you can give him would be great. We're piloting a textbook series right now, and I only have one set of books, so they can't go home with the kids. I'm having all my students take notes in a special science notebook. I gave Steven one today."

"Yes, he showed it to me," she said.

I glanced down at the textbook on the shelf below the student desk, thinking about how I could support Steven. "I know he's is not strong at notetaking, but Steven's an attentive listener. I actually have extra texts. I could give you one if you'd like to add some extra support."

"Yes, that would be good. I can have my aide work with him."

Judy followed me to the other side of the demo counter. I slid open the whiteboard door to expose the cupboard behind it and picked out one of the remaining four new books. "We don't use this book every day. There are labs and lots of supplemental materials I'm trying out with the kids, but the basics are here. Right now, we're just beginning the chapter about cells. In December I'll be assigning a big project to make a model of a cell. I'll let you know when we do that."

"Just keep me informed about any concerns you might have, Jan."

"Steven's a good kid. I'm glad he ended up in your Special Day Class, Judy. He seems much calmer, more settled, and that's got to make a difference with his ability to learn."

"Thank you, Jan." She took the book from me and walked toward the door, then turned and said, "You know, I've been thinking, it might be smart to put Mark into one of your classes. Mainstreaming would do him some good, and I know you had him in fifth grade too. What do you think?"

I flashed back on the first day of fifth grade when Mark had a tantrum and threw a desk across the classroom. His mother and I struggled that year to figure out what was going on with him.

"Mark was quite a challenge in fifth grade," I said, "but yes, I'd be happy to have Mark join one of my classes. Has he finally gotten medication to successfully control those angry outbursts?"

"Once they got the bipolar diagnosis, he's been on a couple of different medications. I think the one he's on now is working pretty well for him. Let's give him another couple of weeks before making this decision," she said.

"Okay. You could walk Mark over just to chat with me."

"Sounds good, Jan. Thank you for taking on my students."

"Good heavens! We're a good team. Thank YOU for being their safety net."

After she left, I paused in the silent classroom, thinking about Steven. I could hear Stacey in the supply room, washing out beakers. I grabbed my stack of notes from the day and headed across the room to join her.

"What was that all about?" Stacey asked.

"Oh, not much. I just got a new student from Judy, and she was checking on him." I set my notes down next to my computer. "Actually, he's not new to me. I had Steven in my fifth-grade class." I walked over and stood next to Stacey, while she continued to wash beakers.

"We used to do oral book reports, once a month. Every month was a different genre. Steven did NOT like to speak aloud in class. At first, he just hung his head and ignored me until I called on the next student. I figured his low reading level was a problem, so I helped him choose books he might like and could manage. He still wouldn't give an oral book report." I picked up the towel and started drying beakers for Stacey. I set them on the counter in neat rows, ready to be returned to the storage shelves.

Caught in memories of the struggles he'd had, I rambled on. "One day he proudly showed me a book he had chosen at the library. It was a really hard book, and it took me a moment to realize its importance. The book was the original, long version of a song I played during some of our writing periods, Lorena McKennitt's 'Highwayman.' He loved that poem set to music and somehow found it in a book. He stuck with that thing, trying to read it, for weeks."

"I think it's easier to teach science to eighth graders," Stacey commented.

I smiled in response and went on, "But there's often a reward for patience at any age. With Steven, I tried every single month to get him to give a book report, never gave up on him. Eventually he did stand up in front of the class, even though he hardly said a word. At the very end of the year, he finally did it; he gave his first oral book report. I was so proud of him."

Without responding, Stacey finished washing the last beaker. I dried and set it down.

"Listen to me, blabbering on. I'd better get back to work, or I'll be here all night."

"Thanks for drying the beakers, Jan."

"You're welcome. Thanks for listening."

I sat down at my computer with a smile and added Steven's name to the list of students in my fifth period class.

Two weeks later, at the end of fifth period, Steven hung back, taking his time, allowing all the other students to leave the classroom before him. I knew he had seen something I had missed, and he wanted to tell me about it.

"Mrs. Wright," he said when he made his way to the front of the room.

"Yes, Steven," I said as I cleaned up the plastic sheets I used on the overhead projector.

He held the silence for a moment, watching me work, and then said, "Could I help you with that?"

"Oh, Steven, that's very thoughtful of you. Thank you, but I'm done with this for today." I set the plastic sheets aside.

"You know, I just had an idea. This next period is my prep period; I don't have any students. Would you like to stay after class for a few minutes some days to be my assistant? We could ask Ms. Costello if that would be okay with her," I said.

"She won't mind," he said.

The late passing bell rang.

"Why don't I walk you back to your teacher, so you don't get a tardy from her, and we'll ask her permission for you to assist me."

"Sure, Mrs. Wright," he said.

I grabbed my key out of the drawer in the demo counter. We walked out of the room, and I locked it behind us.

We walked across campus toward the Special Day Class. After a few moments of silence between us, he said, "I saw Jeremy getting into your drawer yesterday when you weren't looking during the lab period."

"You mean the drawer where I keep my keys?" I asked.

He nodded. "He took his bouncy ball you confiscated from him last week." He paused and then added, "He was really mad at you then."

"I knew he was angry, Steven. I told him he could have it back next week."

Gosh, I hadn't even noticed the ball was missing. In fact, I forgot all about that ball. Steven sure picks the right time to tell me his observations, when no other kids know he's telling on them.

After a moment of silence, Steven said in a deep, quiet voice, "You're too easy on him, Mrs. Wright."

Sounds like he's criticizing me. Oh . . . but maybe he's right.

"Maybe so," I said, adding, "Thank you for letting me know, Steven. I'll handle it."

Chapter 33
Circle of the Muse

Asticky note hung on my mailbox. It read: *Jan, would you please be in my office after school today at 3:30? Thanks, Katherine.* No hint of a topic. No name of an upset parent. No scheduled committee meeting. No sticky notes on other teachers' mailboxes. My curiosity was piqued, but I would have to wait through the day to find out what it meant.

❧❧❧

I cleaned up after the last science lab class, put away materials in the storage room, and then checked my watch. Time to see what the principal had in store for me. I hurried across campus.

In the office foyer, Katherine chatted with a guest I did not recognize. The woman wore a flowing dark green cape-like jacket over a lighter shade of green slacks. She had a classy silk scarf in varying greens and oranges around her neck, tied to one side. A riotous mass of shoulder length, brown hair came alive with hints of red in the sunlight. She held what looked like a roll of architect plans; her manicured nails flashed bright orange polish. Like a peacock among drab peahens, her flamboyance made everyone else look rather mousey by comparison.

She didn't seem like a parent coming to talk about a student, and the mystery of her visit intensified as Carol gave me a quick grin and a wink from across the office.

When Katherine saw me approaching them, she turned to the woman and said, "Oh, here she is. This is Mrs. Wright, our art teacher." I tried not to show surprise at being introduced as the art teacher instead of the science teacher. "Jan, this is Ms. Sorenson from the group that was commissioned to create the Circle of the Muse."

In an attempt to appear equal to the title Katherine had given me, I straightened my posture and shook hands with the woman. "Welcome to Crittenden," I said, noticing her sparkling green eyes.

"Thank you. We always feel so welcome when we come here. I think it was Mrs. Sanz and her art students we worked with before?"

"Yes, Mrs. Sanz was the part-time art teacher last year," Katherine explained as she led us across the room. "Let's go into the fishbowl. That's our affectionate name for this glassed-in corner of the front office."

We circled the table as the woman set down the large roll of papers in the center and unrolled it, beginning to explain. "These are the plans for the Circle of the Muse. We would like to work with students to design and create a broken tile mosaic for the center." Her voice held onto the sounds, drawing out each word, adding to a sense of her control and obvious confidence.

She pointed to the space in the very middle of the drawing of the structure. A trill of anticipation hit me; I hoped this meant she would involve *my* art students in the project.

She smiled and said, "We like to involve students in our creations."

"Like the poem on the metal panels," I said.

"Yes," she replied.

"Will this be the final piece of the project, then?" I asked.

"Yes, we'd like to complete the structure in the next few months, and we'd like to work with your art class on this last part."

There it was. *My* students would create this visible piece of public art.

Beaming with pleasure, I said, "My students and I would be honored to work on this project. When would you like to get started?"

"How about next Wednesday?"

"That would be fine. We're just finishing up a project, and we'll be ready for you."

To make sure she understood our time constraints, I explained the timing for the art period, and Katherine handed her a copy of the bell schedule. We were all set to work together.

I checked my watch, again. Our guest was late. Students fidgeted. I sensed the impatience in the room and realized I needed to improvise a lesson plan until she arrived, *if* she arrived. I lowered my shoulders in a conscious attempt to reduce my feeling of tension.

I shifted into teaching mode and handed out plain white paper.

"Please take out a pencil. How would you like to learn a simple way to draw round objects to include a sense of depth?" I started, working to keep the sound of irritation out of my voice. I saw some heads nod. Without elaborating, I picked up a green marker and sketched a birthday cake on a plate on the whiteboard, then I added some shading.

"Let me start over. This time, you follow me," I said. "Start with a football shape."

I continued adding lines with students following my instructions, until the classroom door opened. We turned to look at the intruder.

"Mrs. Sanz?" asked the young man wearing jeans and a dark pull-over sweater.

"No, I'm Mrs. Wright. I'm the elective art teacher," I said, striding toward him.

"Oh, I was told I'd be working with Mrs. Sanz on a design for a mosaic?" He remained by the door, hesitant to enter.

"Mrs. Sanz does not teach at Crittenden this year," I said, noting the visitor sticker stuck on his chest but feeling a little puzzled to have this stranger walking into my class. "Welcome. Come on in. This is the art class who'll be working on the mosaic. And you are Mr. . . . .?"

"I'm Eric. Just Eric," he said, walking toward the front of the room with me.

"Okay, Eric." I paused hoping he would continue with an explanation. When he remained silent instead, I said, "We've been waiting for Ms. Sorenson. I thought we'd be working with her."

"She'll be here in a couple of minutes," he said.

We waited long, quiet seconds, until I couldn't stand the awkwardness and rushed on, "Class, Eric is going to work with us on the mosaic I told you about." I paused to think of what to say, how to fill the time. Finally, I asked them, "Do you have any questions for Eric about the Circle of the Muse?"

"How come there's rusty metal on it?" asked Chris with a challenging grin.

"I don't know," he said. "I'm just working on this part."

Silence again.

I continued, "Okay, Eric, can you tell us what you do?"

"I do metal construction from designs I'm given. I've worked on a few mosaics using metal as the frame that gets filled in with broken tiles, which is what we're planning for this project," he said.

At last, the door flew open, and Ms. Sorenson made her grand entrance, her arms full.

"Hello," I said starting toward her. "Class, this is Ms. Sorenson."

"Hellooo students," she replied with dramatic inflection. I heard a few giggles from the kids.

With a smile that lit up her face, she asked, "Where can I set these down?"

I pointed to the table next to the windows at the front of the room.

She rushed across the room, her charcoal gray cape flew, revealing the red satin lining beneath. She deposited her bright red purse, a large satchel, and the roll of design papers onto the end of the table. She reached up to her neckline, undid the bright red Chinese frog fastener, and slipped off her cape, draping it over an empty chair. Then she took center stage, facing the class. The kids and I gawked at her fashionable attire: dark gray wool slacks, red cashmere sweater, red high heeled shoes, bold gray and red necklace with matching earrings. The bright red of her lipstick glistened as she smiled at the class. What a stunning, colorful sight!

"Let me see, where shall I begin?" she said.

The kids stared at her, wide-eyed. She had captured their full attention.

Eric seemed to fade into the corner of the room.

"Oh. Yes. Your class has been selected to complete the design for the Circle of the Muse. Does anyone know what's going to be placed in the center of this art plaza?"

Blank looks from the students gave her pause.

"The time capsule goes in the center. You know? You chose items to put into it with your science classes to be opened fifty years from now?" She gave them a confused look, as if trying to pull the answer she wanted from them.

I interjected, "Ms. Sorenson, these kids were in fifth grade. They didn't get to participate."

Ms. Sorenson looked puzzled, but moved on, perching on the edge of a table while she continued to address us.

"Well, we're going to design and create the mosaic art piece that will surround the metal time capsule, which we plan to embed in the very center."

"Is that what's going in that hole?" asked Marisol.

"Yes," she said. "And you will complete the central part of the Circle of the Muse. Does anyone know what a muse is?"

Chris raised his hand, and I nodded to him. "It's a Greek or Roman god or something?"

"Doesn't it mean something about inspiring a writer or an artist?" added Marisol.

"Yes, you're both right," said Ms. Sorenson. "There were nine goddesses in mythology who were the daughters of Zeus. They presided over the arts and sciences. In today's usage of the word, we'd call a muse a spirit or a source of inspiration for an artist's creativity."

I looked at the faces of my students. Her dramatic voice held them enthralled, the very embodiment of a muse, herself.

"To start your thinking for our project, let me explain the art concept. We want this piece to be a welcoming sight to those who enter the campus. It should be a gathering place, a place of inspiration. You've all seen the poem on the steel panels in the six different languages, giving a sense of inclusion to people of different backgrounds. That poem won the school-wide poetry contest." She paused. "Oh, maybe you weren't included in that," she said, looking at me.

I shook my head. "They were sixth graders then, but the poetry contest only included seventh and eighth grades."

"Well, you will be included now," she told them. "Eric, would you unroll the plans, please?" He stepped forward, opened the tube, and pulled out what looked like blueprints.

"The poems, cut out of modernistic steel panels, are hung from rusted metal frames, to represent new and old working together." She stood up and rifled through the drawings, pulling out the design for one of the panels.

"Did you notice the points at the tops of the frames?" She pointed to the drawing. "They reflect the points in the concrete that face the cardinal points of the compass: north, south, east, and west."

Chris raised his hand.

"Yes, Chris. Do you have a question?" I asked.

He nodded. "Is that why we have those small, pointed steps? Because it's all just a big compass?"

"Yes." She handed the first drawing to Eric. I helped him attach it to the whiteboard using magnets to hold it up while she pulled out another drawing, showing the concrete points within and just outside the circular steps. "The idea is that education can take you anywhere in the world. Knowledge connects the past, the present, and the future," she said, handing that drawing to us to display too.

Ahh, now I was beginning to understand this creation.

"My challenge for you is to design this central part." She pointed.

"Let's start with colors. We can use tiles of any colors you choose. Let's limit our choices to two or three, plus maybe black or white."

Toni raised her hand. "How about using blue like the sky and brown and green like the earth?"

"Oooo, I like your thinking on this," said Ms. Sorenson. Toni blushed under her compliment.

Marisol raised her hand. "How about red, white, and blue like the windsocks we tied onto the panels on September 11? That French president said, 'We're all Americans.'"

"We made the windsocks before anyone said that," interrupted Chris.

"It's still a worthy idea to think about," said Ms. Sorenson.

"I know!" said Brittany. "School colors, blue and yellow. It's a welcome to our school, and it's about us getting a good education, isn't it?"

"Oh, I like that," enthused Ms. Sorenson.

She continued to work through designs with the students, using colored markers to sketch designs on another large piece of paper, and pulling ideas from them until they all agreed upon the final picture of a compass radiating from the time capsule, done in blue, yellow, and white, with black accents, including black letters for the cardinal compass directions. I sat in awe of her skillful encouragement and interpretation of their ideas. We all felt excited about art and the process of creating it.

The bell rang to change classes before we knew it. I did my best to scurry our guests out, so I could get myself across campus and back to my fourth period science class. My head buzzed with thoughts about the Circle of the Muse as I raced past it, appreciating it more than I ever had before. Yes, I would say I liked it, and some day, I would point with pride at the artwork of my students.

Chapter 34
Football

Brilliant white light bathed the athletic field across from my classroom. The grassy area filled with people, older kids donning uniforms, younger kids chasing each other, and parents setting out blankets and folding chairs. My nose picked up the aromas of picnic dinners: hamburgers, hot dogs, Kentucky fried chicken, burritos, tacos . . . my mouth watered. Announcements blasted on a loudspeaker, punctuated by the shrieks of children playing and parents hollering to them. Football had taken over the park property our school shared with the City of Mountain View.

Walking past the field on my way out to my car in the adjacent parking lot, now filled with cars, I recognized some of my students and their families. I gave a wave, a nod or two, or a cheery "hello," all I could manage at 6:00 PM, time for me to go home from work.

As I started up my car, I began to think about the extravagance of this sports phenomena. The cost of all the lighting, the maintenance of the field, the balls, and equipment. My thoughts turned to the expenses for the families: uniforms with all the padding, helmets, and specialized shoes. More than that, the commitment made by those families to be present for their kids grabbed me.

What if this display of family attention and money could be focused on academics? What if they valued science in the same way they do football? I have to do my part to address this imbalance.

My musings continued on my long commute across the southern end of San Francisco Bay in the darkening sky. I reached home, brimming with thoughts I had to share with my husband.

Walking into the house, the enticing garlic smell of dinner didn't stop me from barraging Jerry with all my newly hatched plans. "Jerry,

I've been thinking about our science fair. NASA is right across the highway from our school. We could use our connections with those scientists to recruit our judges. Cool, huh?"

"That sounds like a good idea," he said, serving noodles onto our dinner plates, followed by chicken in a spicy tomato sauce. My stomach growled with hunger. I continued to talk, as I put my purse in the closet.

"When I started the science fair at Crittenden last year, I did my best, but later, when I went to that county science fair training, I saw all kinds of possibilities for improvement. For one thing, I discovered our winners could move on to the county's science fair if we scheduled ours just a little earlier in the spring."

We settled into our meal at the dining room table. Jerry listened as I carried on, knowing I would have to run out of steam before I could stop. "This year, I want students to practice being docents to explain the exhibits. You know, the best way to learn is to teach.

"I could have my students write letters to invite the superintendent, the district staff, and the school board. How about the mayor of Mountain View?" With barely a moment to take a bite of food, I continued. "And we could ask news reporters to cover the event when families come to see all the projects set up in the multi-use room. Our science fair has to be even better than last year. I want to make science a big deal!"

"What got you so wound up about the science fair tonight?" he asked me.

"Football," I took a mouthful of chicken. "Mmmm, this is good, Jerry."

"What? Football?" he said between bites, looking at me with one eyebrow lifted.

I smiled. "Yeah, I walked past the field on the way to my car tonight. They were getting ready to play football."

Jerry listened as I went on to explain my thinking. I could always count on him to be my sounding board.

Later, at the sink, we cleaned up the kitchen together. I set the dish towel down and put my arms around my husband, snuggling into his embrace.

"I'm so grateful for your patience and support, Jerry. Thank you."

"You don't have to thank me, Jan. What you're doing is important."

"I'm lucky to have you," I said, giving him an extra squeeze.

I stepped back and gave him a teasing look, "And, I'm glad you like science better than football."

Chapter 35
Mosaic

Three weeks had passed since the planning day with Ms. Sorenson when Eric surprised me in the middle of a lesson. He walked into the art room carrying a huge metal tray. Inside the tray, two-inch-high metal dividers outlined the shapes the class had created for the mosaic.

"Wow, is that our design?" asked Marisol.

The kids spontaneously clapped, causing Eric to blush while he set the metal tray on a table at the back of the room. "I'm sorry to interrupt, Mrs. Sanz."

"That's Mrs. Wright," corrected Chris.

"Oh, sorry," Eric replied, looking down at the floor as his cheeks flushed.

"That's fine, Eric. We've been waiting to start the mosaic," I said. "Is Ms. Sorenson coming today?"

"I don't think so," he answered.

He shifted his weight from one foot to the other, and he said, "I need to go out and get the tiles we're going to use. I'll be right back."

As soon as the door shut, I turned to my class and said, "Okay, you can get up and go take a look."

"Yay!"

"It's just like we drew it on the whiteboard, isn't it?" said Marisol.

"It looks so cool in metal," said Chris.

Eric returned with two huge boxes of tiles. I pointed to a spot on the floor and said, "Those look heavy. Could you put the tiles over here under the window? Thank you."

With an "ooof," he set the weighty boxes down onto the floor. He pulled at the flaps to open the first box, revealing blue tiles. Then he opened the second box. Yellow tiles. "I've got to get more tiles and some tools," he said as he turned to leave.

"That'll be the white and black tiles," said Marisol, grinning.

"Let's go back to our seats and continue our lesson," I said.

"Awww, don't we get to start the mosaic now?" asked Chris.

"When Eric is ready for us, we'll stop what we're doing," I said, knowing I would not regain their full attention anyway.

By the fourth trip, Eric stood beside the supplies and looked across the room at me. I paused and said, "Yes, Eric? What would you'd like us to do?"

"Ummm," he mumbled. "Can I show the kids how to break the tiles and glue them into place?"

I could see the eyes light up on several students at the thought of breaking tiles. I set down the marker I had been using and said, "Yes, of course."

Eric held up the tile cutter tool.

"Hey, that looks like a pair of sharp pliers," offered Macy.

I saw a little grin cross Eric's face.

He said, "It's called a nipper or a tile cutter." He demonstrated how to use the tool and then showed us the color labels on the bottom of the tray in each design section where each piece would be glued. Eric then asked me to choose two students to work with him. All hands went up in the class. Everyone wanted to be chosen.

I grabbed the cup that held a class set of tongue depressors, each one with a student name written on it. Without looking, I chose two sticks and read aloud the student names.

"Belinda and Jorge will go first."

They jumped up and made a beeline to Eric.

Disappointment painted the faces of the rest of the class.

"Everyone will get a turn. I'll set my timer for five minutes," I announced.

After giving a few moments to watch them get started with the tile, I returned to the lesson in progress. We continued amidst the distraction of the sounds of tiles breaking.

At the end of the period, several students had taken five-minute turns with Eric.

"I know some of you haven't yet had a chance to work with the tiles. I'll save your name sticks, and you'll get your turn the next time," I said, heading off complaints before I announced clean up time.

As the bell rang at the end of the period, Eric and I walked out of the room together. I locked the door, saying to him, "So, when will you be back to work with the rest of my class?"

"Uh, I'm not sure. I left the nippers for you to use."

I turned to look at Eric, a question in my eyes, not sure what to say.

"They can cut up the rest of the tiles and glue them into the frame when I'm not here," he went on.

"Oh. All right."

I'll have to figure out how I can supervise them while I teach the rest of the class. These art people really have no idea what it takes to be a teacher.

We walked on toward the Circle of the Muse. Before he left me, I said, "Thanks for working with the kids, Eric. Could you let me know when you'll be back again, so we can prepare for your visit?"

"Sure," he mumbled, heading off toward the parking lot in the front of the school.

In the next few days, my students finished the tiles. We didn't see Eric for several weeks. We had almost forgotten the project. It gathered dust in the back of the art room.

Finally, I received a phone message telling me Eric would be installing the mosaic and grouting it the following Wednesday. I planned a flexible lesson for that day, something with very little set-up or clean-up time.

Wednesday arrived with a surprise for the whole school. Eric started the installation of the mosaic that morning, without my art class. Kids poured into the courtyard for their fifteen-minute break, just before third period, and discovered him working in the center of the Circle of the Muse. A crowd gathered to watch him as he worked. By the time I figured out what was happening, he had installed the metal framework with the glued-in tiles and was halfway through grouting the entire mosaic. The bell rang to start third period.

I approached Eric and said, "Good morning, Eric. Do you mind if the art class stays to watch?"

He looked up at me and said, "That's fine, but I have to keep at this so it won't dry too fast." He bent back to his work.

I shooed a reluctant group of students back to their respective classes, while my art students stayed, crowding around the circle to watch the completion of their project. Eric worked on without engaging in conversation.

"That's the W for West. I did that!" said Jorge, pointing.

"I worked on that blue circle in the middle," added Chris.

"What's that empty hole in the center for?" asked Marisol.

"That's for the time capsule. Don't you remember?" said Chris.

We watched Eric use a squeegee to fill the spaces between the tile pieces with light colored grout. Then he used a damp sponge to wipe and re-wipe the surface. He finished about twenty minutes into the period and began to clean up.

"Class, let's thank Eric for his work with us," I said to the group.

"Thank you, Eric," they said in slow unison.

Eric gave them a small grin and ducked his head.

I led my class back to the art room with half the period left in which to do a modified lesson plan. I pulled out a quick sketch lesson, building upon skills I had already taught them.

In the days that followed, the grout dried and the caution tape encompassing the Circle of the Muse came down. The empty hole in the middle filled up with bits of trash.

We never saw Eric or Ms. Sorenson again. Weeks later, one of my students came to tell me the time capsule had been secured into the hole, at last. The project was complete.

When an article came out in the local newspaper, it gave credit to the firm who had built and installed the artwork, along with the art teacher, Mrs. Sanz, and her art students.

Article about Circle of the Muse by Artik:
https://www.artika3.com/index.php?id=71

My art class created the mosaic in the center of the Circle of the Muse in 2001.

Chapter 36
Gumdrops

The grocery store carried colored gumdrops. I tried to gauge how many bags I would need for five classes of science students to make DNA models, if students worked in pairs.

Are there enough different colors for each of the four nucleic acid bases plus the sugar and phosphate molecules? Six colors. Yes, more than six. Good. Maybe five bags per class, twenty-five total? Plus one extra. Does this store have that many to sell? Can I get more of the same in another store?

How much will this cost me? I'll turn in the receipts, but anything over the meager allowance we have for supplies, I'll be paying for myself, like most teachers do.

Oh, and I'll need boxes of those sturdy, round tooth picks too. And, maybe straws for the sides? What can we use as a base to hold the models, so we can twist them into the double helix shape?

"When I tell you to open the bags, you will sort the gumdrops by colors using the paper plates at each lab table," I told the fifth period class. "You will notice each plate has a name in the center: Adenine, Thymine, Guanine, and Cytosine for the bases. Notice the color of the gum drop drawn under the names? Place all the gumdrops of that color on the plate. Then there are sugar and phosphate plates with their own colors. The last plate, the blank one, is for any other colors of gumdrops. If you do a good job and do not eat any of the gumdrops as you construct the model, you will be allowed to share and eat the leftovers." I looked at them with my serious teacher face.

"Did I make that clear? If you refrain from sampling, you get the reward at the end. If you are caught sneaking gumdrops before I give permission, you will be excused at the end of the period to sit at a desk while the others eat gumdrops and you watch from afar." I raised my eyebrows and I said, "This can be fun, but don't test me or you will lose the privilege."

For some students, the best part of the modeling lesson had to be the treat of eating candy in class. However, I also knew that making a color-coded model would help students better understand the structure of DNA as we knew it. Besides, model-making met part of the new state standards for science in seventh grade.

At the end of fifth period, Steven stayed behind. I knew what he wanted to tell me. I headed him off with, "Steven, there are no chores for you today, but I'd like to visit your classroom. How about if I walk back with you?"

"Sure, Mrs. Wright," he said.

I grabbed the paper lunch bag I had hidden behind the whiteboards. It contained the extra bag of gumdrops.

Steven waited for me to lock up and then shuffled beside me across campus. We remained silent until about half way there.

"Mrs. Wright?"

"Yes, Steven," I smiled and nodded.

"Tony ate some of the gumdrops when you weren't looking."

"I suspected that, Steven. What happened when he did that?"

"The kids at his table told him not to."

"And then what happened when I gave permission to eat them?"

"His group gave him less," said Steven.

I smiled. "Good, Steven. That made it fair, didn't it?"

"I guess so," he replied. "But he should have been sent to his desk, like you said."

We let that hang between us. I had accomplished my goal with class behavior, but I felt I had failed to live up to Steven's keen sense of justice.

When we reached his Special Day Class room, Judy, greeted me with warmth. I handed her the paper bag of gumdrops I had brought and whispered to her, "You can give these out to your students when it's appropriate. Steven can explain what we did with them in class today."

Judy set the bag on a nearby counter, faced her students, and said aloud, "Welcome to our classroom, Mrs. Wright. Thank you for coming to visit. Class, say 'Hello' to Mrs. Wright."

"Hello, Mrs. Wright," came out in a staggered choral response from the nine students whose desks were scattered around the edges of the room. The room seemed cluttered with materials ranging from balls to dolls to food containers. There were building blocks, head phones and tape recorders, bean bag chairs, and blankets. A few ragged looking books sat in haphazard piles along with crayons, markers, and an assortment of papers.

"I didn't mean to interrupt. I just wanted to visit for a few minutes to see how you are all doing today," I said.

"I'm fine," said Dora, coming over to hold my hand. "I'm Dora. I like your dress."

"Thank you, Dora," I replied. "I like your dress, too."

"Emilio is not having a good day," she told me.

"Leave me alone!" he yelled back at her, throwing a couple of pink pencils onto the floor in her direction.

"Emilio, you need to be kind to Dora. Just move over to this corner and finish your work with Ms. Patel," cajoled Judy.

"Make yourself at home, Mrs. Wright," she said glancing back at me on her way to Emilio.

"I'll only stay a few minutes," I replied.

Dora dropped my hand and ran to pick up the pencils, holding them close to her chest. "Mine!" she barked, moving to another corner of the room and placing the pencils in her overflowing pencil box. She began to arrange and rearrange the items covering most of the surface of her desk.

Mark, sitting at a desk with a book, caught my eye. I walked over to him to look at his reading material, a book on science fair projects.

"Mark, I'm so glad you joined my science class. Are you already planning what you'll do for your science fair project this year?" I asked.

"Yeah," he answered as he flipped the pages of his book.

"If you want some help, you know you can ask me, Mark. I want this to be something you'll enjoy doing this time." I thought about the tantrum he'd had the previous year over the science fair project he did for Mr. Doren. I would give him extra guidance this year, even if he didn't ask me for it. In fact, I made a mental note to call his mother about this year's project.

Emilio's voice raised, and he shoved a pile of books onto the floor. "I don't want to work with Ms. Patel anymore!"

I figured it was time for me to make an exit while Judy dealt with his outburst.

"See you tomorrow in class, Mark," I said to him.

Dora scooted back to my side, clasping my hand tightly, possessively, in hers again.

"Dora, it was good to meet you," I smiled at her. "I need to go now."

I disconnected my hand from hers and began to walk toward the door, passing Steven seated at his desk, leaning back into his seat, his arms folded behind his head, observing the chaos in the room. I nodded to him and said, "Thank you again, Steven. See you tomorrow."

"Good-bye, Mrs. Wright," yelled Dora, waving as I approached the door to leave.

I waved good-bye to the class and to Judy and took a last glance around the room noticing all the student behaviors Steven was observing and keeping track of for Judy. Then I leaned in toward him and said to him with a grin, "Be sure to remind your teacher about the bag I brought."

He grinned back at me and said, "Yeah. Don't worry. I'll tell them about making DNA molecules."

Smart kid. He knew I'd brought gumdrops in the paper bag.

Chapter 37
I Don't Care

Thung. My iMac computer came to life.

I selected the "test maker" CD from its case, inserted the disc into the computer, and waited for the screen to come up. Fulfilling my charge to try out every possible facet of our new pilot series, I found the chapter I needed and settled in to read the selections for multiple-choice test questions, something I rarely used in tests I created myself. I could see the advantage of saving time in grading so many papers if this worked well, but I had my doubts about the quality of this assessment style for all of my students. The good readers would have little trouble, but my language learners would struggle. I wanted to assess science learning, not just reading ability.

I read through the first five questions. I noted the same concept addressed in three of them, but with different wording. I chose one to include in the test template. Another question asked about an unimportant detail. I rejected that question. Ninety minutes later, I had selected a list of thirty multiple choice questions and placed them in the testing template.

I moved on to the short answer and essay question portion of the test making CD. Checking my watch, I realized I needed to finish up and get ready for tomorrow's lesson, so I could get home in time for dinner with my husband. I would give myself another fifteen minutes to work on the test.

Half an hour later, after reading and thinking through all the options, I had chosen five questions. I clicked on the instruction to save and then print the test. I listened to the hum of the small printer on the counter as it spit out my first "pre-made" science test. It had taken a lot longer to put together than I had hoped, but I had begun to learn how to use this new testing tool and expected the next time would go quicker. Hopefully, scoring the tests would save a significant chunk of time. I could use the scanning machine I had discovered in the staff work room to read the answers, at least for the multiple-choice section of the test.

"How many questions will there be?" asked Aaron as his seventh period classmates listened intently. "Will it take the entire period?"

"There are thirty multiple-choice questions," I began.

"Easy," said Aaron under his breath, glancing at Billy and rolling his eyes.

"And five short answer questions," I finished.

Aaron perked up. "Wait, you mean fill-in-the blank questions or essays?"

"Good question, Aaron. This time there are five questions that will require about a paragraph to answer," I said, smiling at his intensity.

I continued, "You may use all the notes in your science notebook to study. If you've been absent at all during this unit, please be sure you get the notes from a friend or from me."

Tran raised his hand.

"Yes, Tran?"

"Mrs. Wright, will there be anything we need to draw on this test?" he asked.

I grinned at him, "No, Tran, not this time, but you might have to identify some parts of a drawing. Hint, hint."

Thursday, the day of the test arrived. As students walked into class, I stood at the doorway and handed each one a sharpened #2 pencil with a good eraser.

"Your ticket out the door today will be that pencil I just gave you," I said to start class. I would use the same set throughout the day, and Steven could sharpen them for me after his class.

I demonstrated how to use the "bubble-in" answer sheets and explained the short answer questions. Then I laid out my test-taking procedure.

"It's important for you to do your own work, without talking. Your eyes must stay on your own paper. You may not look at anyone else's paper." I paused. "My rules for taking tests are strict, just like the state-mandated standard testing we do in the spring. My goal is to give you practice with how we will do testing then, to make you more comfortable with the process and therefore more successful. You will be ready to do well on those tests.

"You can have the whole period to work on the test, if you need it. Please turn your test papers over when you're done, so I'll know you have finished. We'll stop when everyone has completed the test.

"Since you have placed on your desk a book to read or a paper for drawing, you have something to do if you finish earlier than the others. You may not get up, talk, or disturb others. Let's make sure everyone can concentrate and do their best on this test."

After the test began, I watched as they worked, a rare, low energy day for me. I enjoyed the quiet time to observe my students.

As soon as the final bell of the day rang, I hurried off to the staff room with my stack of answer sheets from the multiple-choice part of the test. I reread the directions for the scanning machine, then I placed my answer key into the slot and pushed the button marked "Key." The paper slid through and came out the bottom with small red marks by each of the question numbers, indicating the machine had captured the marks on my answer key.

To score the student papers, I then set the stack of answer sheets from my first period class into the tray and pushed the scoring button. Within seconds, they ran through the machine and came out at the bottom with scores. Encouraged, I put the next set into the machine. It worked. Within minutes, I walked back to my classroom with scored answer sheets, humming to myself.

Seated at my computer, I clicked on the grading program and began to enter the scores from this part of the test. They seemed unusually low. I took a look at some of the answer sheets and noticed the machine had scored stray pencil marks and erased choices as wrong answers on some papers. By the time I recorded all the scores on this section, my concern had grown. I knew I needed to recheck all the multiple-choice answers with human eyes. I still had the short answer questions to personally read and score.

"Mrs. Wright, do you have our tests graded?" asked Jose when I opened the door to let my first period students into the room.

I smiled at him. "I do indeed have some of the tests scored, but it's going to take a little longer for me to grade the whole thing."

He looked disappointed.

I held up the stack of machine scored answer sheets. "I'd like to go over the multiple-choice questions and answers from yesterday's test, so you'll know how you did. This will also give you a chance to learn from any mistakes you might have made."

I paused and decided to go on, "And, I need your help. The machine made some errors because of stray pencil marks on some of the papers. If you find anything you think is a mistake, please circle it."

We soon discovered more scoring errors.

The stack of papers with mistakes continued to grow throughout the day. Disheartened, I began to suspect a few incidents of cheating, too. After school I sat down again at my computer to review and revise the scores. An easy task had turned into a drawn out, unpleasant chore.

Finally, I returned to reading and scoring the short answer part of the tests. Shadows stretched out long across the floor as the sunlight coming through the single window in my room gave way to the diffuse light of dusk. Friday evening dragged on; I moved slowly from paper to paper, tired at the end of a long week. I wanted to quit and go home to my family.

I calculated how long it would take me to grade all the tests. If it took me two minutes per student paper, for 150 students it would take me 300 minutes, five hours, not including breaks. If I took any longer per student, it would add hours to the process.

Five hours. Or longer.

I decided to take the stack of tests home with me to finish grading over the weekend. Hopefully, Jerry wouldn't mind too much if I holed up to do my grading instead of helping him with our kitchen remodeling project. Our younger son, Brian, would be there to work with him this weekend anyway.

Saturday morning, after a slow start to the day, including a long, leisurely breakfast, a stalling tactic on my part, I sat at my dining room table working on a stack of test papers.

After several hours of grading, I came across a unique answer. "How dare she write this?" I said aloud to myself, feeling indignant.

I picked up the test paper and marched into the kitchen where my husband was installing a new cabinet with our son.

"Listen to what one of my students wrote as her answer to the last question on my test." I read aloud in a mocking tone of voice, "I don't know, and I don't care."

They continued to work. I fumed. "Brian, what do you think of that?" I asked.

"Well, Mom, maybe she just didn't understand why it was important for her to learn that concept you were testing."

I turned around with a "huff" and went back to the dining table, stewing on the frustration of spending more time on grading than these kids spent on learning, feeling sorry for myself.

Then, a moment of clarity, an "aha!" moment, hit me.

I walked back into the kitchen and said, "I just realized you're right, Brian. I've been teaching about cells, but I never clearly explained why students need to know this information, what makes any of this subject valuable to them. Thank you for giving me a new perspective on my work."

It took me until Tuesday morning to get all the grading completed and recorded. Finally, I could return the tests with their grades.

I waited at the door, watching as she approached, chatting with a group of girls. "Angelica, I'm so glad you're here today," I said.

Without responding, her eyes shifted to me and then quickly darted away. She dashed past me and plopped down in her seat. I continued to greet arriving second period students.

"I'm handing back the rest of the test papers today," I announced, once the period began. I held up the stack of test papers and said, "And, I want to tell you something I learned from one of you while I was grading these." I paused, looking at the blank stares from my students.

With a serious expression on my face, I continued. "One of you wrote as an answer to the last question, 'I don't know, and I don't care.'" I heard a few gasps. Angelica averted her eyes from me and looked up at the ceiling, and I avoided looking directly at her.

I let the silence hang in the air, looking from student to student. They stared at me, concern crossing their faces.

"How can I expect you to take this seriously, to learn what you need to know, if you don't understand why it's important?" Again, I paused.

"We're talking about *your* life. *You* will make decisions as adults that need to be based on the knowledge *you* acquire now, *this year*, in seventh grade."

I held up a newspaper, "Do you see the headline on this page? There's a huge controversy going on about the use of stem cells in research. Should we allow them to be used for research or not? Do you know what this means? Most people don't understand anything about this. But, only four or five years from now, you will be considered adults, and you may be asked to make decisions, to vote, based on issues like these. Your parents didn't even learn about this when they were in school, because this body of scientific knowledge is all new. You're studying about cells now, and this year you will learn enough to go home to your parents and explain. Imagine that! You need to teach them. It is important for you to learn, so you can make informed choices for you and your family."

I smiled at Angelica, and then I tacked up the newspaper article on the bulletin board. My impassioned speech might make a minor impact on these students today, but I vowed to make a renewed, conscious effort to connect each day, each lesson, with meaning for my students.

Chapter 38
Rodney

An expectant hush settled in the room. I moved to the end of a row of desks and counted out papers. Continuing to talk while I delivered stacks of papers, I explained, "This next assignment is the one you've been waiting for, the cell model. It's worth 80 points toward your science grade."

A murmur ran through the class. Papers passed along the rows. Binders clicked.

"These are the directions you'll need. Please put your name on the top of the page."

I returned to the demo counter and read aloud the directions on the page, stopping for questions between sections.

"You'll work on your model at home, but I will also have materials here for after school sessions for anyone who wants to work at school instead. And I'll be here to answer questions."

"Be creative with your materials and accurate with your labeling. Oh, and I will be choosing some of the best of this year's models to add to our display case."

My science classroom door was propped open in the late afternoon sunshine. A variety of colored paper and trays of plastic shapes, fabric, cardboard, beans, macaroni, popsicle sticks, markers, and glue covered one of the lab tables. Rodney walked into the room and dropped his backpack on a desk.

"Hey, Mrs. Wright," he said.

I looked up from a stack of papers I was working on. "Hi Rodney, I'm glad to see you here."

With his hands in his pockets, he said, "I need to work on my cell model."

"You came to the right place, Rodney."

He sauntered over to the materials table and sat on a stool. "Got a lot of stuff here."

"Tell me again which cell you chose to model."

"Animal." He ran his hand through a bowl of macaroni.

"Have you started already, or is this your first time to work on it?" I asked.

"I don't have anything at home to use," he paused. "Mrs. Sherman told me to come here to get some help."

"Good. Why don't you get a textbook? Take a look at the animal cell picture to get some ideas. You can also look at the samples in the display case over here, Rodney."

He pushed the stool back and moved to the display case near me. He stood there looking at the samples for a moment. "Looks like a lot of work."

"Yes, it does take some time to make a model, but I think you'll find it's worth doing. Making a model really helps you learn about the structures inside the cell, and most kids like it better than just reading about cells. It's important to know what living things are made of, to know how these tiny pieces of us work."

Rodney walked to the closest row of desks and picked up a book from the shelf beneath it. He carried the book to the materials table and set it down. I continued to work on my papers.

After a few minutes, Dion and Antonio entered the room. "Hi Mrs. Wright," said Dion. "We just finished working with Miss Martin. Can we work on our models today?"

"Yes, of course," I said. "Come on in. I'll get the models you two started on Monday."

"Hey, Rodney. You making a model too?" Antonio asked.

"All seventh graders are making cell models, dummy!" said Dion, poking Antonio in the arm.

"I haven't really done anything on it yet," said Rodney.

"They're due next week," said Dion.

I set the beginnings of their models on the table. The boys started gathering materials to use, talking as they worked.

When I finished scoring papers, I carried them into the storage room and set them down beside my computer, ready to record the grades later.

I could hear Stacey gathering supplies. She came around the corner and said to me, "You've got kids with you again today."

"Only three today."

I washed my hands in the sink and then opened the cupboard next to the door. I took out a stack of napkins, a box of crackers, a jar of peanut butter, and a knife and carried them into the lab.

"How would you boys like a snack?" I asked, setting things down on the table.

"Cool. Thanks, Mrs. Wright," said Dion.

"Yeah, thanks," echoed Antonio.

Rodney reached the table first. He took a stack of crackers out of the package, placed them on a napkin, and picked up the peanut butter jar. "I like this kind of peanut butter," he said.

"Me too," I replied, smiling.

The boys ate and worked on their models. At last, Dion asked, "What time is it?"

"It's almost 4:30," said Antonio.

"I'm closing the lab in five minutes," I said.

Dion and Antonio piled supplies on top of their half-finished models.

"These are looking good, boys. You coming in tomorrow?"

"Yeah, thanks," answered Antonio.

They took their backpacks and walked out of the room, leaving Rodney sitting at the table.

"Could I have some more crackers and peanut butter?" he asked. "I didn't have any lunch today."

"Yes, help yourself, Rodney." I handed him the peanut butter, and he spread it on a few more crackers. "Why didn't you eat lunch today?"

"Mom forgot to put money in my account," he answered, munching on the crackers.

"You can still get a meal at the cafeteria without money in your account, though."

"Mmm hmmm. I don't like to ask." He paused. "Sometimes Mrs. Sherman lets me come into her classroom at lunch time. She gives me a sandwich." A little quieter, he said, "Mom gets paid this Friday."

After he'd eaten several more, I said, "I've got to close up. Can you come back and work on your model again tomorrow?"

"I think so."

Rodney replaced the textbook and picked up his backpack.

I yelled back into the storage room, "Stacey, I'll be back in a few minutes. I'm going to walk over to the office with Rodney."

"Okay, I'll be here for a while yet," she replied.

Rodney and I walked toward the door together. I stepped outside with him, shut the door and locked it. Shadows stretched from the trees.

"The days are getting shorter," I said.

"Yeah, it gets dark early now."

"How are you getting home tonight, Rodney?"

"Mom's boyfriend." We walked a few more steps in silence, then Rodney said, "He just got out of prison and doesn't have a job yet, so he's coming to get me."

I nodded, taking in the information he'd shared with me, wondering if he was worried.

"Are you sure your mother wants you to go home with this man?" I asked.

He shrugged, "Mom says he's done his time, paid his dues."

We reached the sidewalk. No one in sight.

I waited with him for a few minutes.

"He'll be here soon," said Rodney.

"I'll be inside the office for a few minutes, and I'll check on you when I'm done," I said. "I want to make sure you get home before dark, Rodney."

I left him outside and walked around the corner to the back door of the office where I met Carol.

"I was just coming to lock that door," she said.

"Is Katherine here? I need to keep an eye on my student who's waiting for his ride home."

Carol locked the door behind me. I pulled a few papers from my mailbox and followed her back to the front office. Rodney was still standing out front, waiting.

"That's Rodney," she said. "He usually walks home, and he lives a long way from here."

"He's been in my classroom working on his cell model."

Katherine walked out of her office.

"Rodney just told me he's being picked up by his mother's boyfriend who just got out of prison," I said.

"That kid had a rough start to the year. I've talked with his mother several times already. Carrie has taken him under her wing," said Katherine.

A battered van pulled into the parking lot and came to a sputtering stop. Rodney dragged his backpack over to it as an unshaven, tattoo-covered guy with a mean scowl on his face came around to open the side door of the van. *Is that man staggering?*

The man appeared to say something and then took a swipe at Rodney, missing. Rodney seemed upset, talking back to him.

"I think I'll go out and talk with them," said Katherine.

"You be careful," said Carol.

As Katherine opened the door, we heard the man yell, "Get in the van, you little shit!"

Katherine dashed out the door toward them with determined steps, calling out as she went, "What's going on? Rodney, are you okay?"

I followed Katherine out to the sidewalk, my adrenalin pumping. Seeing the two of us, the man backed off, raising his hands.

Katherine controlled a tense conversation, asking him questions about who he was and where he intended to take Rodney. I stayed close, watching Rodney's sullen facial expressions, his shoulders slumped in resignation. Glancing over at the office, I could see Carol through the windows. She stood at attention next to the phone, ready to call 911, if necessary.

"Everything's okay here," said the man in a gruff voice. "Just need to get the boy home now."

"Rodney, are you all right?" Katherine asked again.

"Yeah, yeah. I'm going," said Rodney. He threw his backpack into the back of the van and jumped in. The man slammed the door shut.

"Taking him straight home right now," the man said loudly. He walked around the front of the van and hoisted his bulk into the driver's seat. Katherine stood there for a moment. He revved up the engine and backed out of the parking space. Watching them depart, she walked back toward me.

"I don't trust that guy," I told her.

"Get the license number," said Katherine.

We repeated it aloud to each other while we walked back to the office where Carol waited, holding the door open for us. Katherine grabbed a piece of paper from the counter and wrote down the license number. "A silver Dodge van, right?"

"Yes, I think so," I said.

"I didn't get close enough to smell if he was drunk, but before he slammed the door shut, I could see a couple of shotguns in the van. That's got to be a probation violation. I need to do a police report," said Katherine, walking around the counter to the phone.

Carol and I exchanged glances. Katherine picked up the phone and dialed.

"Oh dear, I didn't notice the guns," I said, shaking my head.

"This could take a while," said Carol.

I waited while Katherine made the call. Carol looked up Rodney's emergency card and made a Xerox copy of it. We reviewed the details of what we'd seen and what we knew about Rodney until the police arrived minutes later. After a few quick questions, they took off in the squad car.

"I'll stay here until we find out if Rodney arrived home," said Katherine. "You may as well leave, Jan. Might be a long night."

I looked at Carol, not sure if I should go. Without hesitation she said, "Don't worry. You go. I'm staying here with Katherine."

"Okay. I'll go back to my room to finish up a few more things, but I'll check in with you before I leave for home," I said. "Call me if you hear anything."

I walked back to my classroom, unlocked the door, switched on the lights, and relocked the door before I walked back to my desk area. The lights had been turned off on Stacey's side of the room. She'd already left.

I opened the drawer, pulled out my purse and dug into the side pocket to find my phone. I sat down on my office chair, flipped open my phone and dialed my husband. I wouldn't go home until I knew Rodney was safe.

⸙⸙⸙⸙⸙

Thursday of the following week, after school let out for the day, Stacey came into my room and walked around the tables to take a look at the completed models that had been turned in.

"These are good, Jan. I think they're even better than last year."

"I agree. It helps to keep the best for the next year's examples. It challenges the students to do better when they see what can be done."

"So, did Rodney turn in a model?"

"Mmm hmmm, here it is. I can see it's not complete, but he did get something turned in on time. I think he's feeling pretty good about that."

"How did things work out after all that police stuff happened last week?"

"Well, the cops arrested the mother's boyfriend, as you know, and I think Katherine has to testify at a hearing next week. Since I didn't actually see the guns, I'm not involved. They're expecting the guy will go back to prison for a while. Meanwhile, Rodney seems to be doing okay with it all. The seventh-grade teaching team is keeping close track of him. Both Katherine and Carrie have talked with his mother. We just do what we can to take care of our kids while they're with us."

"Yup. And now, you have a ton of models to grade."

"I'll be busy, for sure. I've got the score sheets ready. I'll do what I can after school, but I know I can't get it all done, and I'll have to come in during the weekend. It's the one downside of this assignment. I've even calculated it. If I spend only five minutes per model, it will take me about 14 hours to grade them all. I try not to think about it, because the kids just love seeing all the variety. Best of all, they really learn about cells. The bonus is that making the models meets a couple of state science standards too."

"If you're going to be here this weekend, I'll come in for a couple of hours on Saturday too. We could go out to a restaurant for lunch."

"Like regular people! Yes, I'd like that. It gets to be a long weekend being here alone."

"Well, have fun, Jan," she said with a hint of sarcasm.

"Right. Fun. See you tomorrow, Stacey."

She left the room and I wandered through the tables, enjoying the student work on display. Excellent models stood out as choices for next year's samples.

By Friday, several of the kids had asked me if I had finished grading the models. They were proud of their projects, and they had no idea how long the grading process took me. I never released grades until I had completed all five classes. I promised the kids I'd have the grades ready by Monday, giving myself the extra pressure to complete the marathon grading weekend. At least I could look forward to having a leisurely lunch with Stacey, a rare treat.

Chapter 39
Cooperative Learning

"Where do you want these, Mrs. Wright?" asked Javier, my custodian, pushing a large, heavily laden cart through the door.

"Oh good! They're here!" Walking toward him, I clapped my hands. "Let's stand them up right there, next to the wall by the door. The kids will be so happy to see these in the morning. Thank you, Javier."

The arrival of tri-fold display boards made science fair projects come to life in a way that drew in even the most resistant students.

As soon as Javier left, I sat down at my computer, pulled up the template for the Pick-Up-Your-Science-Board announcement letter for families and plugged in the dates for the end of this week. I sent a copy to the other two science teachers, so they could use it for their own grade levels. Then I hit the print button to make 190 copies, enough for each of my seventh-grade students.

I liked to ramp up the interest for this event, to get kids to talk with their families about their projects. I encouraged parental support, but I didn't want them to do the work *for* my students, a message I included in every letter home.

My letter to parents also explained cooperative learning. Since I would not be able to differentiate individual participation, all students in a group would receive the same grade, based on the final project. To make it easier, I encouraged groups of two, but recognizing differences in personalities and social strengths, I also allowed trios and singles. I emphasized strategies and roles for sharing the workload within the group, especially when they worked on the projects at home. I offered to share materials and opened my classroom as a workspace before and after school.

I spent class time helping students choose appropriate topics and set up their groups. I gave the scoring rubric for the science fair projects to each student. I asked the rest of our school staff to encourage, remind, and offer help.

I thought I had all the bases covered.

I never liked yard duty or bus duty of any kind or duration. In all the years of teaching, I had never become the strict disciplinarian Cora Lee had been in Norfolk. Although I had developed the necessary skills, I still did not enjoy being the stern rule enforcer, especially in unstructured settings for kids I did not know well. Besides, yard duty always meant losing a bathroom break.

When the last kid stepped up onto the bus, the doors closed with a *hiss*. I felt relieved. Then I remembered what I had to do next, a parent conference with the principal and vice principal in attendance. I shook my head in resignation.

I made a quick stop to pick up a few papers, used the bathroom for the first time since lunch, and strode across the breezeway from the staff room to the office.

"They're waiting for you," said Carol as I passed her desk.

I rolled my eyes.

She grinned at me. "Good luck," she whispered.

Standing at the end of the hallway, I could see the crowded conference room through the glass wall. The parents were seated at the table, next to each other, with their backs to me. Bonnie sat across from them, around the corner from Katherine who sat at the end of the table by the open door. Rachel, the student in question, was not in attendance. *Darn. This is a missed opportunity.*

I paused long enough to take a deep breath to center myself, attempting to push down the resentment I felt about this confrontation. *I've already wasted time in two long conversations with Mrs. Fredricks.*

Now she thinks she can overrule me by bringing in her husband and the school administrators. I marched down the hall and into the conference room.

"Good. Mrs. Wright is here," said Katherine, smiling in an attempt to relax the tension.

"Hello, Mr. and Mrs. Fredricks," I said, while I slipped around Katherine at the end of the table to the far side of the room. "Ms. Murphy, Ms. Duval." I nodded to each of them.

"I'm sorry to keep you waiting. I had bus duty." I stopped short of telling them I needed a bathroom break too. I set the project board against the wall, pulled out a chair to sit down across from the parents, and placed the folder filled with papers on the table in front of me, trying hard to keep my facial expression neutral.

I asked, "Where's Rachel? Won't she be joining us to talk about her project?" *I already know the answer, but I want to make a point about the student's responsibility for her own role in the project.*

Katherine and Bonnie had their "make-nice" faces on. The parents, with pasted-on smiles, eyebrows up, and shoulders raised, were not disarmed. I felt their animosity.

"No. She will NOT be here," replied Mrs. Fredricks with a sneer.

Aiming a polite, controlled smile at the parents, Katherine said, "Thank you all for being here this afternoon. As I understand it, we're here to discuss a concern you have about your daughter's science fair project grade. First, let me say, we were all so proud of the work our students did to achieve the huge success of our science fair that Mrs. Wright has organized for the past two years. I hope you had an opportunity to see the articles in the local newspapers. We received accolades from Mayor Kasperzak and from the NASA volunteers who helped out with judging. Our School Board has sent special commendations to our school. Of course, we're thrilled with the level of parent participation in this event." She paused.

Mrs. Fredricks squirmed in her seat; the fire in her eyes and the intensity of her facial expression did not lessen with Katherine's attempt to put any kind of positive spin on the discussion to follow.

Giving it up for a lost cause, Katherine said, "Mr. and Mrs. Fredricks, would you like to start by explaining your concerns to us?"

Mr. Fredricks spoke up, his eyes narrowing to accusing little slits, scanning the seated group, "My wife tells me she's gotten nowhere in her talks with Mrs. Wright concerning our daughter's science fair project grade."

Mrs. Fredricks perked up, sitting forward on her seat, she glanced at her husband with a self-satisfied smile. He leaned back into the chair and folded his arms across his chest, tilting his head as if daring me to oppose them.

"Yes, I've called her twice, and she won't budge on this, so I've had to go above her head," she said. "I think it's unfair." She raised her chin, reminding me of a tattling, spoiled, little girl who hadn't gotten her way.

I seethed inside and redoubled my effort to keep my face as blank as possible.

Bonnie spoke up. "Mrs. Fredricks, would you please tell us what you believe is unfair about this grade."

Without hesitating, Mrs. Fredricks spewed out her indignance. "I don't see why the whole group should get the same grade. Our daughter, Rachel, did all the work on this project. Those two other girls in her group didn't do much at all."

Katherine and Bonnie nodded, encouraging her to go on. I had already heard her argument, twice.

Mrs. Fredricks, gathering speed and volume, rattled on, "Rachel brought the science fair project board home and set up meetings to work on it at our house. That Mexican girl, Linda, only came once. She sat around complaining. She hardly lifted a finger to help Rachel. The white girl, Christine, seemed nice at first. She showed up a couple of times, but she didn't do much work, either. Basically, we did all the work. We were the ones who stayed up late getting it done so Rachel could bring it back to school on the due date. I just don't think it's fair that those other two girls got the same grade as Rachel. I've already talked with Mrs. Wright about this and she doesn't agree." With a final loud huff, she looked across the table with daggers in her eyes.

The room remained silent in response, waiting for her next comment.

"Besides, I think she deserves an A on this project," she pouted and sat back into her chair.

"Mrs. Wright, would you like to respond?" said Katherine, looking at me with one of her most professional looks, belying the underlying friendship we shared.

"Yes, of course," I replied, in my teacher-mode persona.

"First of all, I'm glad you came in to see us in person, Mr. and Mrs. Fredricks. I have a few things I'd like to share with you both."

I opened the folder in front of me and picked up the top sheet of paper. I held it up.

"Do you remember receiving this blue paper I sent home with all the students on January 15th?" I passed it across the table to them. "It's the overview of what I expected, with all the due dates listed."

The parents studied the paper. I waited.

"I don't remember seeing this one," said Mrs. Fredricks.

"How about this one?" I asked, sliding over a yellow paper.

"I'm not sure," she said.

"This yellow paper lists suggestions for how to choose a topic."

"Oh, maybe we did see this," she said.

"Please take a look at the other side of the page," I said.

She flipped it over.

"As you can see, these are the guidelines for working in cooperative groups. Take a look at the top section. I explain how to choose group mates. I encouraged students to work in twos, but I also allowed them to work alone, if they chose to. As you well know, your daughter did not choose those options. I allowed groups of three when all three students came to me to request it and agreed that they would try to do an equal amount of work. Which your daughter, Linda, and Christine did."

I reached across the table to point at the bold print.

"See the highlighted statement in that paragraph? It says all members of a group will receive the same grade, since I could not fairly know how much each one had contributed."

"But, *I'm* telling you my Rachel did all the work. Shouldn't that make a difference?" Mrs. Fredricks asked, defiance obvious in the sound of her voice.

"I'm sorry, Mrs. Fredricks. It would not be fair to all the rest of my students to make an exception to the rules for a single student. Your daughter knows this, which is why I hoped she would be here today, as I requested."

I picked up another page, a pink one. "This one is a reminder about making their group and topic choices. There at the bottom of the page is another reminder that the students are to do their own work, not their parents. It lists all the times I opened the science room before school and after school for three weeks to allow groups to meet there to work and ask me for help with their projects or cooperative group roles."

Finally, I handed over a green paper, saying, "You'll notice each paper is a different color. I did that on purpose to make them stand out from all the other papers students carry home in their backpacks.

"This page explains the rubric, or scoring system, I used on the projects. Before they ever started, my students knew exactly what was expected of them, how to get the grade they wanted. Again, there is a reminder to do their fair share of the work and that parents are not allowed to do the project for them.

"Mr. and Mrs. Fredricks, I know very well that your daughter worked hard on this project. You can be proud of her accomplishment."

Mrs. Fredricks shoulders slumped. When she looked up at me, I saw a last bit of resistance surface in her face.

"So why did she only get a B+ on it instead of an A? I think it looks great," said Mrs. Fredricks.

Katherine and Bonnie looked at me. I rose from my seat and grabbed the project board I had stashed behind my chair. "I thought it might help if I showed you a project that did earn an A." I set the trifold board up at the end of the table. I had taped over the names to keep the students anonymous.

"If you'll take the green page and follow along, I'll point out the areas that were scored on this one," I continued. With the assembled group following along I led them through the scoring process. Pointing out areas I knew had not scored as well on Rachel's group project. I could see understanding coming to light in her mother's eyes as I spoke.

At last, a look of resignation registered on Mrs. Fredricks face.

"Is there anything else you'd like to say?" asked Katherine, turning to the parents.

"No, I guess not. It looks like I can't change your minds," said Mrs. Fredricks. She stood up, followed by her husband. "I still think we did a great job on this science fair project, and those other girls shouldn't get credit for it."

At this point, my own anger had dissipated, and I now understood where her anger had come from. Despite my admonitions for students to do their own work, this mother was upset because she herself had worked on the project with her daughter. She saw the grade as a judgment of her work, as well as Rachel's.

"I'm truly sorry this science fair project has caused you so much concern," I said to her.

As I walked back to my classroom, the campus appeared empty. I still had to prepare for the next day of classes, and I felt exhausted after an exceptionally long couple of weeks with kids before and after school, evenings with science fair judges, a weekend spent grading projects at school, and putting on the grand, school-wide science fair event for families and special guests on Tuesday night. I'd hardly slept. Dealing with upset parents had sapped the last of my energy.

I began to wonder if the whole science fair had been worth all my extra time, effort, and aggravation. I'd spent more time to score some of the projects than the students had spent in making them. And Rachel's parents had challenged one of the huge drawbacks I saw in cooperative learning: individual accountability. I had to admit that no matter how hard I worked to communicate the guidelines, besides the obvious inequity of parent support for projects done out of class time, group grades didn't seem fair to me either.

Exhaustion and self-pity began to drag me down. I wandered through my classroom, too drained to get anything productive accomplished. Feeling disheartened, I decided to go home.

I crawled into bed and fell asleep by 7:30 that evening.

Art students painted the sign for our school-wide
Science Fair in school colors, blue on yellow.

I checked preparations for the evening event.

Families explored science fair projects in the multi-use room.

Chapter 40
Spring is in the Air

With flowers blooming and sunshine the rule of the day, Mrs. Chambers showed up on campus. The former seventh-grade social studies teacher had retired the previous year, but as part of her contract, the district required a certain number of days of her service. For this she had devised a bold project for Crittenden Middle School. Little did I know how that involvement would affect me in particular.

"I'd like to welcome back Clarice Chambers," announced Katherine to hearty applause.

The teaching staff sat in students' chairs clustered around tables in Toby's math classroom.

"Clarice, why don't you tell us a little about the project you have planned for us?" Katherine urged.

"Oh, it's nothing much," said Clarice as she leaned against the counter at the side of the room. Her shoulder length, gray hair frizzled out in all directions, more unkempt than ever. I envied her casual appearance in soiled jeans and a large, faded, plaid work shirt, a sure sign of her more relaxed days at home. Beside her sat a tower of egg cartons, containing what I knew to be multicolored eggs from her hens and geese.

She straightened up and began to explain. "We're going to paint a mural." She looked around the room of familiar faces. "Every student in the school will have an opportunity to participate in painting it."

She paused and then continued in her understated tone. "I want the staff to get involved too. Everyone will get to paint something on the wall outside the cafeteria. I'll do the background and give suggestions; you can do the animals."

Animals? We looked at each other. Heads shook and doubt crossed several faces.

What's she getting us into? Me? Paint an animal?

"I was inspired by the colorful paper garden wall you created for my retirement last year. So, we're going to paint a jungle scene." With that she leaned back into the counter, placed a hand on the stack of egg cartons, and said, "Oh, and I brought eggs for anyone who wants them."

We sat in stunned silence for a moment. Finally, Katherine said, "Are there any questions for Clarice?"

Carrie raised her hand.

"What about those of us who have no artistic talent?" Carrie laughed, and most of us chuckled with her.

"Oh, don't you worry about that," replied Clarice. "I'll have lots of pictures for you to choose from, and I'll help anyone who wants my help. If you don't want to do an animal, you can paint flowers. Each of you will be successful. I have no doubt."

Later, I walked out of the staff meeting with Nicole, the new teacher who had taken Clarice's place on the seventh-grade team. "That flower garden display Clarice spoke about," she paused. "I saw it on the wall across from the Circle of the Muse when I interviewed for her job. It was one of the reasons I chose this school."

"Wow, I didn't know that, Nicole." I smiled, remembering the project. It turned out to be a spectacular, fitting tribute for a creative teacher who had worked at the school for over thirty years.

"Who organized it?" she asked.

"The construction of the paper garden was easy," I began. "I just asked the grade level science teachers to let all our students trace and cut out their handprints from colored construction paper, which I provided. These became the petals of the flowers. Students each wrote their name and a note of thanks to Mrs. Chambers on their handprint. My elective class traced and cut out the green leaves, and I put them in the staff mailboxes, so every staff member could write their own notes. My class then taped the paper handprints onto the wall in designs that made flowers. I cut out the stems, and we made the green grass. Then, for the sign that read, 'Happy Retirement, Mrs. Chambers,' I traced out the words and students filled in the letters with paint."

Realizing I had said more than she needed to hear, I ended with, "It was actually a lot of fun to do. I'm so glad it helped you choose to teach here at Crittenden with us, Nicole."

She smiled and held the door to the workroom open. "I'm not surprised it was you, Jan."

I walked through the door, followed by Nicole.

"Now we're all supposed to paint a jungle scene. I'm not so sure about this," she said.

"I think it's a great idea, but painting animals is a lot tougher than cutting out handprints. I guess we'll just have to see how it all turns out." I picked up a stack of copies from the Xerox machine. Nicole and I sorted the pages into piles on the work table. During the day, teachers would send a print message to this central machine that could handle large jobs of multiple copies. When any of us had a moment, we'd pull out the accumulated orders and stack them on the adjacent table. Finding our own sets of copied pages, we gathered them up and headed back to our classrooms.

Several days later, I walked into the art room to begin the art elective class. Cans of paint, brushes, sponges, and trays covered one of the tables. Another couple of tables were blanketed in pictures of animals and all kinds of jungle scenes and plants. Clarice had been at work here and apparently didn't realize I used the room for my art class. My students helped me gather the mural materials and set them on a single table, so we could use the rest of the room for our art lesson. I left a note for Clarice, explaining our use of the room during third period.

The following week, the mural began to appear. A backdrop of vines and trees started creeping along the cafeteria wall. Students gathered in curious clusters to watch the scene taking shape. I loved the suspense of the reveal, igniting visual imagination. Kids talked about which animals might appear and who would be painting them. I began to think about my own choice. Could I paint a monkey?

In the next few weeks, I found traces of Clarice's work in the art room, causing me to clean up her things before I could teach my class. I tried to catch her to talk about it, but she usually arrived in the middle of the day and left before the last bell. At first, I let it go, and it got worse. Later, I left notes for her. She would leave a cleaner room for a few days, and then I'd find another messy room to deal with.

A couple of weeks into the project, I arrived at school early to set up for my art class before school started. When I walked into the art room, I was shocked to see the disarray: used paint supplies and spills on the tables, splashes of cut-out pictures from magazines on a couple of the tables, heaps of tarps on the floor. The deep sink in the back of the room was covered in greens and browns with paint-filled brushes soaking in buckets everywhere. The more I looked, the more distressed I became. I could not use the art room for my class at this point. In a huff, I turned around and marched out the door and down to the principal's office.

"Katherine, could I interrupt you for a moment?" I asked.

"Sure Jan, what's up?" she said. "You look upset."

"I *am* upset. I just walked into the art room to set up for my class. I know Clarice is a very creative soul, but that gorgeous art room is now a complete disaster! Clarice made a total mess with all the mural paints and brushes in there. In fact, the brushes look like they've been ruined because they haven't been cleaned. That's wasteful and expensive. I'm sorry; I don't mean to be a complainer, but I seldom see Clarice, so I haven't been able to talk with her. I've left her notes about the shared use of this room. I don't know what else to do about it, but I can't use the room for my art class the way it is right now."

"Let me take a look, Jan. I know Clarice can be a little scattered. Can you take your class to another space for today?" she said.

"I'll figure something out for my class," I answered. "Katherine, it's going to take a lot of work to clean up all the paint in those deep sinks. She can't continue to use the space like that."

"Don't worry, Jan. I'll take care of it."

Katherine got up from her desk and headed out toward the art room while I returned to my science classroom to make a new lesson plan for the day.

Thinking as I walked, I had an inspiration. I could take the kids outside to sketch, using some of the perspective techniques I had taught them the previous week. We could use the set of clip boards I had acquired during my years of teaching fifth grade. I would look through my stored boxes in the science supply room to find them. This was not the lesson I had planned, but I reasoned that I could also point out the various shades of greens in the trees and bushes while we sketched. I could coordinate my last-minute art lesson with the jungle scene that had begun to entangle us.

Katherine sent me a note explaining that she had designated a smaller room with a sink for Clarice and her mural project. That seemed like a workable solution for me.

Clarice showed up more often during the school days now; work began in earnest on the mural. Small groups of students could be seen with her, painting flowers and a variety of leaves and vines. Animals began to appear to the delight of all. Talented students painted lions, parrots, giraffes, and an elephant, all under Clarice's guiding council. Once in a while, on my lunch break, I stopped to check on the progress.

"Jan, I'm sorry to have left a mess in the art room. Katherine gave me a room where I can keep all the supplies now," she said when I had a chance to chat with her one day.

I acknowledged her apology and went on to praise the glorious mural taking shape.

"You said you'd like to paint a monkey?" she asked.

"I'm not sure how well it might turn out," I said. "I don't have a clear picture in my mind of what one looks like."

"That's not a problem. I can give you an assortment of monkey pictures. I'll set aside this door for your monkey. Come and see me right after school gets out today," she encouraged. "I'll show you my new room and the stash of pictures I've torn out of magazines for months now."

I met Clarice after school that day for a tour of her exclusive work space. She got me started painting the monkey, and we worked together for days. But since Clarice still had the key to the art room, I sometimes found evidence of her continued use of the space that interfered with my art class projects.

Several weeks into the mural project, I walked into the art room at the beginning of third period to find my stacks of prepared, cut-out colored construction paper shapes spilled onto the floor. Three cans of paint had dripped over their sides and spilled onto one of the tables. Dirty brushes and paint-filled sponges filled the sinks in buckets that overflowed into rivers of colors. The night before, I had left the room clean and set up for the day's lesson which I could no longer accomplish.

After the last bell, I found Clarice still painting as she sat on a paint-splattered tarp, wearing clothes covered in almost as much paint as the wall she was working on.

"This is the crocodile I told you about," she said to me as I squatted down next to her.

"Clarice, the mural is really taking shape, and we all love it." I took a breath and went on. "Could I talk to you for a few minutes about the art room?"

"Oh, I know I left a mess again. I couldn't find my key to the storage room, and I couldn't find the custodian, so I had to use the art room instead. At least that key was on my key ring. I'll clean it up later."

"Clarice, I couldn't teach my class today because of the condition you left the art room in."

"I'm sorry. By the time I finished last night, it was so late. I was just too tired to clean it all up. I'll get to it this afternoon. I promise."

I didn't know what else to say to this creative and inspiring woman, but I couldn't keep trying to share the art room space with her.

It would soon be time to begin of a new series of elective classes, so I decided to change my offering from general art to designing tessellations. I could use my science room then and relieve a lot of pressure. Besides, I'd have time to take a small break before third period, like everyone else.

Still, the fate of that beautiful art room worried me.

The monkey I painted, along with the entire mural, appeared perfectly intact eighteen years after the events in this chapter.

Chapter 41
Sex Education

Science teachers at Crittenden Middle School devoted the last two weeks of school to sex education, partly because the topic held students' attention and partly because the three of us who taught science put it off until we could no longer avoid it. Professionally, I would say we waited until students were the most mature and until we knew the students well enough to have a strong relationship with them for such a delicate subject.

In fifth grade, we separated the boys and girls for these classes and talked about puberty. It was always a nervous time for teachers, as well as students. Teaching seventh-grade sex education was a different story altogether. Seventh graders were not the naïve children they had been two years before. This time, I had to teach boys and girls together, as a group, in their regular science classes and include the topics of human reproductive systems, insemination, pregnancy, and sexually transmitted diseases.

My main source of advice and direction came from conversations with the former seventh-grade teacher, Charlene. There were no explicit district curriculum guidelines, just a folder marked SEX ED in the science file cabinet in the storage room and a list of videos I could order. The P.E. teachers didn't take kindly to my suggestion that they could teach the unit during their health classes. Nope, I was stuck doing the duty.

We always sent out information notices to parents, explaining our course of study. They had the choice to opt out and have their children sent to study hall instead. Few made that choice. I wondered how many students conveniently forgot to give the notes to their parents, anticipating an opt-out from them.

Charlene advised me over the phone when I called to ask how to proceed. She said to put out a question box for any student who wanted to ask a question; she told me NOT to take questions aloud during class. That method was designed to reduce embarrassment for students and teacher alike. It should also give me time to prepare an adequate response.

The other edict from Charlene was to start sex ed with a listing of all the names students could think of for the male sex organ. I would start by writing "penis" on the overhead projector, then read it aloud. My students would then supply all the rest of the names for the same body part. It was supposed to lessen the stigma of talking about the "unmentionable" subject.

In truth, seventh-grade boys were only too happy to offer words for our list, once the ice was broken. Many girls sat in silence during this list making. Once we had exhausted the entire list of student responses, along with their guffaws, giggles, and reddened cheeks, I was supposed to tell them we would use only the scientific word, "penis," for the rest of all the classes.

Personally, I had almost never said "penis" aloud, let alone in front of students. I was fifty-three years old the first time I taught this unit, and I had been brought up not even saying the word "sex" aloud. It was a bit for me to get used to, trying to be the solid educator who added nothing of a personal nature to the discussion, to create a trusting atmosphere, without embarrassment, when I myself was just a touch uncomfortable. I learned a few words I had not known before as the boys poured out their lists. I'm quite sure many of my students did too. I questioned this technique, wondering if I was teaching the "wrong" thing by listing all the possible names for penis. However, the technique worked, at least for me; I was able to say "penis" quite easily after five science classes in a row that first year.

At this point, I handed out a piece of construction paper to each student. I told them to fold it in half and write their name on the upper corner to make a folder in which to keep their notes. Then I handed out a diagram to label with the scientific names for the male reproductive system. Students were to keep their notes in the folders I collected at the end of each class.

I told students NOT to discuss anything outside of class, except with their parents. Of course, I enlisted the help of the other staff members to squelch the conversations I knew were happening regardless of the guidelines I set up. How could a bunch of middle schoolers not talk about this topic?

Once we started on female anatomy, the initial lesson began with the same technique. I would start with uterus and list the alternate names. Then came the female reproductive system diagrams and labels for the various parts.

This year, I had taken a workshop on organizing written notes with students. One suggestion I liked was to recycle paper by using the back sides of old papers for note taking. The instructor introduced me to t-charts, a great way to set up a vocabulary lesson. I demonstrated how to draw a giant T on a piece of paper. One side I labeled vocabulary words and the other side I labeled definitions. On the left column, we wrote each of the scientific names for all the male reproductive parts, starting with penis. On the right side, we printed the definitions.

The lessons ran smoothly until I got to seventh period. These were my least inhibited, most verbal students. I made the innocent mistake of handing out rulers to make the lines of the t-charts. I actually gave thirteen-year-old boys rulers to do a lesson about penises. A few of the boys in the back of the room began to snicker and make motions to measure their own body parts. The snickers spread as students nearby caught on. Being the teacher in charge, I had to say, "Boys, that's not the intention of those rulers. Please use them only to make the lines on your t-chart." At which, everyone burst out laughing, and I could not help but join them.

"Look at Mrs. Wright! Her face is bright red," pointed out Doug.

Their laughter increased. Mine too.

"Okay, okay. You got me. Now hand in the rulers. We've done enough with these," I said at last, trying hard to regain my composure.

Responses in the question box revealed a wide range of previous knowledge about sexual behaviors. There were innocent questions, opportunities to correct misinformation, and obvious challenges from sexually experienced students. Stacey was teaching sex ed with eighth graders at the same time, so we often conferred on how to explain answers and which questions to ignore. One day, when asked the average size of an erect penis, I deferred to an internet search. It didn't occur to me that I would be wading into a massive amount of unfiltered internet porn on my school computer. Oh my!

Guidelines for teaching anything about contraception were minimal, so I kept my lesson brief. However, I did end the unit by sending kids home for the summer break with full knowledge about sexually transmitted diseases, an attempt to discourage sexual experimentation by these young teens.

The lessons ended with only a single day left in the school year. Those students who had been excluded from sex ed were returned to class, and the embarrassing topic was set aside for another year; at least that was the plan. Unfortunately, I had forgotten to return the sex ed folders on the last day of those classes. I also had all of the science notebooks to return to students, along with a few other saved assignments, so on the final day of school, I would hand everything back to students and remind them to keep the sex ed folders in their backpacks until they got home. They were not to share any of those pages with other students.

When each class of students arrived for science that last, shortened school day, I asked them to share memories, to tell what had been important to them, from our year of study together. We brainstormed, writing the lists on the whiteboard.

Then, I asked students to write a letter to me, telling me what they would remember most from this year in science. At this point in second period, Angelica burst out, "Mrs. Wright, I'm so sorry I wrote that comment on my test paper about not knowing and not caring." She pointed to our memories on the whiteboard and then to the bulletin board with all the news articles we had gathered during the year. "Now I know EVERYTHING is important!"

The kids in her class and I laughed together. It was a moment of joyful vindication for me. I could believe I had made science meaningful for my students, at least some of the time.

The letters, though often general and repetitious, always made me smile, cry, and miss my students. School year endings were exhausting.

The last day of the middle school year was less structured than any other day of the year with parties, movies, or games going on in most classes. This particular year ended with someone getting wind of a possible fight as students were to leave the campus. A hand-delivered note alerted the staff. Told not to spread the news to alarm our students, Katherine asked us to patrol the exits.

The last order of the day was to hand out final report cards. Any student who had an outstanding bill or missing textbook would not receive one until things were settled with the office, which would remain open for the next couple of weeks.

Many classrooms barely contained their students as the time for the last bell approached. My students knew they would remain seated until then. Planning the perfect timing to control student behavior was tricky. I watched the clock.

The final bell rang. I dismissed my seventh period science class to cheers. The classroom door burst open, and they poured out into the loud sounds of adolescents departing for summer vacation. Anxious to disengage myself from lingering farewell conversations without alerting my students about the possible fight, my trained ears picked up the sounds of an angry commotion near the edge of the field by the parking lot.

I raced toward the sounds while several of students hurried back to me yelling, "Mrs. Wright, Mrs. Wright, Rodney's really mad. He's screaming swear words and throwing his papers all over the yard."

I could see him slamming his backpack into the ground and yelling, "I'm glad this fucking year is over! I hate school!"

"Dion, go tell Ms. Falco to call the office to let them know what's going on," I said in a rush, heading toward Rodney. I could see several students stopping to watch his tantrum. Some tried to talk him into calming down.

"Cool it, Rodney!"

"Let it go."

He was having none of that and continued his tirade, smashing and smashing his backpack until the strap tore off in his hands.

"Rodney," I raised my voice, trying to be heard over the pandemonium as I approached him. "Rodney, please stop."

"I don't give a fuck!" he yelled scooping up papers from the ground and tossing them into the air as he fled, sidestepping away from the school buildings and me.

From the far side of the field, Mr. Simon, the P.E. teacher, sprinted in our direction, followed by a growing group of kids, eager to see what was going on. Rodney spotted them, and with one last toss of his backpack, turned and ran, leaving campus with stunned students in his wake.

Seeing Rodney's exit, Mr. Simon did an about-face, taking his followers with him to the opposite side of the field.

The papers Rodney had strewn around contained all the sex education diagrams and notes I had handed back to him during fifth period. I was mortified to see these highly sensitive papers released indiscriminately into the view of all and any who passed by. Besides all the middle school kids, including sixth graders who had not been exposed to the more mature sex ed classes, there were parents and younger children here to pick up students. It was supposed to be a joyful day of celebration.

I scooped up papers as fast as I could manage. Christina and Dolores stopped to help me.

"Mrs. Wright, Rodney didn't listen to what you said about these papers," said Christina, speaking aloud the obvious, shaking her head.

"I think he's mad because he didn't get his report card," said Dolores, handing me a stack of papers she had gathered.

I thought she had a good guess about what had set him off; I also knew there was a lot more to this boy's story. I felt devastated and helpless, yet I knew his outrage heralded a scream for help.

What can I do to help that poor boy? I'll go talk with Katherine about him before I leave.

"Thank you for helping me capture all these papers, girls," I told them as I took the last batch of papers from Christina. "You go on and have a wonderful summer vacation."

I looked out across the lawn and saw students milling around on the far side of the field, closest to the gymnasium. A few kids ran toward the group, and I heard one boy yell, "Let's go see the fight!"

Cripes, the fight was still a concern.

I deposited Rodney's papers in my classroom trash can and called the office. Carol told me Katherine and Bonnie were out on the field talking with the kids who had come to fight. I watched from my doorway as the crowd began to disperse, heading off campus in various directions. I began to walk out toward the field to make sure things were settled. I could hear sirens in the distance and wondered if the police were about to arrive.

By the time I got half way across the athletic field, Katherine and Bonnie were headed back toward the office. I stopped and watched as all the tension between students evaporated. Those two administrators were fabulous at conflict resolution. The wail of the sirens diminished into the distance.

I returned to my classroom just as the "All Clear" sounded on the classroom intercoms. I leaned over the demo counter, and with a huge sigh, I gently rested my forehead on the cool surface for a few seconds. Then I stood up and surveyed the empty desks, absorbing the quiet of the room now devoid of students. My gaze ended at the stack of letters from my students. I would read them later.

Endings and Beginnings

Mountain View, California
August 2002 – June 2003

Chapter 42
Getting Ready

"**D**id you know that right now, in 2002, people are working on mapping the human genome? Can you imagine what the future holds for us once we understand the blueprints that create a human being? What a great time to be a life science teacher!"

Carol chuckled at my enthusiasm.

"I don't mean to rush you, Carol, but I was wondering if you have the class lists done yet?"

"Yes, and I've already put copies in your mailbox. We may have a few changes yet, but this is what we've got for now," Carol answered. "And, you do have your keys for Room 210 and 302 from last year, right?"

With a grin, I nodded my head as I pulled the keys out of my pocket to show her.

She grinned back at me, "Just let me check them off on my list now."

While she pulled out the key list I continued, "I plan to get my computer grading system set up today, but first I want to unpack the new texts and supplies, if they're here."

"I think Javier is at your room right now with a huge load of boxes," she said as she checked off my name. Nobody was better than Carol at keeping track of all of us.

"Thank you, Carol. I'll get out of your hair now. See you later today."

I left Carol sitting at her desk and strode down the hallway to the mail room. I picked up my class lists and scanned the unfamiliar names. The last of my former fifth graders were now in eighth grade. This year's seventh-grade science students would be all new for me.

How long will it take me to learn all of the new names? I had always been good at memorizing names, but this year would be the ultimate challenge.

With class lists in hand, I pushed open the door to the courtyard and headed across campus. I could see a district truck backed up next to my classroom door, so I made a beeline past the Circle of the Muse without a second glance.

"Hola, Javier. ¿Como está?" I hailed him, arriving breathless as he pushed the hand truck toward the open back of the delivery truck.

He turned toward me and answered with a twinkle in his eyes, "Muy bien, señora. Y tu, mi amiga?"

"I'm great, Javier," afraid to try any more of my halting Spanish. "It's so good to see you! Look at all the boxes. Wow!"

"Yes, you have a big load here. I put the supplies in the storage room already." He pushed the hand truck deftly up the ramp and into the truck.

"Wonderful, Javier. Thank you, that's perfect." I stared up at him.

He pointed at a stack of boxes inside the truck. "Where would you like these? It looks like they're full of textbooks."

"Umm . . . let's put them at the far end of the room, by the lab tables," I replied.

He loaded up the boxes, tilted the hand truck back and maneuvered it down the ramp. I walked ahead of him to show him where to place the stack.

Turning around, I surveyed the room.

"Oh, the room is so clean and beautiful! Look how that floor shines. It's such a joy to see it like this, all clean and fresh before students return in the fall. You are the best custodian I have ever had the pleasure to work with, Javier."

"Thank you, señora. I just do my job," he said quietly, tilting his head down just a touch.

"You do it very well," I smiled in deep appreciation, knowing my praise was welcome, but making him uncomfortable.

My thoughts ran through the years of other classrooms and other custodians. I remembered one in particular, early in my career, who spent more time sleeping in his little supply room or chatting with the other teachers than doing his job. When he did come into my room, he didn't use clean water to wash my classroom floor, making it even dirtier than before he "washed" it. I did a lot of my own cleaning that year.

Not wanting to embarrass Javier further with my praise, I moved on to an easier topic for him. "How's the family, Javier? Are they all ready to start school this year?"

We chatted with ease, but within moments Javier said, "Please excuse me, señora. There is much work to be done today, and I must be going."

"Of course, Javier. Have a good day! It's so good to see you."

"And you too," he smiled broadly as he departed.

I walked into the science storage room and set my class lists next to my computer. I glanced at the stacks of boxes filled with supplies and materials that had come with our new textbook series. It would be quite a project to integrate them with the existing bounty of science supplies. Stacey would be in later, and we would figure it out together.

This year, for the first time ever, we would be using textbooks to teach science, one per student. I had felt honored to be chosen to pilot this series the previous year even though it meant a lot of extra work for me, figuring out how to share one set of books with all five of my science classes and learning how to use a multitude of resource materials.

Too excited to work on the class lists, I went back to the lab and started opening boxes. I unpacked the books onto the lab tables, found my black permanent marker in the demo counter drawer, and began to number each text inside the front cover. Each student would be assigned a specific number, so I could track the books and make sure each one was returned at the end of the year, ready for the following year's students.

As I stacked the texts on the lab tables, I realized how heavy they were. I thought about students carrying them in their backpacks with all their other textbooks.

We won't need to use these science books every day. Maybe I should just send these texts home with students for homework and use the classroom set the way I did last year. If I send the books home, some may get lost and never be returned. I'll have to make a big deal about expecting the books back and be conscientious about using it for homework often enough to make sure it's needed.

Thinking of all the money spent on these books and the new supplies to go with them, I shook my head. *Darn. I need to make copies of the first few workbook pages for next week. Better put that task on my list of things to do.*

As predicted, the district did not spend a cent on what we called the disposable workbook, the piece I'd found most valuable. Money appeared in the budget for copy machines and paper, but not for continuous purchase of workbooks. Besides, unlimited teacher time spent copying didn't cost the district anything.

A voice coming from the supply room behind me called out, "Jan, are you in here?"

I walked toward the sound, "Yes, Stacey I'm here!"

I heard her joyfully yell, "Aaaaa, we're back!"

"Welcome back," I replied with a hug. Stepping back, I looked up at her, noticing her height in a way I seldom did at other times. "You look terrific, and so relaxed. Where did you get that tan?"

"I worked at the pool as a lifeguard most of the summer." She grinned. "And I dated a few guys." She tossed her hair back and turned to re-enter the supply room that connected her classroom with mine.

I followed her, saying with a chuckle, "Now, that sounds like you. I want to hear everything about them."

"I'll give you the details at lunch." She turned to face me, hand on her hip and a saucy look on her face. "You know I dumped most of those boys after one date."

"Why am I not surprised, Stacey? The right one just hasn't come along yet. You'll find him, don't give up."

She shook her head, "I haven't yet."

We leaned on the counter beside each other in the middle of the room, our backs to the window with the summer sunlight streaming into the room, staring at the stack of boxes we had to unpack.

Stacey said, "We'll have to get this put away today, but I want to do my textbooks first. Let's take a break at 11:30 and go out for lunch. Then we can work on supplies when we get back."

I didn't hesitate, "Burritos at La Bamba!"

"Of course."

I returned to the lab tables in my classroom, opened another box, and found a treasure trove of teacher materials. Carrying them back to my desk space in the storage room, I sat down and picked up the packet of computer resources. I took a CD out of its plastic sleeve and slipped it into the slot on the front of my computer. From the menu on the screen, I chose the first chapter of the textbook.

The possibilities entranced me. It would be fabulous to use these video clips with my students, but I was stumped. *How can I manage that? Maybe I could write a grant to get a projection machine to share with the other science classes.*

Even then, in the enthusiastic glow of summer renewal, I knew I'd never find the time to do that during the school year.

An hour later, the plethora of teaching materials I had investigated threatened to overwhelm me, so I pushed down the feeling of stress beginning to overtake my optimism. I needed to return to the more familiar tasks of getting the classroom ready for students: finish numbering textbooks, clear out the display cases, and prepare the walls for student work.

Chapter 43
Planning for Success

S oil covered the lab table where students had spilled it. Rosemary, Adrianna, and Dylan packed up their things to head home after helping me with the trays of newly planted seeds.

"Thank you for doing such a great job of organizing all those cups to fit neatly on that ledge in front of the window," I told them. "Nice work on the signs separating the investigation sections."

"I hope my plant grows really tall," said Dylan.

"Mine too," added Adrianna, hefting her backpack onto her back.

"I can help clean up that dirt, Mrs. Wright," said Rosemary.

"That's okay, Rosemary. I'll take care of it. I don't want any of you to be late getting home."

"Bye, Ms. Wright," they chorused when they walked out the door.

Just as I finished cleaning the soil off the tables Judy walked into my room.

"Well, what brings our esteemed Special Day Class teacher to this end of the campus today?"

"Hi Jan, I just wanted to touch base with you about John."

"Come, sit at a lab table. I just cleaned them off. We planted seeds today for an experiment. I've never done this with so many kids before, especially with only a small window for light. Let me put this bag of soil away, and I'll grab John's latest lab worksheet."

Sitting on a stool across from Judy, I pulled John's paper out of the fifth period folder. Judy pulled her glasses down from the top of her head and took a look at the partially filled worksheet.

I said, "I've noticed he's a little noise sensitive."

"Yes, he can't tolerate much commotion, and you know we tend to have a few outbursts in my classroom. I just got a set of earphones for him to put on when he needs to soften the sounds. That seems to help."

Nodding, I said, "You can see John didn't complete the written work, but he did make an attempt. I think he understands more than he can produce in writing."

"I'd agree with you. When he comes back to me from your class, he can often tell me a lot about what you've done."

"That's good. Socially, I know he prefers to keep to himself most of the time. I've paired him with a few different students for partner work. He's not a very active partner, but he hasn't gotten upset, yet."

"Good. If he gets to be too much, you just let me know, Jan."

We eased off of the stools and started back through the room, moving toward the door.

"I heard you're on the District Strategic Planning Committee, Jan."

"Yeah," I said. I knew most teachers didn't enjoy this sort of thing, but I considered it a compliment to be invited to participate. With Whisman and Mountain View districts newly merged, we would take several days to set unifying goals, something I truly enjoyed. "I think it's important work to be done, even though I don't like being out of the classroom and having a substitute."

She smiled at me, heading toward the door to leave. "I'm glad it's you instead of me. Come visit our SDC classroom again. You're welcome, any time."

"Thanks, I will. I'd really like to check in on Steven again."

I smiled, thinking about Steven. I didn't have the connection with John yet that I'd hoped for, but I knew to be patient and persistent with him. I just hoped I could get the other students in fifth period to be the same. It seemed much harder to get to know kids I only saw one period a day, especially this year, when seventh grade was not populated with students I'd already had in fifth grade.

I went back to work, returning trays of materials from the lab to the storage room.

Stacey came bustling in from her side carrying supplies to put away. "How did it go today, Stacey?" I asked.

"Fine. No problems. I like teaching physics. Hey, do you remember

Aaron Sheldon?"

"Of course. I had him in seventh and fifth. He giving you trouble?"

"He's such a smarty pants. He's always challenging me in class." She dropped a handful of batteries into their plastic container and shoved it back onto the shelf.

From the other side of the shelf set, I chuckled, "Yeah, he'll do that until he figures out you know what you're talking about. It will make you a better teacher, bring your 'A-game,' around him. At least, it did for me." I stacked Styrofoam cups into their container.

"As long as he doesn't sass me. I won't take that." She walked back to pick up circuit boards from her classroom.

Placing packets of unused seeds in a container, I said loud enough for her to hear me, "No, you should never tolerate sass or back-talk from him, or any student."

"Don't worry. I don't," she said as she returned and dumped the circuit boards into a container. She walked over to the sink and began washing her hands.

"What do you think of Kimberly? Isn't she extraordinary? I kept several pieces of her work as samples for this year's class." I returned the seed tray to its place on the counter.

"Yeah, she's a great kid." She dried her hands and walked toward her desk corner.

"I miss those kids! Can't believe they'll be graduating from eighth grade in June," I said, walking back toward my lab to gather the last of the planting materials. "Hey, I just got a new student today, Dmitri, who only speaks Russian. Bonnie says he's very bright so she put him in my seventh period. That's a tough class for someone who's struggling to learn a new language." At this point, I knew I was talking to myself.

From the far end of the storage room, I heard Stacey yell to me, "I'm done for the night. Going home. See you in the morning, Jan."

"Okay. Good night, Stacey," I hollered back to her.

I walked over to the cups filled with seeds we had planted during the day. I wasn't at all sure how this investigation would turn out, but

I wanted to give it a try, using the materials from our new text series. I hoped all the energy and time we put into it would yield worthwhile scientific results. No matter. I'd send the plants home at the end of the experiment with students who wanted them. I knew some kids would learn something about living things and most would enjoy watching their plants grow. With my poor track record for keeping houseplants alive, I'd consider it a success if anything grew at all.

Chapter 44
Tiffany

First period ended, and I opened the door for departing students. October chill hung in the air, reminding us the end of daylight savings time was not far off.

The next group of students began to flow into my room. I returned to my demo counter and reorganized my materials and notes to begin the lesson again with my second period class. I squirted water on the clear plastic sheets and cleaned them with a piece of paper towel, ready to use them again on the overhead projector.

Her strident voice carried over the normal commotion of middle schoolers transitioning between classes. "I don't want your stinkin' invitation!"

Turmoil followed the group of girls through the door and into my classroom. At the center of the whirlwind was Tiffany, fire spitting from her eyes. "Who'd want to go to your stupid party anyway?" she yelled.

"It's going to be cool, and you're not coming," taunted Jessica.

"Eat my shorts!" sneered Tiffany.

I set down the paper towels and walked around the demo counter toward the girls.

"What's going on?" I asked.

"Leticia's having a party," answered Jessica with a toss of her hair.

"Tiffany's all mad because she's not invited," explained Mai Ly.

"I just invited a few close friends, that's all," said Leticia brushing by the girls to reach her seat.

"Like I even care!" said Tiffany, throwing her backpack on the floor. She slammed her body down into the desk chair so hard she knocked into the desk next to hers.

"Hey, leave me out of this!" protested Martin, scooting his desk away.

"Nobody wants your ugly face in this anyway, "Tiffany retorted with a toss of her long hair.

"Okay, girls it's time to settle down and leave this discussion for later. Have a seat. Jessica . . . Leticia . . . Mai Ly . . . Tiffany."

Muttering discontent, the girls sat down. Looks passed between them. They weren't going to learn much with all the emotional upheaval I saw brewing. I returned to the overhead projector on the demo counter, turned it on, and placed a clean plastic sheet on the glass. Picking up a green marker, I began to write. The words projected on the screen behind me.

Please take out your science notebook and pencil. Write your name and date on the upper right-hand corner of the next available page.

The room quieted as I wrote, saying nothing to the group as a whole. I flipped open the attendance binder and noted there were no absences in this period. Good.

I continued writing silent directions on the overhead.

Turn to Page 54 in the textbook.

Students reached for the books on the shelves beneath the desks. Tiffany banged hers down and drew the attention she desired from the other students.

I kept writing directions without acknowledging her actions.

Draw the outline of the animal cell you see in the diagram. Make it large enough to fit the entire page.

"The whole paper?" Isaac questioned.

Without speaking, I underlined *entire page.*

The class complied and started sketching. I remembered a day ten years before, when I was teaching fifth grade in Placerville. I came dressed as a mime and didn't speak a word to my students, all day. I never intended to go through the entire day without speaking, but it worked so well, I carried it through to the end. It was the most amazing, peacefully quiet, school day I'd ever experienced as a teacher.

Using silent directions began to change the energy level in this class

273

of pubescent seventh graders; they responded with their own quietness.

I took the directions off the overhead projector, saving them for the next class, and placed the next clean plastic sheet on the glass. Using my copy of the science text, I too sketched the outline of the cell. Then I drew the nucleus and labeled it. Looking up at my students, I said, "Read the page silently until you discover what this part of the cell does. Put your finger on the words and look up at me, so I'll know you've found it."

At the end of the period, students left calmly, but I wondered when trouble would erupt again with Tiffany. I didn't have any time to deal with those thoughts, though, because the next period was my art elective class at the opposite end of the campus. The fifteen-minute break between second and third period allowed students to eat a snack. I left the science room all set up for the next class, locked the door, walked briskly across campus to the staff room, and made a quick bathroom stop. I arrived at the art room just as the bell to start the period rang. I unlocked the door and stepped aside to allow students to enter, glad I had set up the materials for this art class before school.

One of the last students to arrive, Tiffany finished eating her cinnamon roll, licking her fingers. Although she struggled with academic skills and she could display quite an attitude in science class, I had discovered her gift, a tremendous talent in art. The turmoil of her emotions from the beginning of second period seemed to have subsided, at least for now.

"How are you doing, Tiffany?" I asked.

Avoiding eye contact, she said, "I'm fine, Mrs. Wright." She passed me to take a seat by herself at a back table. Knowing her words were far from the truth, I would keep a watchful eye on her.

This art period sometimes gave me the opportunity to connect with students in ways that didn't present themselves in science. For Tiffany, it was a real blessing. She could relax and do what she loved without all the pressure of the rest of the academic day, and her natural artistic ability left the other students in awe of her talent.

The lesson for this day involved the elements of symmetry and asymmetry. "These prints are all masters," I began, pointing to the prints I had set up on the whiteboard. "Take a look at each one and think about how much energy it portrays. Does it make you feel calm, quiet, rested? Does it make you feel excited, full of energy?" I almost said, ". . . like a party's going on," but, looking at Tiffany, I caught myself and realized the poor choice of words. I ended with, ". . . like bouncing around or dancing?"

We analyzed the art prints and then began our project to create examples of symmetrical and asymmetrical designs. Once the materials were distributed, I wandered through the class watching them work, stopping to chat with some students. At first, Tiffany started to brush her hair, looking in a mirror she had pulled out of her bag. She was a beautiful girl who often wore her shoulder length, shiny brown hair in different styles. Without speaking I gave her a look from across the room. She rolled her eyes at me and put the brush and mirror away.

Taking her time to get started, Tiffany worked independently, choosing her colors and cutting her shape designs, stacking them in a neat pile in front of her. When I finally made my way to her end of the classroom, I stopped beside her for a moment. She seemed content to work silently, so I let her have the space and the quiet time to herself.

Before I knew it, the alarm on my watch rang. Forty-three minutes for class periods seemed mighty short some days. "Time to clean up," I announced. "We need to leave the rest for tomorrow. Any unfinished pieces can be stacked on top of your work. Please be sure you wrote your name on the back."

We always seemed to push the time limit, just getting the final piece done. I hurried the last student out the door and locked it. Not quite running, I zipped across the campus back to my science room where students jostled in a playful mob, waiting for me to arrive. I unlocked the door and students streamed into the room just as the five-minute passing bell rang. Fourth period underway, my brain switched back into science teaching mode, concerns about Tiffany dissipated in the faces of the next class of thirty-three seventh graders.

I placed the silent directions from second period on the overhead projector and turned it on. While students complied, I took roll, noting the few names I still confused in this period. I vowed to get them right today.

I picked up the next sheet of plastic, set it on the projector, and began to sketch the outline of an animal cell.

One week later, Tiffany was absent from second period science class. Ten minutes after the start of third period art class, she came through the door with a tardy slip. And a really short hair style. The entire art class stared at her.

"Tiffany, your hair . . ." said Brittany, mouth agape.

"Wow, what happened to you?!" said Dylan when she sat down at the table behind him.

"I don't want to talk about it," she said dropping her book bag on the floor and crossing her arms, defiantly daring the others to comment.

I continued giving directions for the art assignment, writing them on the whiteboard as I went. Tiffany bent her head down and raised her hand to smooth the back of her head, grabbing and pulling at what was left of her hair, as if trying to make it longer.

Once the class was involved in the project for the day, I made my way through the class, chatting with students about their work, and at last I came to Tiffany, who had barely made an effort to get started.

I bent down close to her and quietly said, "Are you all right?"

"I was late to class because my mother took me to a beauty salon," she replied.

I faced her, turning my back to the rest of the class and said in a quiet voice, "That seems like an unusual thing to do on a school day."

In a small voice, with her head hung in shame, she answered me, "Yeah, my dad was so upset with me for screwing up at school, he chopped my hair off last night."

"Oh," I replied, waiting for her to say more.

"I was really mad at my dad," she said lowering her eyes and her voice even more. "My hair was a mess. I didn't want anyone to see me like that, so my mother took me to the beauty salon this morning."

She just sat there. I waited. She remained silent.

"Your hair really does look cute, no matter how short or long it is. You are a beautiful young lady, in so many ways, Tiffany."

She sighed.

I moved on and left her to figure out what she wanted to do with the class time that remained.

Chapter 45
Grade Level Meeting

I grabbed my folder from the cabinet above my computer and dashed across campus. Checking my watch, I saw I had five minutes to spare, so I made a quick stop at the office to check my mailbox and then zipped into the staff room to pick up some paper. Then I hurried to Carrie's classroom. Melanie, Nicole, and Gretchen were already there, seated around a rectangular table at the front of the room.

Carrie stood at the head of the table; her smile radiated warmth to each person in the group. She turned to me. "Hi, Jan. I was just showing the others our latest accordion book creations. They're turning out rather spectacularly, I think." She seemed to glow with pride for her students and their work.

I put my things on the table and sat down. Carrie handed me a stack of student-made books, their pages neatly folded back and forth like pleats, filled with student-written poetry and illustrations. Unfolding the books and admiring the work of students we shared, I said, "Oh, these look amazing, Carrie." I kept to myself my memories of making this same kind of book with my students, years before, the pattern lost in the hodgepodge of my old fifth grade files.

Pamela was the last to arrive, her arms full of materials which she set down on a nearby desk.

"Sorry I'm late. I was talking with Katherine and Bonnie about Tiffany." Pamela sat down at the table. "She's getting herself into a lot of trouble, and I'm worried about her."

Nicole spoke up, "She was having a bad day in social studies. I don't put up with that, so I sent her out to see Bonnie."

"Yeah, what's gotten into her?" Gretchen asked. "She refused to dress for P.E. today. Did you see her hair?"

"I talked with her during art class," I said. "She came to school late, third period. She had a fight with her father last night, and he took the scissors to her hair. To straighten out the mess he made of her hair, her mother let her go to a salon before she came to school."

"Her father cut her hair? That's just awful. Poor girl," said Carrie.

"I talked with Tiffany's mother last week about missing math assignments," said Melanie. "Both Mom and Dad work. They leave the sisters home by themselves a lot, and the girls tend to get into trouble then. I offered to let Tiffany be a part of my Monday/Wednesday afterschool homework club."

"That's a really good suggestion, Melanie," I said.

Pamela said, "And, I could take her after school on Tuesdays and Thursdays with a small study group."

"Sounds like a plan. Let's put Tiffany on the agenda for next meeting to check on her progress," said Carrie. "Speaking of the agenda, time to get to it. It's October already, so let's discuss Halloween. How about wearing coordinating costumes this year? Any ideas?"

"I know. Let's each dress as something that represents what we teach," said Pamela.

"Oh, I like that," I said. "I could be a skeleton, since I teach about the human body."

"Easy for you," laughed Melanie. "I'd have to come as a math equation."

Once we'd finished our plans for Halloween, Carrie moved on to the next agenda item. "We need to talk about our annual parent conferences next. Jan, you had something to suggest."

"As you know, I'm on the District Strategic Planning Committee with Myrtle Rae." I looked at Nicole's puzzled face. Knowing she was new to the district, I added, "She's the Assistant Superintendent, Nicole." She smiled and nodded in response.

I continued, "Myrtle recently shared an interesting idea about student-led conferences. If kids explain their own work, they become more accountable for it. So, while we sit with them, we let students share samples of their assignments with their parents."

"I like this idea," said Nicole. "We started student-led conferences in my last school, and they were very successful."

Melanie added, "Yes, I began to do something similar with my sixth-graders last year. It gives students a chance to sit down and actually talk with their parents." She sat back into her chair and sipped on a cup of tea. "Often, kids don't really spend time as the center of their parents' attention."

"You're so right, Melanie," Pamela said.

I nodded and said, "We could use my science room, allowing us to spread out far enough for several conferences to go on at once. If we color code our folders by subject matter, we can use them as visual clues to see when we're needed to move to the next conference."

We paused for a moment in thought.

Then Carrie said, "It looks like we're in agreement to try this style of conferencing?" Heads nodded around the group. "Okay. Let's try it."

We continued to work through our agenda, a long one, but typical at this time of the year.

"Before we finish up today," I said, at last. "I'd like to propose a big change from last year." The group eyed me. I rushed on, "Instead of doing the science fair, I'd like to suggest a seventh-grade field trip to the Exploratorium in San Francisco. I'd like us to work together on a study guide and a culminating assignment upon our return. I would handle the science part, language arts teachers would work with the writing assignment, math could be involved with math-centered problems from specific exhibits. What do you think of this?"

"Great idea, Jan. I think the kids are ready for a change after two years of science fair projects," said Melanie. "And, I like the collaborative approach to integrate the subjects."

"Jan, will you see if we can set up a date? It might be too late to get enough buses."

"Sure. I'll do that."

Carrie closed our meeting with, "I see on our rotation schedule that

Nicole will host the next meeting. Hey, we got a lot done today, folks. Happy October, everyone!"

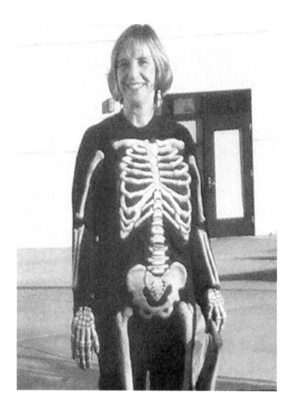

The caption in the yearbook read: There are no bones about it –
Mrs. Wright shows us what she's made of on Halloween.

Chapter 46
Microscopes

"Today we're going to use the microscopes to look at cells. The colors you'll see are not natural. The cells have been professionally stained to create contrast, so we can see the different parts. I'm handing out plain white paper for you to record drawings of what you'll see."

I passed out the paper to my second period students, then walked back to the demo counter.

"Take the paper and fold it in half lengthwise, hotdog style. Like this." I demonstrated with a piece of paper. I waited while they folded.

"Now, fold it in half the other way." I turned my paper and folded.

"You should now have four rectangles." I unfolded and held up my paper. Then I sketched the page with the four divisions on the overhead projector. "You'll draw what you see on four different microscope slides, two will be filled with plant cells and two will have animal cells. Draw a line at the bottom of each rectangle. This is where you will write the label to tell which type of cells you have drawn." I drew the lines on my example.

"I'll keep track of the time and give you a warning to let you know when you should be moving on to the next type of slide viewing, so you can take enough time on each one to do a decent job drawing all the shapes and details you see in each one."

Murmurs of protest reached my ears.

"I know we're not all artists, but it's important to do your very best job to record what you see, with accuracy. When you look through the microscope you see a big circle, right? So, draw a large circle in each of the rectangles. Then, when you get your slides, fill in each circle by drawing exactly what you see."

I held up two completed papers. "Take a look at these two pages from former students. You can see which one shows the most effort, which one shows the differences between the types of cells.

I held out the poorly done paper. "What could be improved on this page? Gabriella, what do you see?"

"All the cells are round, but some should have corners, like squares."

"Right. Do you need to be an artist to do that?"

"No, I guess not."

"What else do you see, Raven?"

"No labels?"

"Yes. That's an easy fix, right?"

She nodded.

"Okay, what else?"

Felix raised his hand, "Ahhh, there's almost no details inside the cells on that one?"

"Yes, good observation. Can anyone tell me what you need to do to earn ten points on this assignment, compared to something like this one that earned a mere three points?"

"You have to draw good!" laughed Jose.

"What does that mean?" I countered.

"It means to take the time to do a better job," he said.

"Yes, and what else besides time do you need?" I pushed.

"Well, you told us to add details. Like the day you dressed up in the lab coat. We need to observe and draw what we see."

"Excellent, Jose. You're right. Take your time to draw exactly what you see. Be careful with your observation. Look for the details and differences." I pointed to the class rules chart above the door. "That's following class rule number three. Ask yourself: Is it your best?"

Jose looked pleased, I hoped he would take his own advice, since he was often one to rush and do less than required.

"When you finish the four required drawings on the front side of your paper, you and your partner may choose any slide from the wooden case I have set up here on the counter." I pointed to the box of slides. "These are one-of-a-kind slides. After you look at any of these slides you need to return them to the case in the slot with the matching number. We have of all sorts of things to see, like butterfly wings, fly legs, small water animals, and a whole lot more."

Charles' eyebrows went up, and a smile spread across his face. Gabriella and Anna exchanged glances with nods of their heads. I knew many of them would be eager to explore.

"One last review on how to use the microscope." I demonstrated how to change lenses and focus the microscope.

"I'll test you, individually, on how to focus the microscope when we have the quiz this week, so don't just rely on your partner to set it up. If you have any questions, be sure to get help from your partner or ask me during this lab period."

I had set up our sixteen microscopes on the lab tables. I wished it could have been one for each student, but I felt lucky we had this many. Students knew they had to take turns and share to complete the assignment. I let them choose their own partners today and watched to see who chose to work together and who was left out. I partnered those who were slow to find someone.

I placed the see-through calculator/timer on the overhead projector and set the time to five minutes. Students could see the time counting down as they worked. Then I walked through the lab, checking on my students.

"Mrs. Wright, are these cells still alive?" asked Raven.

"No, they were alive once, but not now. They have been preserved so we could see and study them," I said.

"Sort of like mummies, dead things we can study, right?"

"Never thought of it that way, but I can see the similarity." I thought for a moment. "Would you like to see some live cells?" I asked.

Without hesitating, Raven answered, "Well, yeah!"

"Okay," I smiled. "I'll bring in some water from a pond near my house. We'll see if we can find some living one-celled animals to observe."

"Rad!"

I moved to the next table to review Cody's drawing. "Let me see what you are looking at, Cody."

He moved over to let me peer into the microscope. I lifted my head and said to him, "Try counting how many rectangular shapes you see in that top row."

We traded places, and he began to count.

"Oh, I didn't draw enough, did I?"

"Good observation. You know what to do to improve your drawing."

Cody began to sketch. I moved on to the next pair.

"Is this really what an onion looks like?" asked Juan.

"Yes, indeed. All living things are made up of these tiny building blocks, cells."

Beep. Beep. Beep.

"You have one more minute to finish the first drawing. Don't forget to take an occasional look at the timer to see how you're managing your time."

Toward the end of the period, Charles walked up to the extra box of slides. He looked through the list and chose one, taking it back to the microscope he shared with Antonio. He set the slide beneath the lens, snapped the clips into place, and focused.

"Wow! That's so cool. You've gotta see this fly leg!" He stepped aside, so Antonio could view the slide.

"I want to see it," said Gabriella. "Can I look too?"

The boys moved, so she could take a peek.

"Ewwww, that's gross."

"I want to pick the next one," said Antonio.

"Here's a bee wing! And a human hair," said Tamika.

"We have five more minutes to work. Please be sure you have completed the four required drawings," I announced.

"Awww, we just got started looking at the good stuff over here," complained Charles.

I got the same reaction from most of my classes. Introducing students to a world they had never seen always thrilled me. Of course, a few of my students already had exposure to microscopes. Others just had no interest, but, for the most, this was a new and "eye-opening" experience.

"Yeah, I want to see the dragonfly mouth parts!" said Jose.

"How about if I schedule another lab period to explore all these extra slides?" I asked.

"Yeah!" said several students.

"I promised Raven I'd bring in some water from the pond in the park near my house, so we can use the microscopes to see some that are still alive. They will be more difficult to see, because they won't be stained, but they will be moving. Your microscope skills have improved enough, you can manage it."

Their looks of anticipation and sense of accomplishment made my heart sing.

Chapter 47
Partners

J ohn waited in the shade, by the corner of the building near my door, a scowl on his face, his eyes downcast. I knew he didn't want me to acknowledge his presence, so I unlocked the door and opened it wide, setting the stand down with my foot to keep the door open. With two minutes until the first bell after lunch, I walked into the classroom. He would follow when he was ready. He liked the relative quiet before all the other fifth period students arrived.

I busied myself preparing for class. John slipped into the room, hesitated for a moment staring at the rearranged desks, and then took his seat.

Talking amongst themselves, a small group of girls wandered in after him.

"Hey, Mrs. Wright, you moved the desks," said Aracely when she noticed them, looking to me for explanation.

"I did indeed," I responded with a smile, leaving her indirect question hanging.

Seconds later, we heard raucous laughter headed in our direction.

"That's Pavani!" Aracely laughed.

The girl in question ran through the doorway, squealing with delight, with Jamal and Juan Luis on her heels. The three of them came to an abrupt halt when they saw me glaring at them. "Oh, sorry, Mrs. Wright. I know, I know. I'll calm down," she said with a giant grin. Juan Luis reached out to tickle her waist and peals of laughter spilled from Pavani. She pranced across the room to her seat, boys in tow.

John sat with his fingers in his ears.

"Make a large t-chart on your paper. Label one side Animal Cell and the other side Plant Cell." I demonstrated on the overhead projector. "We've been learning about the structure of these cells for a couple of weeks. List as many characteristics, traits, or descriptions as you can think of in the animal cell column. You have sixty seconds. Go."

I set my watch timer and walked around to the student side of the demo counter. Observing students' work, I walked through the room. Some worked rapidly; others tended to take their time, but I could see everyone writing something. As sixty seconds neared, several had stopped and were looking up at the ceiling or staring at the paper in front of them.

Beep, beep, beep.

"Stop. Put your pencils down," I said in a calm voice. "Count how many different things you wrote about animal cells." I paused. They counted.

"Raise your hand if you got five or more." Most of the class had their hands up. "Good job! Keep your hand up if you've got seven or more." Several hands went down. "All right. You've got a great start. Keep it up."

Back at the overhead projector, I pointed at the second column. "As I'm sure you expected, the next task is to make another list on the plant cell side of your t-chart. Try to match similarities by listing them across from each other. Do the same with differences; list them directly across from each other." I illustrated with my pen. "You have sixty seconds again. Ready? Go."

I walked past John. I had originally seated him close to the door, against the wall, the second desk back in the column. This morning I moved the desks so that two columns touched each other, forming pairs of desks across the rows. John was partnered with Victor. I hoped that would work well for both of them.

Beep, beep, beep.

"Stop again. Pencils down."

"I'm not done," complained Ryan.

"That's okay, you'll have more time in a few minutes," I said.

"You may have noticed I changed the desk arrangement today. You are seated next to a partner for the next part of this activity."

"Oh no, do I have to work with Jennifer?" said Nathan.

"Yes, you do. Think of it this way," I paused, raised my eyebrows and raised both of my hands in the air. "Oh no, does SHE have to work with YOU?!"

"Zing! Mrs. Wright got you!" said Vijay laughing.

"Okay, okay, I guess she did," laughed Nathan.

"You know. I've told all of you. You will work with several different partners and groups in this class. It's important to be respectful to each other. You don't have to like them; you just have to work with them. Like in the real world. You can't always choose who you have to deal with. No one wants to hear, 'Eww, do I have to work with you?' Everyone is different, so look for the gifts we each bring to the experience. What's that second rule?" I pointed to the sign above the door. "Read it aloud with me."

"Is it polite?" they chorused with me.

"Enough said?" I asked.

Some nodded and some rolled eyes amidst grumbles of agreement.

"Okay. Your assignment is to work with your new partner. I see we have an even number in this period, so that's good. Everyone has a partner.

"Using soft voices, you will share the lists you made. Add to your lists anything you both agree needs to be on them. Make sure you agree about everything on both lists. Cross out anything that does not fit. Start with the animal side of your chart. The person to talk first is the youngest. Then switch roles and the older student will share the rest of their chart. Keep talking until you've covered everything on both lists. Any questions? Okay. Remember to use quiet voices. Stop when I turn off the lights. Now, figure out who's the youngest. Go."

The class began to talk. I knew I needed to keep a watch on John, since this would be a noisy activity, so I stayed near him while I scanned the rest of the room to see how things were going.

Victor asked John his birthdate. John hung his head and scowled in return. "Okay, well my birthday is in August, I'm 12. Are you older than me?" Getting no definite response, Victor continued. "Well, since I'm probably younger, I'll start."

Victor read his list. John remained impassive.

I moved in and suggested, "Why don't you both check to see if John has the same items you do, Victor? Start with that first one you have, 'nucleus.' John, do you have that on your list?" He nodded.

I moved away, letting them work it out, checking on other partners to make sure they were cooperating. By the time I got back to Victor and John, they were silent again. I could see several other pairs were finished, too. I reached for the switch and turned the lights off. The room got quiet.

I turned on the lights and said, "Nice work."

Madison raised her hand. "Yes, Madison?"

"Mrs. Wright, could we check our list with the textbook?"

"Great suggestion. Yes. Actually, I'd like everyone to do that. Check your lists and see how you did. Work with your partner on this."

After several minutes, I turned off the lights. Again, the room quieted. "Thank you for responding to our quiet signal." I turned the light on. "You need to put this page of notes in the science section of your notebook. You have time to do that now."

The class filled with the sound of students taking binders out of backpacks, clicking them open and shut, talking to each other.

While they chatted, I walked to the back corner of the room. "If you can hear me, get quiet and put your hand up," I said in a normal voice. A few of the closest students heard me and followed directions. I said it again. "If you can hear me, get quiet and put your hand up." The quiet spread across the room and before long, I had their attention.

"In this display case are samples of excellent student work," I said. I opened the glass doors and pulled out a plant cell model. Then I chose an animal cell model and lifted it out of the cabinet.

Pavani raised her hand.

"Yes, Pavani."

"Mrs. Wright, are we going to make models this year, too?"

I smiled. "Yes, you are. In a couple of weeks, I will hand out all the directions for the model project. By December 12, you will create a model of a cell with materials you choose. It's good to start thinking about what you might do, which materials you might use. You can see these are made from all kinds of materials. All of them have easy-to-read, accurate labels for each of the parts." I started to walk toward the front of the room, holding the cells so the students could see them.

"Pavani, would you choose two more models to bring to the front of the room with me?" I returned to the demo counter and set them down. Pavani did the same.

"Meanwhile, on Friday, we'll have a quiz, so you need to study this chapter on cells. Use your at-home textbooks this week and read for the details you may have forgotten. You know how tricky these quizzes can be, right?"

I could see John hanging his head, and I knew I would need to talk with Judy about the coming quiz and the model project. He would need help to be successful.

"The bell's going to ring in a minute. I'm going to do a notebook check at the end of next week, and you will get points for the t-chart we just worked, as well as other notes we have done."

Ring!

"Have a good afternoon. See you tomorrow."

Chapter 48
Creative Solutions

Just as my prep period began, Bonnie walked into my room.

"Hi, Ms. Vice Principal. What brings you to this end of the campus?" I said in greeting.

"I'd like to talk to you about Tiffany," she said.

"Yes, she's had a rough time. Come, have a seat with me at a lab table."

"She's been getting into a lot of trouble with a particular group of girls," she started. We pulled out stools to sit on. "And, you know about the incident with her haircut a while back."

"Um hmm," I nodded.

"Katherine and I have conferenced with her math and language arts teachers and her mother. We've tried a few things that didn't seem to make a difference for her, so I had an idea."

Why she did she come to see me?

She continued, "I'd like to move her out of the group she's with for most of her classes. I think we should try changing her schedule."

"That might work," I said.

"I'd like to put her into first and second period language arts with Carrie."

"She's in my second period science right now," I said.

"Yeah, I'd like to move her into your seventh period science."

"Ahhhh, you know, my seventh period science class consists of high achievers. They're high academic and rather articulate students," I said. "Tiffany would be a fish out of water in that period."

"I know, but it might change Tiffany's behavior," Bonnie insisted.

"She might feel isolated and overwhelmed. She could give up and fail because she'll think she can't compete," I countered.

"Maybe so, Jan, but I think she's made of tougher stuff than that. I'd like to give it a try and keep an eye on her."

"Okay, if you say so. I remember your work with those alternative kids. I trust your instincts."

"Thanks, Jan." She got up to leave. "Carpool tomorrow?"

"Sure thing. It's more fun driving in together, especially when we sing." I smiled.

Seventh period took the news of a coming test seriously. Several students were looking forward to the challenge, with one major exception, Tiffany. She scrunched down into her seat when I made the announcement, as if making herself disappear would protect her from facing the inevitable test.

At the end of the period, Tiffany packed up to leave. I stopped her at the door and said, "Tiffany, could you stay for just a moment?"

"I have to get to the after-school homework session," she mumbled, but she moved to the side to wait for the others to leave.

"I'll give the teacher a call to let her know I've kept you a few minutes," I said. "Tiffany, I know you've missed some of the notes. Do you have someone you'd like to ask for them, or would you like me to help you get caught up?"

"I've got it covered," she said, shifting her weight from foot to foot, looking down at the floor.

"Well, if you change your mind, just let me know."

She didn't respond, so I went on. "Tiffany, how are you getting along with the change in your schedule?"

"I don't like it. I miss my friends." She looked up at me. "I want to go back to what it was."

"I think you'll have to stop fighting with those girls, first. You'd have to convince Ms. Duval and Ms. Murphy that you can get along with them . . . and get all your schoolwork done. You have to start coming to school every day."

"Yeah, I know," she said, shifting her weight and staring at the floor.

"You know we care about you, Tiffany."

She looked up at me and said, "Yeah, I know. Thanks, Mrs. Wright."

She hefted her backpack over her shoulder. I watched her depart, wishing I could do more to help her feel better about herself and take an interest in her own education. I wondered about the choices she'd make and knew I could only do my small part to encourage her at this time in her life.

Several weeks later, I arrived early in anticipation of an exciting day. I opened the classroom door half an hour before the first bell. Kyra waited there with her mother. Angelica and Martin arrived right behind them. The kids had their arms filled with cell models.

"Good morning! Come on in. Find the lab table with your period number and leave your model there," I said, walking into the room.

"Thank you for letting us drop these off early, Mrs. Wright," said Kyra.

"Yeah, I didn't want mine to get all messed up, carrying it around all day," said Martin.

"Mrs. Wright, this is my mother, Mrs. Camarena," Kyra said in a sweet, child-like voice.

"Hello Mrs. Wright," she said as she nodded her head to me.

"Welcome to our classroom," I replied. I looked at her daughter and said, "Kyra, you may show your mother around after you put your model down. Be sure to show her your microscope lab paper that's up on the wall."

She nodded, her head bent and cheeks a bit more rosy than usual.

I heard her tell her mother, "Mrs. Wright always puts up our best work on the walls."

I smiled.

More students and parents arrived with cell models. I greeted them each at the door and directed them to the lab tables where they eagerly looked at the models beginning to fill the tables.

Gabriella took her dad to deposit her model on the table. I watched her take him over to point out her work displayed on the wall. When they made their way back to the door where I stood, her dad said to me, "Thank you, Mrs. Wright. Gabriella loves science this year."

"That's good to hear."

"Have a good day, mi corazón," Gabriella's dad said to her as they parted just outside my door. I smiled at the affectionate name he'd called her.

By the time the first bell rang, the kids had covered all the lab tables with models. My first period class clustered around them.

"Ooo, look at that one! She used candy in her model!"

"See the shoelaces and buttons."

"Look how he made the labels."

"Wow, how did he make that nucleus see-through with the tiny DNA strands inside?"

"This one's really nifty. It's so big!"

I let them look and talk for a few minutes and finally called them back to their seats so I could take attendance.

With each period, the excitement grew along with the size of the display. As seventh period began, the last of the models came in with the students. One of the last to arrive, Tiffany pulled her model out of a large paper bag and placed it on the lab table for the others to see.

"Wow! Look what Tiffany did," said Sean. Students began to crowd around Tiffany and her model.

"It looks like you made the cell wall out of clay. How did you get it that deep green color?"

"Ooooo, that's jewelry for the chloroplasts. Nice."

"It's so creative! I couldn't think of anything like this."

Her instant celebrity with this tough crowd put a satisfied smile on Tiffany's face. She excelled in art, and this was the perfect project to give her some positive attention, for once. It reminded me, once again, that each student has unique gifts; we just need to look for them.

Bonnie walked in after school while I was working on grading the first period models. "I've heard a lot about these cell models. I thought I'd come take a look at them."

"Yes, they're looking mighty good this year." I walked to the seventh period table. Bonnie followed me. "Look what Tiffany did."

"Well, will you look at that," said Bonnie. "I'm impressed."

"Me too. But more importantly, she impressed the entire seventh-period class when she walked in with it today. You know I wasn't sure how moving her to seventh period science would work out. She is decidedly quieter in that class. I think she's a bit intimidated by them, but she really earned some positive feedback with her cell model. I'm glad she had an opportunity to shine."

"Good to hear that. I was just reaching for any kind of non-punitive solution for her when I decided to mix up her schedule. The home situation hasn't changed much, but she's a good kid at the core."

"I think she knows you have her best interests at heart, Bonnie. You may never know your impact on her, but she may surprise you some day."

Student-made cell models fill the lab tables.

296

Chapter 49
Eyeballs

Some students giggled; some primped. Some made faces, and some looked puzzled. Some ignored the mirror I handed to each one of them. Normal first period behavior.

"Please place your mirror on the desk, in front of you," I began. "I'm going to turn the lights off for a minute. Just sit quietly in the dark. Mirror on the desk, please."

I turned off the lights and waited, counting to thirty in my head. "Now, pick up the mirror and look at your eyes."

"But, Mrs. Wright, it's dark in here," said Jorge.

"There's enough light for you to see your eyes," I said.

"Oh, yeah. I can see them," said Elena.

"Stare at your eyes. Look right in the middle of your eyes. Keep looking, keep looking. I'm going to turn on the lights, but I want you to keep looking at your own eyes. Ready?" I flipped the light switch on.

Audible gasps filled the room.

"Ooooo . . ." said several of my students.

"Wow! Did you see that? Did you see how small the black part got?"

"That's your pupil, silly."

"I didn't know your eye could do that. Not like that!"

"Do it again, Mrs. Wright. Do it again."

Incredibly, some kids had never seen their pupils react to the change in light. Teaching, at its very best, occurs with a moment of discovery. Of course, I turned the lights on and off a few more times for them, for pure joy.

I planned a deliberate path to the ultimate lesson. First, we read and studied the textbook with its illustrations. Then, I asked my students to draw and label a diagram of an eye. Next, I held up the giant professional 3D model of an eye and took it apart to show my students the inside structures. We played a game I created with the names and functions of the parts. Each lesson added another layer of understanding and brought them closer to the real thing: dissecting actual eyeballs.

Wearing a lab apron, latex gloves, and goggles, I opened the dissection kit and held up forceps, scissors, probe, scalpel, and specimen pins, explaining the functions of each and my expected safety measures. I referred to the three posted class rules, yet again. I used the first one often, asking kids, "Is it safe?"

Next, I showed them a specimen tray, an aluminum baking pan filled with black wax about one inch thick on the bottom. I demonstrated how to use the pins to anchor a specimen in place.

Then I announced, "Now I have a real eye to show you. I'll go get it."

"Ewww . . ."

"A real eyeball???"

"Yuck, I don't want to see it."

I walked into the storage room and retrieved a tray covered with a cloth. Chatter in the room increased, but I had their rapt attention as I walked back to the demonstration counter.

"You have learned a lot about the structure of the eye. Now it's time to see the real thing."

"Do you have a real human eyeball under that cover?" asked an incredulous Jose.

I grinned, looking at him, "No, . . . it's a cow's eyeball." I heard a sigh of relief. "I'll hold it so you can see it." With that, I pulled away the cover and tilted the tray toward them.

Gasps.

"Ewwww!"

"Cool!"

When they settled down, I said, "In order to see the parts inside, we have to cut the eyeball open with the scalpel." I picked up the scalpel.

"How can you do this, Mrs. Wright?" asked Brittany, pushing back from her desk in revulsion.

"To tell you the truth, the first time I did it, I thought I was going to throw up," I chuckled. "Miss Baron helped me get used to it, like I am doing for you. I really do understand how hard this might be for some of you, but there is nothing better than seeing a real eye if you are to understand how it works."

I loved the drama and students were always attentive during this class, but I added, "Pay close attention to my demonstration today. Tomorrow, you will work in trios to dissect your own cow's eyeball."

I let them react for a few seconds, then I raised my eyebrows and held up the scalpel again. My facial expression said, "Do you want to see me do this?" They got quiet; their focus riveted on my next move.

"You will have a laminated instruction sheet at each station tomorrow. Please keep it clean as you work."

I've stalled long enough. Time to do it.

After the first touch of the eyeball, always the hardest for me, it got easier. I set the scalpel down and picked up the eyeball, holding it in my gloved hand, so the kids could see.

"Ughh."

"Oh, wow."

"This is so icky."

"Can I hold it?"

I let my students express themselves. They settled down when I began to tell them about the next step.

"We use cow eyes because they're very similar to human eyes, only bigger and easier for us to see the parts," I explained.

I explained the tissues, the fat and muscles, surrounding the eye while I used the surgical scissors to cut them off. Students murmured reactions of awe and revulsion. I set these discarded parts aside in the dissection tray. Next, to even louder groans of protest and squeals of delight, I used the scalpel to poke a hole and then make a slit in the side of the eyeball, allowing the aqueous humor to flow out.

"What is the name for this white part of the eye?" I asked.

"It's the sclera," chimed several of the kids.

"Yes, it's the sclera, and it's tough. You have to use a little force with the scalpel to poke through it. Then you need to slip the scissors into the hole and cut around it to open it up, like this." I demonstrated, feeling the thrill of discovery with each step, completely forgetting my initial queasy feeling.

By the end of the demonstration, I knew my students were nearly ready to do this themselves.

Rosemary took her time packing up her things after the last class. Most of the other students left quickly, released by the end of-the-day bell. A small group had gathered around me to see the separated parts of the eyeball. At last, I covered the tray with the cloth and shooed the group out of the classroom.

Rosemary, who had lingered at the back of the room, shouldered her backpack, and trudged slowly toward me at the front of the room, her eyes averted from the demo counter.

"Mrs. Wright, could I talk with you?" she said, looking down at her shoes.

"Yes, of course, Rosemary." I looked at her and surmised her concern about the dissected eyeball I still held in the specimen tray.

"Would you like me to clear this away before we talk?" I asked.

"Oh yes, please," she quickly agreed.

"Okay, Rosemary. I'll be back in a few minutes." Picking up the offending object, I walked out of the classroom and into the storage room.

She waited by the open door, looking out. Her face had a look of distress. She twisted a lock of hair around a finger.

"Did this dissection make you uncomfortable?" I asked when I returned to her.

She nodded in reply.

I waited for her to speak.

Shoulders slumped, she looked up and gave me a piteous look. "Mrs. Wright, I don't think I can do it."

Rosemary, a good student, had never balked at any previous assignment. I recognized her fear.

"You'll be in a group. You don't have to do this by yourself, Rosemary."

"I don't think I can do it." She paused. "Could I just stay in Ms. Sherman's room instead?"

"Truly, I understand the panicky feeling." I nodded. "You remember I told you I thought I was going to throw up?"

She looked up at me with a small grin on her face. "Yeah, it's like that."

We held the silence for a few more seconds.

"What do you think you need to help you be successful tomorrow?" I asked.

"I just can't cut into that eyeball."

"Okay. How about if you don't do any of the cutting? Your partners could do that for you."

She thought about it.

"If you can touch it, do that. If you can watch, just do that. All I ask is that you give it your best effort, Rosemary."

She took a deep breath and sighed. "Okay, Mrs. Wright. I'll try."

301

The next day, I set up two specimen trays at each lab table along with two dissection kits. I assigned students to random trios. They picked up aprons, goggles, and gloves and took their places at the lab tables. I liked to make this lesson dramatic.

The day had gone well so far. I knew my last period students would follow directions quickly and most of them would be eager to get the hands-on experience.

Rosemary had been assigned to work with Patrick and Amber. I stopped to talk with both of them. "You go ahead and get started. I'll bring Rosemary over in a few minutes."

I circled the lab, handing out eyeballs to an excited group of kids, while Rosemary remained at her desk.

After a quick survey of the groups to make sure everyone was set, I walked over to Rosemary. "How about moving a little closer?"

"I want to do this," she said. "I'm really going to try." I left her and continued walking through the lab, answering questions, sharing in the thrill of discoveries.

At last, I could see Rosemary, inching closer, hand over her mouth and nose.

"Ooooo, Mrs. Wright, look at this. The aqueous humor is oozing out of the eye, right onto the scalpel," said Timothy from another side of the lab. "This is so excellent!"

In a flash, Rosemary retreated back to her desk, folded her arms on it, and put her head down.

"Mrs. Wright, look at the lens. I can see you through it," said Vanessa, holding it up to my face.

"Try setting it on the instruction page," I suggested.

"Oh, wow. It magnifies the letters! Look, guys. See what the lens does," she said pulling on the sleeve of the boy next to her.

When clean up time began, Rosemary, up again, stood close to the lab table. I asked Patrick and Amber to leave their eyeball in the tray on the lab table.

To my surprise Rosemary asked, "Can I put on gloves?"

"Yes, of course. The box of gloves it still on the end of the demo counter."

The rest of the class finished putting things away, getting ready to go home for the day. I gave a few parting comments and the bell rang. The room emptied of students. Rosemary remained, holding the surgical gloves in her hands, with Amber and Kyra beside her.

"I'm going to do this, Mrs. Wright," she said staring at the gloves with a determined look on her face.

"I know you can do it, Rosemary," I said, coming to stand at the lab table with them.

She put on the gloves and reached out her right hand toward the tray, then jerked it back.

We just stood in the silence with her. She took a deep breath.

"I'm going to try. I'm going to do this. I'm going to overcome my fear. I can do this. I can do this." With that, she slowly reached out, pointed her finger at the remaining sclera on the tray, and touched it.

"I did it! I did it!"

The girls and I cheered for her.

After another moment of hesitation, Rosemary touched the lens and then, ever so slowly, picked it up. "The lens is sort of squishy and hard, just like you said, Mrs. Wright."

She set it down and backed away from the table, quickly peeling the gloves from her hands.

The girls packed up their things, their happy chatter followed them out of the classroom. Holding the door open, Rosemary turned to face me with a huge grin on her face and yelled, "I can't believe I touched an eyeball!"

"I'm proud of you, Rosemary." I smiled in return.

The door clanged shut, the classroom finally quiet. I paused in the stillness, savoring the moment of victory for this student. Then I twirled around, pumping my fist and sang out loud to myself, "Wahooo! EVERY ONE of them touched the eyeballs!

Chapter 50
Exploratorium

Buses lined the circular driveway in front of the school. A few parent chaperones mingled in clusters, holding coffee cups and chatting with each other in the morning chill of early February. I led my class of eager students, along with five more chaperones, past the Circle of the Muse toward them. More seventh graders and chaperones began to pour out of the other classrooms, laughter and energy shattering the quiet of the quad. We were on our way to the Exploratorium in San Francisco.

I met Nicole coming from the other end of campus, her students and chaperones following behind her. I told her to send her kids to the first bus, where I would ride.

She handed me a stack of permission slips from her class. "They're all here except for these three who need to stay at school with me." She pointed at the names circled on her class list.

"Okay, thanks for offering to stay with those who can't go today," I said.

"I should have a total of about fourteen, depending on absences. I'll make sure we have a good day together," she said.

"Oh, and Tiffany won't be joining you. Her dad sent her to live with Grandma for the rest of the school year," I said with a sigh.

"Maybe that's for the best, Jan."

The buses climbed out of the gridded, asphalt city into the nearby hills. Houses, no longer shoulder to shoulder, were separated by increasing swaths of trees and bushes. The path ahead of us curved along the gentle contours of California's coastal mountain range. Expensive homes began to dot the landscape as we wound our way through the countryside, still green from the winter rains, ascending to the top of the ridge.

Turning into the Highway 280 on-ramp, the buses glided into the sparse mid-morning traffic heading north, up the peninsula toward San Francisco. Vast ranches, fields, and tree-topped hills spread out before us.

Fifteen minutes into our ride, the students had quieted considerably, most of them watching the passing scenery or talking quietly among themselves. Some dozed, lulled by the dull hum of the bus in motion.

"Look! Look! Cows!" shouted Juan Luis, pointing out the left side of the bus.

"Where?"

"There! See the cows?!"

Kids rushed to the left side of the bus to have a look.

Amazed at their interest, I turned toward the kids spilling onto the left side of the bus to see the cows. Using my crowd voice, I directed, "You need to have a seat. No standing while the bus is moving."

"But Mrs. Wright, it's cows!" yelled Angelo.

I pointed to the seats, my eyebrows raised as if to say, "Yes, but you need to sit down."

As she stared out the window from the seat behind me, Maria asked, "Are those real cows, Mrs. Wright?"

"Yes, Maria, they are," I said.

"I've never seen a real one before," she replied wistfully.

"Haven't you ever been up here on this highway, Maria?"

"Nope. I've never been out of Mountain View."

"Me either," said Cody, seated beside me.

At that moment, I realized this field trip was the absolute right choice for this year and these kids. I delighted in being the catalyst for learning, even with something as simple as seeing a real live cow for the first time.

Entering San Francisco awakened the kids in the bus. As we neared the destination, excited voices increased in volume. The buses took the exit ramp into the city. The Palace of Fine Arts, in all its Greco-Roman architectural splendor, came into view.

"Is that where we're going?" asked Juan Luis, his mouth gaping open in wonder.

Built for the 1915 Panama-Pacific Exposition, the exhibit building and the spectacular domed rotunda with its flanking colonnades reflected in the swan-inhabited lagoon had the kids staring out the bus windows in awe. The momentary quiet passed as soon as the bus stopped in front of the entrance to the building. Cheers erupted and the rush to get inside was on. I donned my backpack filled with permission slips, first aid kit, extra worksheets, and my lunch.

As the leader of the field trip, the tension of responsibility buzzed inside me. I gathered the seventh grade at one end of the open air "lobby" to hear an introduction to this incredible, one-of-a-kind science museum. I turned their attention to the young man, the "Explainer," in the orange blazer uniform.

He jumped up on top of a wooden box and used his big voice to tell the crowd, "You become a part of the exhibits. We want you to touch everything. Play, experiment, explore. It's all hands-on. You can't break anything, and nothing will hurt you."

A swell of eagerness bubbled up from the kids. They'd never heard such liberating words in a public venue or school-related activity before now.

After dealing with the tickets, I followed the group into the exhibits.

I hope nothing goes wrong and my students are well behaved today.

I looked down the long, curved interior of the warehouse-like Exploratorium. I couldn't see any of my students, except for one, my Russian student, Dmitri. Alone, he seemed engrossed in turning the knobs and watching the reacting levers on the display, no need to read the English words to keep his attention. I had to ask him twice, "Where's your group, Dmitri?"

With barely a sideways glance at me, he pointed and mumbled, "Over there."

I walked on a bit farther, to a huge bed of nail-like metal rods where I pushed in my handprint next to other designs left by those before me. Continuing on, I found Jason and Jose circling the cloud chamber, a giant plastic cylinder enclosing a misty-looking cyclone. "Where's your chaperone?" I asked them.

"She's over there somewhere," answered Jose, waving his hand toward the walkway.

Across the walk, on the other side, I discovered the missing chaperone with two other boys. Their hands were inside another exhibit, making colored oils move in undulating waves. The chaperone was as fascinated as the boys, and I knew it would be a losing battle to expect the assigned groups to stay close together. I evaluated our surroundings and realized that my kids were in a safe place to explore. They weren't going anywhere else. Staff and chaperones were everywhere. My tension eased down a notch or two.

Juan Luis and Angelo came running toward me, yelling, "Mrs. Wright, Mrs. Wright, there's a cow's eye dissection demonstration! Come see!"

I let them pull me down the hallway to the kidney shaped table surrounded by kids, some mine and some from other schools. An orange-jacketed "Explainer" with a large Afro-style hairdo held them enthralled as she cut into the eyeball, talking about the parts and answering questions from the group.

Throughout the cavernous hall, kids did exactly as they were told: they played, they experimented, and they explored. They touched everything.

I found Kyra and Amber standing at a long metal tray filled with bubble solution. A metal pole suspended horizontally between two vertical poles could be raised by pullies on either side, bringing with it a wall of bubble material. Kids blew on it to form a giant bubble that extended into the room, rising toward the ceiling to delighted squeals.

Kyra moved to another bubble tray and dipped a giant metal circle into the liquid. Then she spun around making an oblong bubble shape that enveloped her. "Mrs. Wright, try this!" she said, eyes sparkling. She handed the circle shape to me and picked up a triangle for herself. Amber blew a bubble from a square shape into the bubbles Kyra and I created. Their looks of joy and wonder warmed my heart.

I connected with students and chaperones throughout the day, marveling at the variety of interests and interactions I saw. There was quite literally something for everyone here.

At one point, Jose ran up to me and said, "I've lost my science folder, Mrs. Wright. Do you have another one I could have?"

"I can give you another worksheet, Jose, but I don't have any more folders or pencils."

"Oh, that's okay. I can borrow a pencil," he replied.

I dug into my backpack to pull out a paper, just as Charles and Cody arrived.

"Could I have one too?" asked Charles.

I smiled at them, handed out the papers, and shook my head, thinking I should never have insisted on the study guide in the first place. This amazing place did not need a study guide to augment all the learning going on. For many students, the folder and its worksheets had become a burden.

Then there was Vanessa, happily writing the answers to all the questions, using the back sides of the pages to capture her thoughts. Vinh, a gifted artist, sat on a bench looking out at the lagoon through the colonnade, sketching what he could see. Patrick stayed at engineering exhibits on the mezzanine for hours, lost in thought, puzzling over the challenges posed, jotting equations on his folder.

For a while I sat on a bench in the center of a large open area, eating my lunch, just observing. Rosemary and Amber played in the sound area, trying out the echo stations, pounding on the circular wooden xylophones, and creating magical musical melodies together. I watched Felix sitting on a spinning seat holding onto the axle of a spinning bicycle wheel, tilting it in various ways, learning to control the speed of centrifugal force. I could see Angelo in the snack bar area as he snuck up to grab a french fry from Raven. With laughter she swung around and smacked the back of his head. He circled the table and grabbed a french fry from Maria next. She giggled in response, delighted with his attention.

At the far end of the hall, I discovered a shadow room. I moved closer to see what was going on inside. Juan Luis, Eduardo, and Vijay were absorbed with forming poses and watching the countdown to time their jumps to the flash of light that created shadows on the white wall behind them. When they saw me watching them play, Juan Luis hollered, "Come join us, Mrs. Wright."

Vijay added, "Yeah, come on, Mrs. Wright, make shadows with us."

I joined them to play. I gave Juan Luis unexpected shadow bunny ears. We laughed at the results. Then I squatted low and the boys gave me a halo of hands. We moved together in interlocking shadows to create visual images. We simply had fun.

By the end of the day, busloads of tired, happy kids and adults arrived safely back at the school. A day well spent. This was going to be a hard act to follow with regular classes the next morning.

**Science Field Trip
S.F. Exploratorium**

The 7th grade students traveled to San Francisco for a day of Science and Fun at the Exploratorium.

57

A page from the 2002 – 2003 yearbook.

Chapter 51
Observation Fiasco

RINGGGGGGGGG!

The bell screamed through my over-sensitive ears, causing me to flinch in pain. The onset of a migraine had lured me into a dark corner of the room at the end of my prep period for a quiet moment with eyes closed.

Only one more period to teach, and then I can go home. Ahhhh.

My eyes flew open. *Oh, no. Scott hasn't returned the film projector. That's my whole lesson for this next period. Maybe he's on his way?*

I dashed through the room and out the door, surprising a waiting group of students. Not seeing Scott or the projector coming toward my room, I said, "Stay here. I'll be right back."

I rounded the corner of the building, brushed past students entering the sixth-grade science room. Scott stood next to the projector, deep in conversation with a student, his film still on the reel. He did not notice my entrance.

Brusquer than I intended to sound, I said, "Scott, I need the projector for this period."

He looked up at me. "Oh, sorry Jan, I forgot to send it back. You can take it."

He turned back to the student and continued his conversation.

No time to unwind his film here, since the first bell has already rung and my class is standing outside my door. I'll just have to take it with me.

The sound of student chatter magnified my tension. I pushed the cart through the aisle. A steady flow of students blocked my exit as they entered the room. In frustration, I tried not to bark at them. "Excuse me, excuse me."

I never should have let Scott talk me into borrowing the movie projector during my prep period. It's too much trouble to get it back and set up again for my next class. Will I ever learn to say "no"?

I pushed the cart over the rough asphalt back to my classroom. A mob of kids waited for me outside the closed door. Engrossed in their own conversations, they seemed oblivious to my pleas to move aside. "Let me through, please," I said for the third time.

The late bell rang, piercing my head with pain once again.

I hate having to rush like this. I hope we don't run out of time.

I pushed the cart into my classroom; boisterous students flowed around me, throwing down backpacks, claiming their seats, taking out notebooks, intent on their own conversations.

At the back of the room, I plugged in the projector. I detached Scott's film, put it in the film can he'd left on the lower shelf of the cart, repositioned the empty reel, and began to thread my film into the machine.

"Mrs. Wright, Mrs. Wright. We've got visitors," said Rosemary above the din in the room.

I looked up to see the assistant superintendent in charge of curriculum standing in the doorway, wearing a pale blue suit and high heels, her flawless blonde hair framing her Scandinavian face. Two women and a man waited behind her.

I stopped what I'd been doing with the machine and made my way over to the group.

"Hello, Mrs. Montique. Is there something I can do for you?" We'd worked together on district committees over the years. Even though we were comfortable using first names outside of the classroom, her classy sophistication and exalted district position seemed to hold me in a perpetual state of awe.

"Mrs. Wright, this is Mrs. Green, Ms. Samar, and Mr. Lopez. They are community members of a district advisory committee," explained Sonja. "Would it be all right for us observe your science class?"

What a day for guests! I'm feeling awful, but how can I refuse?

I pasted a smile onto my face and said, "Of course. I'm just setting up for a movie. There's not much teaching to see today, but you're welcome."

"Whatever you're doing is just fine with us," Sonja replied.

"Come on in then." I turned to offer our guests a seat and realized students occupied all the desks, and two more students sat at the lab tables. Thirty-four students didn't leave much room for guests. The adults would have to sit in the lab area.

"Come this way," I said, heading across the front of the room to the far side. Acutely aware of kids talking and interacting with each other, the noise level seemed out-of-control to me. I approached Kyra, who sat at the closest lab table and said to her, "Would you please take your things and sit at the table with Sean?"

I looked to Sean who had spread his jacket, backpack, papers, and books over the table. "Sean, you need to make room at the table for Kyra." I raised my eyebrows and added, "And, please take your feet off the stool."

He grumbled under his breath. In slow motion, he took his feet down and began to slide his things to one end of the table. Kyra rolled her eyes, as she waited beside the table, tapping her toe.

I turned to our guests and stated the obvious, "This is a rather large class; you're welcome to sit anywhere in the lab on the stools."

"Thanks, Jan, I'll just stand," said Sonja. "You don't need to make a fuss about us; we'll just watch."

Of all days to watch. I'm struggling here!

The class chatter had increased to a dull roar. I needed to get their attention and get the lesson underway. I walked back across the room to the door and turned the light switch off. The class slowly settled into silence. I turned the lights back on and stood behind the demo counter, facing the class.

After introducing our guests, I said to the class, "As you can tell, we're going to see a movie today. The subject is genetics. We've been learning about inherited traits: genes, alleles, genotypes, and phenotypes. This film will set us up for tomorrow when we'll do an activity that will help us to understand the variations in some of the traits humans inherit."

I held up a plain white piece of paper, folded it in half and then in half again. Then I unfolded it showing the resulting four sections. "We've done this before to take notes on films. You will fill each square, front and back, with a quick sketch from the movie and write an appropriate caption under each one. The assignment is worth ten points. Make sure you choose important points from the movie to illustrate."

I asked two students to hand out the paper, then turned around and pulled down the movie screen behind me. Instead of catching at the bottom and locking into place, the screen screeched back into its casing. CAAAA-CHING BANG!

I jumped at the sound. Students laughed.

My whole body clenched in pain. Agonizing migraine pain.

I pulled the screen down again, working to secure the latch. I stood up to scattered applause from the class, and then trudged to the back of the room to continue threading the movie into the projector. Once all the students received drawing paper and I'd finished with the machine, I gave a final reminder, "Remember to choose important ideas to capture with your notes. You'll have time to finish sketching after the film ends. Any questions?" I glanced at the clock, my tension rising. *These kids might not have time to work on their sketches after the film.*

Seeing no hands raised, I said, "Damon, would you please turn the lights off?"

I turned on the movie projector; the film started turning, but no light came on to project the picture. A rumble of discontent ran through the class. I turned the machine off and then on again. Nothing.

"Damon, please turn the lights back on," I said, my headache pounding at the back of my eyes.

"Awwww!" the kids responded in disappointment.

"Don't we get to see the movie?" asked Adriana.

I looked over the projector, checking the parts, feeling a bit of panic. *The filament in the light bulb must have broken when I rolled the cart back to my room. Darn. I've got a room full of antsy kids and guests from the district observing me. Now what am I going to do?*

In desperation, I tried once more. No luck.

"Sorry kids, it looks like the light bulb has broken. No movie today."

I won't have the projector tomorrow, so this class will be out of sync with the other classes. What am I going to do? Can't do tomorrow's lesson because I don't have the worksheet ready.

I returned to the demo counter through a class of chattering students. My head hurt. I felt exhausted and worse, unimaginative. Trying to think of what to do, knowing the district folks were watching me, I said, "Okay, take out the textbook from under your seat."

"Awww, do we have to?" Kayla seemed to speak for all of us.

Embarrassed to have our guests hear them balk at the use of our new texts, I just nodded and flipped through the pages, looking for something appropriate to work on for the rest of the period. I found the section on genetics and inherited traits in the current unit of study.

"Please turn to page 236. We'll read a few paragraphs aloud and use the paper to take notes on key vocabulary words."

Groans followed these directions.

Why, of all days, do I have visitors watching me make a boring mess of this lesson? Okay, they get to see reality; sometimes that's just the way teaching goes. I felt miserable . . . and embarrassed.

"Who would like to read aloud first," I said, stifling a sigh of resignation.

Did I just see that woman yawn? Guess I haven't made a very good impression today.

Chapter 52
Mentor

The district office building opened into a maze of smaller rooms and cubicles. By this time, I had grown familiar with its occupants and a few of the nooks and crannies of this lofty administrative world.

"Hi, Emily. How are things today?" I asked as I strode past the public barrier counter into the inner sanctum.

"Hi, Jan. Oh, we keep ourselves busy around here. State tests have just arrived and we're hustling to get it all organized," Emily replied, shuffling manuals into piles.

I peeked into Myrtle's corner office since the door stood wide open.

"She's not there," said Emily. "I think she's waiting for you in the back, in the conference room."

I strolled through the central desk area, making my way toward the back. Rounding the corner, I headed into the hallway, glancing into the tidy little kitchen on the right to make sure I didn't miss seeing Myrtle on the way to the conference room. I saw Sonja with her back to me, stirring sugar into a cup of coffee.

"Hi Sonja," I said, stopping in the doorway.

She turned and replied, "Hi, Jan."

"Hey, I meant to apologize for the other day. When you walked in with your guests, everything just seemed to be going wrong. I had planned a lesson around a film, and everything just fell apart."

"It was fine Jan," she said with a tight smile.

In my embarrassment, I rattled on, saying more than necessary, "Oh, not really. That particular day was just awful. The kids got antsy while I struggled with the machine. My mind blanked on coming up with an interesting alternative on the spur of the moment."

"I should have given you warning before we dropped in on you."

Not ready to let it go, I said, "It was definitely not one of my better lessons, and I'm sure that was not what you brought your visitors to see, but I think all teachers ought to be more open to being observed anytime, rather than putting on a rehearsed show for a scheduled observation. So, that's what I try to do, just let people come in to see what we're really doing in class."

"Honest, you did just fine, Jan. I know you've had a lot of people observing you teach this year. Even the most exemplary teachers have 'off' days. Please don't worry about it."

Not knowing what else to say, I simply replied, "Thanks, Sonja. Uh, I need to find Myrtle."

"She's just down the hall, on the left."

I made a hasty retreat and hurried on to the small conference room. Myrtle had stacked several piles of books and papers on the table. She looked up at me as I entered.

"There you are," she said. "Come on in, Jan."

"Looks like you've been busy, Myrtle." I picked up a pamphlet, reading the title aloud, "HIV/AIDS and Other Sexually Transmitted Diseases." I looked up at her and winced. "Myrtle, I never expected to become the 'sex ed expert.'"

"I know, but you've taught this subject at two grade levels now."

From another box, we set out stacks of VCR tapes. I picked up a list of films. "Did I tell you I discovered a very young Beyoncé in a film I borrowed from the county last year? She played one of the kids who asked questions about sex. My students all recognized her; I had no clue. Turns out, they were right, which made the film seem very dated."

"See Jan, that's why you're the right person for this job." She smiled at me, shaking her head from side to side and then went on, "We need a strong, well defined, district curriculum guide for this topic."

We sat down and got to work mapping out a list of topics to be covered at each grade level. It took us about forty-five minutes of discussion. Then we sorted materials into possible grade levels from fifth through eighth grades. At this point, Myrtle said, "We need to check out these materials in more depth. I'd like to add one of the male teachers from the other middle school."

"I think that's a good idea, Myrtle. I'd suggest asking Keith. He's been teaching this subject much longer than Jeff."

"Okay, I'll get Keith over here this week. He can deal with the eighth-grade materials. You can do fifth and seventh, and I'll take a look at sixth. We'll get together as a committee in two weeks, so we can take our proposal back to the Curriculum Advisory Committee next month. Once they approve it, we'll put it on the school board agenda for final approval."

"So, we are looking at getting this completed before we have to teach it at the end of May?"

"Yes, and I'd like you to do the presentation for the board and answer questions with me, Jan."

"I can do that."

As I picked up my purse to leave, she added, "I hear Katherine made you Teacher-in-Charge at Crittenden last week when she and Bonnie were at their leadership conference."

"Yes," I laughed. "It was pretty easy to sit in the office all day and pretend to be principal." But I was thinking about the day I would not be pretending. Katherine and Bonnie had encouraged me to go back to school to get my administrative credential, and now it was going to happen.

"Myrtle, I never dreamed I could be a principal until you suggested it to me." I paused, knowing how much I owed this brave, pioneering woman.

Trusting her to understand, I continued, "It was kind of shocking when I realized I had never even imagined it. As a young girl, I didn't know it was a possible goal for me. Back then, all the principals were men, not women, ever. Girls could be nurses or teachers, not doctors, principals . . . or scientists. Remember all those boring science videos with old white men in white lab coats? That's the picture we saw to define what a scientist looks like. I have girl students now who don't see any of those barriers."

I looked into her eyes and said, "Thank you, again, for your letter of recommendation to the administrative program at UC Hayward."

"I have no doubt you'll do well, Jan."

I had nearly walked through the door when she said, "Jan, there's something else I'd like you to consider."

I turned back to face her.

"Our district is contemplating joining neighboring districts in a new program, the Silicon Valley New Teacher Project. I think you'd make an excellent New Teacher Advisor in this program."

All I could think to say was, "Wow."

She went on, "You would be responsible for working with new teachers at several schools and different grade levels, and you would receive training once a week on how to support them. It would mean leaving your own classroom for a year or two."

Oh, my gosh! She's chosen me to teach other teachers how to teach!

"Sounds like a really interesting and wonderful position. Thank you, Myrtle."

"Of course, you'll need to apply for this position after it's announced. Think about it, Jan."

I thought she was offering me the job, but . . . maybe not? Will I compete with other teachers?

Do I want to leave classroom teaching now, at the end of this year? Leave my kids?

Chapter 53
Medical Emergency

I had just placed a chart on the overhead projector, to explain the light spectrum, when the classroom door flew open. Wide eyed, Jesse raced into the room, followed by Fred.

"Mrs. Wright, Mrs. Wright, we need your help. You gotta come quick. Jason's hurt. Bad." The look on their faces gave me no doubt this was a real emergency.

"Stay seated," I commanded my class. They stared at me following the boys out the door.

"What happened?" I said as they drew me out toward the field.

"Jason's leg is cut real bad," Jesse threw back over his shoulder. We were running toward a small group of boys standing around a boy lying on the ground.

As I approached, the group parted. I read the looks on their blanched faces. Not good. Feeling their panic, I looked down at Jason's leg. His calf splayed open, looked like a gutted fish with not much bleeding at this point. The gaping wound made my stomach turn.

My gaze rose to his pinched face. In an even tone I asked, "Jason, how are you doing? Does your leg hurt?"

"I don't feel much right now, Mrs. Wright," he said in a quavering voice.

The boys backed away as I squatted down next to Jason and placed my hand on his forehead. Clammy. I registered the signs of shock in Jason's pale face. Someone had placed a folded-up sweatshirt under his head.

Remembering my First Aid training, I knew we needed to address the shock quickly. Without moving his injured leg, I needed to raise the other one and lower his head, but first we needed to send for help.

"I want you to lie still and stay calm, Jason."

I turned to look intently at each of the boys. Using a strong, in-control voice I said, "Jesse, go back to my classroom and use the phone to call the office. Tell them it's a medical emergency. Fred, go with him and tell my class to stay inside. Jorge and Cody, you two, run to the office and get Ms. Duval with the big first aid kit, and tell her we may need an ambulance."

They took off running.

"Does anyone have something we can cover Jason with?" I asked.

Felix took off the sports jacket he had tied around his waist and handed it to me. I placed it across Jason's chest.

"We need to raise his other leg a bit. Boys, find something to put under that foot." I held Jason's head in one hand, and with the other hand, pulled on the sweatshirt to flatten it. I gently lowered Jason's head. I sat on the ground next to him and then held his hand in mine. "You're going to get through this Jason. I'm right here with you."

I stroked his forehead, keeping my face deliberately calm and assured. Another sweatshirt appeared, and Rich placed it gently under Jason's "good" foot.

"Tell me what happened," I said, knowing I needed to engage the boys who remained.

"We were running the track around the field. Jason climbed the bike cage and slipped," said Rashad.

"Where's your P.E. teacher?" I asked.

"We don't know. We haven't seen him, but Charles went looking."

"Okay. I need two of you to go find the teacher and tell him what happened."

Rashad and Drew took off.

"Jason, can you tell me how you fell?" I didn't want him to pass out; I wanted to keep him talking and alert.

In a subdued, but steady voice he replied, "I climbed to the top and slipped. My leg caught on something."

"You climbed all the way to the top of that ten-foot-tall fencing?" I asked.

"Almost." He added, "I was trying to get inside the bike cage. I know it was stupid of me."

I nodded and said, "Tell me about the fall."

"My foot slipped into the gap between the gate and the pole. I slid down and my leg got stuck on the latch."

Felix interjected, "We heard him yelling. I saw Jesse and Jorge pull him out."

Just then, Jesse sprinted toward us. Fred stayed back by my classroom, the door wide open with several students standing there, looking out at us, but not venturing farther.

"Carol said Ms. Duval will be right here," said Jesse, squatting down on the other side of Jason.

"How're you doin', man?" Jesse asked.

Jason just looked at him and blinked, his eyes a bit damp from the tears he would not shed.

Before long, we could see Jorge jogging back to us. Ms. Duval followed him with Cody carrying the first aid kit. "We got her," yelled Cody.

I looked down at Jason's face and squeezed his hand. "It's going to be all right, Jason."

I knew Bonnie had been a nurse and worked well under tense situations. She gave everyone around her a feeling of security, just knowing she was in charge. She arrived a bit breathless.

"Thank you for coming so quickly," I said to give her a moment to catch her breath. "Jorge and Cody, you did a good job getting Ms. Duval here." She nodded in response then bent down to look at Jason.

"Well, young man, I hear you've got a wound on your leg," she said.

Jason blinked his eyes as he nodded his head in reply.

"Can you tell me your name?" she asked him in a reassuring, in-charge voice.

"Jason," he replied.

"What's your last name, Jason?"

"Zachery," he said a little louder.

"I'm going to have to take a good look at your leg, Jason," she continued as she squatted down by his feet. She told the boys who had surrounded us to step back and then said to Jason, "I'm just going to take hold of your foot and turn your leg toward me."

As she moved his leg to examine it, I kept my eyes on Jason's face. He bit his lip but held my eyes with his own.

"You can tell us if it hurts," I said. He just stared at me, not speaking a word.

Ms. Duval pulled the walkie talkie that had been clipped to her waist. "Carol, this is Bonnie. Over."

"This is Carol, over," came the reply.

"Call Jason Zachery's emergency contact number and tell them he's had a deep laceration on his leg. Get their permission to call an ambulance. Let them know where we are so they can find us on the campus."

"Will do."

"Bonnie out."

She opened the first aid kit, took out a pair of surgical gloves, and put them on her hands. Then she opened a sterile package containing the largest wound covering I had ever seen.

I took a moment to look down at Jason's leg. She had turned it so I could see the ragged edge of the wound. The meat of his calf muscle gaped open, down to the white of the bone beneath. A wave of nausea swept over me. I breathed in, deeply, forcing myself to remain calm for the boy whose hand I still held.

"Jason, I'm going to need to cut off the bottom of your pants leg so I can place a bandage over the wound," she said. She took a pair of bandage scissors from the kit and began to snip.

When I could trust myself to look at him again, I turned my face back to Jason. He had closed his eyes while Bonnie worked on his leg.

Still worried about shock, I squeezed his hand and said, "Jason, look at me."

He opened his eyes.

"Your mother is on her way. You okay?"

He nodded.

In no time, we heard the sirens from the ambulance. When it arrived in the parking lot next to the athletic field, two uniformed paramedics jogged toward us. Bonnie sent the students back to class and took charge, explaining the situation to the men. I stood up to give them room, feeling torn about staying at the scene with Jason now that help had arrived or returning to my science class, knowing they were unsupervised.

Just as I began to refocus on my other students, I looked up to see Jason's mother running toward us. She came to a halt about ten feet from her son, tears forming in her eyes, a terrified look on her face. I walked toward her. "I'm Mrs. Wright, Jason's science teacher. He's in good hands, Mrs. Zachery. The wound is deep, but he's going to be okay."

I wrapped my arms around her. She held on tight, her body shaking as the tears fell. I worked to keep mine in check.

"Come, let's talk with Ms. Duval and the paramedics. They'll take good care of you and see that your son gets the help he needs." Bonnie took over with Mrs. Zachery, just as the bell rang to end the period.

I walked back toward my classroom. Students streamed out the door, filled with inquiries for me about Jason. I did what I could to reassure them and sent them on their reluctant way to their next period class. Meanwhile, the paramedics loaded Jason onto a gurney, taking his mother with them. When they were on their way, Bonnie joined me, sending curious students to classes. The bell rang. We nodded to each other, and I returned to my classroom, shifting emotional gears, to teach my next science class.

Three weeks later, a chastened Jason returned to class on crutches. He handed me an apology letter from him and a sweet thank you note from his mother.

Chapter 54
Letter from the District

Driving across the gracefully curving Dumbarton Bridge in the pastel colors of dusk, I marveled at the peaceful beauty of the open sky expanse of San Francisco Bay. Salt ponds and low rolling hills bordered the south end of the bay, the twinkling lights of city dwellers tucked farther inland from the coastline edges.

With state-mandated standardized testing of our students completed, the finish line, the end of the school year, began to fill my work horizon. Contentment and anticipation of a weekend to relax with my husband soothed me, along with the mellow music playing on the radio.

"There's some mail for you on the table," Jerry said when I breezed through the family room after hanging up my jacket in the hall closet. He stood at the stove, stirring a pot of vegetables; aromas of a delicious steak dinner wafted through the room.

I picked up the stack of mail and found the letter. "This is odd, Jerry. It's from the Mountain View Whisman School District. Why didn't they send it through the district mail to my school?"

"Open it and find out," he said in his typical, practical manner.

Puzzled, I turned it over in my hand, pulled at the edge, and slit the envelope open with my finger, being careful not to get an annoying paper cut. I pulled out the letter, unfolded the formal looking document, and began to read.

In stunned silence, I read the words, "We are pleased to inform you that you have been selected as the 2003 Mountain View Whisman District Teacher of the Year."

I could get no further. I read the sentence again. Twice.

"Well, what does it say?" asked Jerry, coming to stand beside me.

I handed the letter to him.

He read and then smiled and took me in his arms for a warm embrace. "This calls for a celebration. I'll open a nice bottle of wine."

He handed the letter back to me and took out a couple of wine glasses from the cabinet, setting them on the kitchen island counter in front of me while I read the rest of the letter.

"When do they make the big announcement?" Jerry asked.

"Um, not until the beginning of the next school year."

I sat down on a stool and stared at the letter. "But Jerry, why me? How can this be? I just don't understand. There are so many, many amazingly wonderful teachers in this district."

He opened the wine and poured out two glasses, handing one to me. He picked up his glass in a toast.

"To the Teacher of the Year!" he said, clinking glasses with me. "They got it right."

Chapter 55
Graduation

"Jan, are you coming to graduation practice?" asked Judy standing next to me in the mailroom.

"I teach during those practice times, but I'm ushering tonight, so I'll be there for the actual graduation," I replied, picking through my mail, discarding the ads for science equipment we couldn't afford. "These are the last of the students I taught in fifth grade and again in seventh-grade science. I want to be there to see them move on."

"Good," she said. "See you tonight." With that, she twirled around and made a quick exit through the back door.

Carrie walked into the room. "Hi Jan, are you ushering tonight?"

"Yes, I am," I said to her.

Should I tell her about being chosen as Teacher of the Year? No, I'll just keep it as a surprise until the district announces it in the fall. Right now the focus is on our kids who are graduating.

"I think the whole seventh-grade team will be ushering. They're going to reserve a place for us to sit near the graduates. When they get their diplomas, we'll stand up and make a line to shake their hands," Carrie said.

"I love that idea. Can't wait!" I replied.

If I become a New Teacher Advisor, this may be my graduation too. Wish I knew whether I'll get the job. Now that I know Gwen applied too, I'm not so sure. Darn. This is all happening so late in the school year, I won't even know until school's already out. How can I plan anything?

The slow hours between the final bell of the day and the time to show up to usher for graduation, dragged on. I found myself walking back and forth across the room starting one task that drew me into another, completing nothing, feeling melancholy at the thought of possibly never teaching in this classroom again.

I need to be more productive, use this time to get things done.

What if I never teach in this room again? What if I never have my own students again?

I wandered through the classroom. Lost in thought, I stopped to stare into the display cabinet, looking at students' cell models I had added to the collection this year. I heard Stacey moving around in her office area, and needing a sense of personal connection, I followed the sounds into the supply room.

"Hey Stacey, are you going home for dinner?" I asked, hoping she'd stay here and go out to dinner with me.

"Yeah. I'm going home to change my clothes. I'll grab a bite then," she replied. "Are you staying? I see you are all dressed up already."

"Yeah, it's just too far for me to drive home and come back. I'll just get a few things done here and change into my dress shoes before I head over to the gym," I said with determination, but feeling a sense of disconnection and loss already.

I waited alone at the west entrance to the gym, holding a stack of programs in my hands, willing myself to find the energy I would need to get through this night. I shifted my weight from sore foot to sore foot.

And then they came, changing everything; the quiet ennui of the evening shattered. Decked out in a red, frilly dress covered by an as-yet unzipped graduate's black gown, cap tilted on her head and carrying a bouquet of red carnations, Angelica clip-clopped in on sling-back, black high heels, followed by her younger sister, older brother, and mother all talking at once. I noticed her father with Grandmother on his arm, not far behind. They were swallowed up by an onslaught of excited graduates and families pouring through the bank of doors.

I clicked into greeting mode, handing out programs, one per family. "Welcome!

"So glad to see you tonight.

"Malik, you look so classy in that suit."

Carrie appeared at my side. "I'm glad you're here," I told her. "The programs are in the box over there in the corner. Could you grab another stack for me too, please? Seating for families is on the left side of the gym, graduates on the right." She nodded.

"That's a beautiful corsage, Tanya.

"Chris, please *walk* to your seat on the bleachers. Thank you.

"Have a program.

"Oh my, Doug, is that lei made of ten-dollar bills?

"Restrooms are right over there."

As the arrivals started to thin out, a pain began in my chest. Feeling dizzy, my vision blurred. I felt the sudden adrenalin rush of fear. *Am I having a heart attack?* I squared my feet on the floor to ground myself, gasping to breathe. People streamed around me. I could feel the irregular beating of my racing heart.

The distress passed within seconds, but the sense of panic lingered. I looked around for Carrie. She had wandered off, deep in conversation with a student and her family.

I handed out a program, and another, not speaking, just going through the motions. My mind keyed in on the warning from my doctor.

She told me my blood pressure is too high. She tried to talk me into taking medications, but, noooo, I insisted on doing things my own way. I tried lowering my salt intake, exercising . . . denying the existence of a problem.

In a flash of clarity, I vowed to call the doctor and really listen this time.

I found a folding chair nearby and sat, trying to think. *Should I leave and go home? It's probably not wise to drive right now, but I don't want to be the center of attention by collapsing in the middle of graduation ceremonies, either.* I just sat and worked to control my worry, breathing in, breathing out.

Katherine sat on the platform by the flower-flanked podium, Bonnie at her side. Eighth-grade teachers, district staff, and school board members sat in a row of folding chairs behind them. The mass of thirteen- to fourteen-year-olds squirmed and churned in front of them. Families on the other side of the gym facing them were nearly as chatty and motion-filled.

Teachers and other staff members sat across the aisle, flanking one edge of the block of graduates. Katherine began the tough job of settling everyone down to begin the formal procedure we had all come here to witness.

Feeling "normal" again, I made my way over to the bleachers to take a seat among the seventh-grade teachers. Everyone was excited and engaged by the program; my silence went unnoticed. I took comfort in the proximity of my colleagues.

Katherine began in earnest with accolades and words of encouragement. Graduates responded with cheers and applause, drawing me firmly back to the reality of the present.

Dignitaries came to the podium, one-by-one to give speeches.

I opened the folded program. Aaron, the Valedictorian, would be speaking. And, there, in the middle of the list of names of students who would be speakers, I saw Steven Sanders's name. *My Steven? The one who never gave speeches? No, the program must be in error. Maybe he'll carry something special up to the stage from his class?*

Bonnie began to announce awards, alternating with Katherine. Students made their way through the throngs to gather tokens of acknowledgement. Finally, only a few items remained on the program, students' speeches and handing out diplomas.

At last, Katherine called his name, Steven Sanders. This strong, confident young man walked straight up to the microphone and began to talk. I let out my breath, realizing I had been holding it in from the moment I heard his name.

He spoke clearly about the opportunities provided by Crittenden Middle School and told us he looked to the future with hope. Knowing how difficult school, life, and public speaking had been for this young man, I felt deeply moved. Along with the crowd, I listened to him with rapt attention.

Sitting in the bleachers among the hundreds in attendance, the school dignitaries, the families, his peers, I burst with pride for Steven's stunning achievement.

And then he said, "I would like to thank Mrs. Wright for being such a great teacher. She believed in me and gave me confidence to be able to stand here tonight. I will never forget her."

Tears filled my eyes. The teachers who surrounded me patted me on the back. I caught my breath, thinking about how close I had come to missing this moment.

When the graduates filed past us with their diplomas, teachers formed a line of congratulations. We shook hands. We made heartfelt comments. We hugged, and we teared up. I smiled so deeply my face hurt.

At last, Steven came to me.

We looked at each other with emotion in our eyes.

"Could I give you a hug?" I asked him.

His grin broadened. He nodded his head and without saying a word he hugged me.

I hugged him hard and said, "I am so proud of you, Steven. You . . . are . . . amazing. Your speech was a spectacular achievement. I wish you all the success in the world, Steven. I know you will do well. And, thank you so much for your kind words about me."

He stepped back, still speechless, blushing, and smiling deeply.

Then, he moved on and was gone.

A joyous feeling of pride entangled with the angst of separation left me lost in a turmoil of emotion.

Chapter 56
Last Day

"**M**rs. Wright, what kind of party are we having in here today?" demanded Jorge as he strutted into the science classroom surrounded by bubbly, chatty, seventh graders. Friday, the day after eighth-grade graduation, and the last half day of school before summer vacation, my seventh graders did not expect any work.

I just smiled in response; I had something quite different in mind. A blanket of quiet spread over the group. With affection that nearly took my breath away, I looked at the students awaiting my instructions.

This may be the last time I will ever teach my own group of kids in my own classroom.

My focus turned to the business of the day. "At the end of the school year, it's good to review what we've learned together. Do you remember when we started with the lessons about what a scientist does?"

"Yeah, you dressed up in a lab coat," chuckled Jorge, slouching in his seat.

"Do you remember why I did that?"

"We had to figure out what you changed. I got them all," said Maria pumping her fist in the air to laughter.

"What did that have to do with science?" I persisted.

After a silence, Elena raised her hand.

"Scientists observe?" She paused, checking my response.

I waited, keeping my eyes on her.

"And . . . girls can be scientists too," she said with a smile.

Cheers arose from the feminine voices in the room with several masculine additions to the chorus. My heart smiled at them.

I turned and wrote S-C-I-E-N-C-E in the center of the whiteboard.

Several kids chimed in while I wrote, spelling the word aloud with the sing-song rhythm I always used to teach them how to spell this word correctly.

We continued writing memories from our year together until the whiteboard was filled. Then I turned to them and said, "You are a very special class of students. You may be the last group of kids I ever teach."

I heard gasps, and some faces registered surprise. "What?!"

"I have applied for a position working with new teachers. My job would be to help them become the best possible teachers they can be, and I need your advice. YOU are the experts. You know what works best to help kids learn. So, I have a big favor to ask of you. I would like you to write a letter to me to tell me what you think are the qualities of a great teacher."

I seized a moment of inspiration and continued, "I've decided to write a book about teaching. I want to include some of your letters in my book." Again, audible gasps reached my ears.

After over thirty years of working with children of all ages, these wonderful kids surprised me.

All morning long, while loud parties, games, and movies swirled around us in all the other classrooms on this last day of school, twelve- and thirteen-year-old seventh graders wrote their letters to me in utter silence.

With one final creative whim, I had galvanized the exact behavior I had always sought to achieve: a student-centered desire for excellence in their own work.

They believed their work might be published in a book.

Excerpts from Letters from Seventh-Grade Students

Written on June 13, 2003

These few samples come from the nearly 150 letters written by students on my last day of classroom teaching. They have been copied exactly, with the exception of some minor editing of spelling and punctuation. My students have not seen their letters since the day they were written. I hope some of "my kids" will know I never forgot them.

"Dear Mrs. Wright,

Many people have wanted to become teachers and you had a chance to become one and you did. You are the most enthusiastic teacher I have ever known. Many people should become a teacher just like Mrs. Jan Wright. The thing that I will remember the most about 7th grade science is remembering: S-C-I-E-N-C-E, and all the most interesting thing that I have learned in "science". Though somethings I didn't want to do including dissecting a cow's eye which was pretty disgusting, but I'm glad that I learned about it. I would just like to thank you for everything u taught me and my 2nd period class, and GOOD LUCK on your book. I'll make sure to buy this 1.

Always,

 your Student at Crittenden Middle School

Arlene . . .

P.S. make Sure that u don't ever, ever forget me and my fellow classmates."

"Dear Mrs. Wright, . . . I would tell the new science teacher to be excited or enthusiastic about her/his job."

DJ

"Dear Mrs. Wright, . . . I recommend future teachers should have a sense of humor, but know the boundaries. They should be nice even, if the students are goofing off . . ."

Tyler

"Dear Mrs. Wright, . . . I would advise to be patient and kind with the kids. Always have your schedule planned out. Never let kids get you mad. Remember, patience is the key to a perfect teacher."

Priscilla

"Dear Mrs. Wright, . . . If I was to give advice to a new science teacher it would be that some 7th graders can go wild, and crazy, but a good experiment would catch them calm like the eye ball die section."

Alex

"Dear Mrs. Wright, A new teacher should know to be patient, to listen to what kids have to say. Not to yell at kids a lot. They need to let kids walk around if they need to and let kids socialize once in a while. Teachers also need to make things fun . . . if they don't the kids will lose interest and be bored. So that's all you need to know."

Ally

"Dear Mrs. Wright, . . . The advice I would give to a new teacher would probably be . . . Love your students & understand them because as I grow up, I see so many kids with problems & the teachers don't even know it. That makes me sad, but I know what-ever problems a child may have, all teachers should care."

Natalie

"Dear Mrs. Wright, . . . my advice to new teachers: don't argue with the kids, they're always write."

Unsigned

"Dear Mrs. Wright, . . . I would probably tell a teacher that he/she must go slow on each unit for students to understand. The units are very difficult, so teach well and good luck."

Rebecca

"Dear Mrs. Wright, . . . Just from my point of view, always follow up on the rules."

Jocelyn

"Dear Mrs. Wright, . . . Try to be fun for the first trimester, & in the half of the second be your regular self. Give at least 2 warnings before giving a detention. Then after that give 2 warnings before a suspension or referral. Always smile, & don't give all class detention unless necessary. And don't give up."

Tyler

"Dear Mrs. Wright, . . . Advice for a new teacher will be hold on don't give up I know you can do it. Advice would also be don't be scared to try something new Give it a try. Science teacher try and understand that you must be there when your student needs you. I know Mrs. Wright was there 4 me."

Sincerely

Shanice . . .

Epilogue

On the first official day back to work at the end of summer, the district met as a whole, over 400 of us. I sat next to Principal Katherine Murphy in the midst of the Crittenden staff. Just two weeks before, I had accepted the job of New Teacher Advisor and would be leaving them.

At the end of the opening session, the superintendent made the surprise announcement.

"It is with great pleasure that I announce The Mountain View Whisman Teacher of the Year 2003 . . . Jan Wright."

My colleagues jumped out of their seats, shouted "Hooray," and applauded for me. My cheering school staff slapped me on the back as I made my way through them and up to the stage with my prepared speech.

At the podium I looked out at the audience of my peers. Smiling. Feeling proud and humbled, I spoke.

". . . I do not stand here alone. It isn't just me who is receiving this award.

"I stand on the shoulders of those teachers who came before me. Those teachers who were my teachers when I was a little girl, Miss White in first grade, Mrs. McMullen whom I adored in fourth grade, and even Mrs. Evans in third grade who made us copy all the cursive writing on the board about Indians. I remember their names. And there were all those other teachers I have worked with in the past. Those who shared their methods with me, those whose classrooms I found ideas in, those who processed thoughts with me during workshops, literally hundreds of other teachers I have come across all over the years of my teaching career.

"I stand here now, in the present, surrounded and supported by teachers, you, my colleagues and peers. Together we play a momentous role in our community. And, I mean 'teacher' in the broad sense, because it includes all of you. It includes Javier, my custodian, who teaches me about Spanish and pride in his culture. It includes Carol, our school secretary, who teaches me how to get through the paper maze and why it's important.

"I also stand here looking past myself to those teachers who will come after me, perhaps taking pieces of what I could share with them into the future.

"Take a minute right now to see excellence and achievement. Look around at the people you are standing with, at your colleagues. These are the faces of excellence; these are the faces of achievement. We should acknowledge that. We do this with our students, almost naturally. We acknowledge them and their accomplishments in many ways, why not do this for each other?

"Teacher of the Year is an award that honors the profession of teaching. In that spirit, I stand as a symbol of all of us. We celebrate this honor together.

"On Monday, when school starts, each of us is the Teacher of the Year for the students who are in our classes.

"Thank you!"

I looked out at a standing ovation.

Acknowledgments

My seventh graders who graduated from Crittenden Middle School in Mountain View, California in 2004 inspired this book. I am fulfilling my promise to them after nearly twenty years. My thanks to them for believing me.

Encouraged by my husband for years, the first story I wrote eventually became Chapter Four, Southern Surprises. Dorothy Read critiqued that first story, urged me to stay on the path, and guided my hesitant early steps. She began as my writing cheerleader and returned as my editor extraordinaire. I owe a deep debt of gratitude to my dear friend, Dot, for helping shape the development of this memoir.

Because of Dot, I joined a writers' critique group on Whidbey Island where I met Sue Jensen, a talented mentor who, along with others in the group, pushed my writing to new levels of clarity and honesty. Another member of the group who kept me writing was Pattie Beavens. For a while, she and I were the only two to attend meetings and cheer each other on. Her efforts and determination finally expanded the group into what became Whidbey Writers by the Sea, another eclectic group of writers who encouraged me to reach my goal.

I later joined Whidbey Writers' Group whose consistent critique sessions honed the major part of this book. My thanks to Sandra Ortgies, Mike McNeff, Miriam Johnston, Pat Brunjes, Heather Parsley, Barb Bland, and Ann Adams. A special note of gratitude to Bill Wilson, Avis Rector, and Ben McAdams who walked the final miles of this manuscript on Zoom through the 2020 Covid-19 year.

I am grateful for early readers of the unedited draft of my manuscript. These folks gave me the gifts of their analysis of the book as a whole and offered suggestions that helped to polish the final result. Thank you to my fabulous beta readers: Karen Eaton, Bridget Simon, Dwight Smith, and Sue Nelsen.

During my first year at Crittenden, Sue Nelsen and Joyce Murphree led staff training on writing. With these two, I discovered the joy of writing and became a writing coach myself. As a beta reader, Sue Nelsen, who is also a character in the book, shared her delight in reliving memories with me and made the final product seem worthwhile. Instead of telling, I'm showing!

Also, thank you to Carol Sawyer, Liz Mogin, Joyce Murphree and the late Sanndy Charette who each appear in the book and gave me constructive feedback and support for the Crittenden section.

My appreciation to Terry Hansen for working on the cover design and to Dwight and Judy Smith for sharing their areas of graphic expertise with me.

Thank you to friends who encouraged me along the way. Steve Richwood, who taught with me during the middle years, kept me focused on identifying my audience and defining the theme. Judy Smith listened to chapters, helped me choose the student letters I used, and bolstered my confidence. Ralph Young, often my first audience for early drafts of chapters, expressed enthusiasm for my book, even when I could not see the end in sight. His unwavering support has been invaluable.

Finally, it is with deep appreciation I acknowledge my family. Without their love and perseverance, I could not have been the teacher I became, nor the writer I aspire to be. My younger son, Brian, always gave me solid advice and encouragement to complete this book. My older son, David, is my technology guru and my rock who never doubted my success. My grandson, Kryten, listened to several chapters, and when my stories kept his attention, I knew I was on the right track. He reminded me how seventh graders behave and told me to keep writing, so I did.

I am profoundly grateful for all the helping hands along the way to the completion of *Dear Mrs. Wright, A Teacher's Memoir Inspired by Students' Letters*.

About the Author

Jan Wright spent thirty-one years honing her craft. In 2003 she left classroom teaching to become a New Teacher Advisor with the Silicon Valley New Teacher Project while she earned an administrative credential from California State University in Hayward, California. In 2005 she became a shared vice principal for both Chadbourne Elementary School and Mission Valley Elementary School in Fremont, California. After years of experience in teaching, staff development, and administration, there was just one career capstone left for her to accomplish in retirement: keep her promise to write a book about it. Inspired by students, *Dear Mrs. Wright* fulfills that promise.

Jan currently lives on Whidbey Island in Washington State. Besides writing, in her retirement years she's had the good fortune to fly a helicopter, to go rafting in the Grand Canyon, to swim with whale sharks, and to perform in a musical comedy. As a world traveler, she has photographed wild animals on safari in Africa, hiked Machu Pichu, and learned to speak enough Creole to communicate with children while she helped to build a church and school in Haiti. Always a teacher at heart, she has shared her adventures through writing, annotated photobooks, and group presentations.

For more information about the author, please visit her website:
www.dearmrswright.com

Made in the USA
Monee, IL
02 December 2021

82972593R00208